1789 set
$122.55

MASTERING COACHING AND SUPERVISION

PRINCIPLES OF LEARNING SERIES

MADELINE HUNTER
AND
DOUG   RUSSELL

University of California, Los Angeles

CORWIN PRESS, INC.
A Sage Publications Company
Thousand Oaks, California

Other publications by the same author:

Mastery Teaching
Motivation Theory for Teachers
Retention Theory for Teachers
Discipline That Develops Self-Discipline
Teach More — Faster!
Teach for Transfer
Aide-ing in Education
Improved Instruction
Improving Your Child's Behavior
Parent-Teacher Conferencing

Mastering Coaching and Supervision
© Copyright 1989 by Madeline Hunter
© Copyright 1990 by Madeline Hunter

Printed in the United States of America.

Hunter, Madeline C.
  Mastering coaching and supervision / Madeline Hunter, Doug Russell.
        p.   cm. — (Principles of learning series)
  Includes bibliographical references.
  ISBN 0-8039-6315-7
  1. School supervision. 2. Teachers — Rating of.   I. Russell, Doug.   II. Title.
  III. Series.
LB2806.4.H85   1995

371.1 — dc20   95-7957

        98 99 00 01 02 11 10 9 8 7 6

For information on the complete Madeline Hunter Collection, please contact:

CORWIN PRESS, INC.
A Sage Publications Company
2455 Teller Road
Thousand Oaks, CA 91320-2218
Call: 805-499-9774 Fax: 805-499-0871

This book is an expression of appreciation to
those countless educators and students who
have helped us learn to translate psychological
and educational research into daily practice,
then allowed us to test that practice in a real
world which validates its effectiveness and
develops professional artistry.

M.H.
D.R.

Table of Contents

INTRODUCTION

This book was written in response to supervisors' and coaches' many requests for help in knowing 1) how and what to observe in a classroom, 2) how to analyze that observation, and 3) how to translate those observations into conference feedback and interactions that encourage teachers to continue to enhance their professional effectiveness.

This book was also written to correct the frequent misinterpretations by well meaning educators who seem to have "heard about" but never directly experienced instruction in our work conducted by people qualified to do so. Other educators may have taken a "course" but have not had the opportunity to develop the performance behaviors required for effective coaching and supervising. As a result, many school districts, state systems and legislatures have developed check lists of "indicators" of excellence in teaching. *Nothing could be farther removed from our intent!*

You will read again and again in this book that the only thing a teacher must always do is THINK and the only thing a teacher must never do is cause a student to lose dignity. Those are the only two absolutes in teaching. All other teaching and learning behaviors are determined in relation to their effectiveness with particular students in specific situations.

The skills and behaviors identified in this book are deceptively simple in their description, incredibly complex in their implementation. To know them is one thing. To be able to implement them effectively and artistically in a growth evoking conference requires the highest degree of professional proficiency: something that is acquired only with a great deal of practice and with expert coaching. After a quarter of a century of practice, the authors of this book are still learning.

You will find many redundancies in the book because some things need to be said, read, and heard again and again. The following four ideas are essential to becoming a skilled coach or supervisor.

1. Coaching and supervising must be built on the observer's solid foundation of knowledge of instructional theory *not* on a check list of what "should" be in a lesson.

2. Initial training time (typically 25-30 hours for instructional theory and an additional 25-30 hours for coaching) is adequate *only* to build a base of understanding for beginning application to the observations and conferences of supportive, volunteer teachers. The primary purpose of initial observations and conferences is to develop the observer's skills rather than to contribute to the professional growth of the teacher. Additional, intensive training is necessary before the observer will be competent in routine coaching or supervising, let alone working with more challenging teachers. While

this book provides an introduction to the skills of coaching and supervision, it does not supply the basic instructional theory which is prerequisite to effective use of those skills.* This book also can serve as a reference for follow-up and practice of coaching and supervisory skills: activities which are essential to continuing professional growth.

3. There are no formulas for designing an effective instructional conference. While there are some general guidelines, each conference is specifically designed for an individual teacher in terms of the objective and interaction which would be most growth evoking at that time. Planning and conducting a conference is situational and relativistic in the same way that all teaching is situational and relativistic. There are no absolutes or recipes!

4. Evaluation of educators without adequate staff development and supervision (coaching) can be very costly in time, energy and money with little, if any, professional growth by teachers. That professional growth is the major purpose of all coaching, supervision and evaluation.

The first section of this book (Chapters 1, 2, 3) develops a rationale for the current emphasis on coaching and supervising. This rationale is followed by a description and discussion of the activities and skills essential to conducting a growth evoking, instructional conference (Chapters 4-11). The concluding section suggests strategies and time lines for a staff development program that results in enhanced teaching effectiveness.

After reading this book and implementing the understandings and skills described, we invite you to join us in an international effort to make all members of our profession increasingly effective with all learners, in all content areas, in all nations.

Madeline Hunter
Doug Russell

---

* See TIP Publications, P.O. Box 514, El Segundo, CA 90245

EDUCATION AS A PROFESSION

Education now qualifies as a true profession. 1) a body of research based knowledge, not possessed by those outside the profession, exists and has been articulated for use by educators. 2) Performance in education requires synthesis of that knowledge with additional knowledge about current situation and client which results in professional decision making rather than following a set of fixed procedures. 3) An educator must continue to add new insights, research based skills and understandings to performance throughout that professional's career.

Research based knowledge usually begins with experience which then is subjected to rigorous investigation to be validated or impeached. At the beginning of this century the belief existed that Latin and mathematics "trained the mind" and transferred to make learning other subjects easier. That general notion was impeached by research. Another belief emerging at that same time was that when learnings were similar, knowledge of one transferred either positively on negatively into learning the other. That belief was validated by subsequent research.

Knowledge about teaching/learning also is generated by extrapolation and inference from psychological research. An example would be the extrapolations from attribution theory which suggest that a teacher reinforce a student's effort as a primary cause of achievement. Such a reinforcer has high probability of causing a student to attribute success to factors within the student, his/her ability and effort, rather than to factors outside the student such as difficulty of assigned task or luck.

When a profession, such as education or medicine, deals with humans, cause-effect relationships are always expressed as probabilities, never certainties. (Even physics has a principle of uncertainty.) Consequently, *there are no absolutes in teaching.* Education is a relativistic, situational profession which requires a constant stream of decisions on the part of the teacher. There is nothing an excellent teacher always does (except think) or never does (except abuse a student). Every other teaching behavior is appropriate in some situations, not appropriate in others.

We currently define teaching as a constant stream of decisions which, when appropriately implemented, can increase the probability of learning. Students learn more when they are well taught, and teaching is the reason for the clinical practice of education. Beyond learning basic skills, it is important to remember that excellent teaching also increases the probability of the student becoming a creative, thinking, independent learner.

Professional competence in teaching is a sensitive and volatile issue. Beyond competence exists the art of teaching. That art, however, is a beautiful manifestation, not a violation of basic principles of human learning. Cause-effect relationships between teaching and learning have been researched more in the last two decades than in all the preceding centuries. As a result, we now possess a considerable body of articulated knowledge about what formerly was only the experience or intuition of effective teachers.

Intuition, which is highly operant but non-articulated knowledge, belongs in every profession but it should be used to augment research or experientially based knowledge, not in lieu of it. Unfortunately, intuition dies with its possessor. Until it is articulated it cannot be effectively and validly transmitted to other professionals. The capacity to explain is critical and successful transmittal.

It is also important to remember that no matter how skilled the educator (or physician), learning a profession is a never-ending process. As experience and/or research reveals new findings, effective educators must consistently add those understandings and skills to their professional repertoire for the benefit of students. Even champions have coaches!

Coaching and supervision have the power to escalate teaching effectiveness by 1) reinforcing and extending a teacher's productive practice, 2) adding new understandings and skills to a teacher's pharmacy of teaching alternatives, 3) remediating or developing alternatives for less effective practice, 4) keeping a highly skilled teacher growing in instructional effectiveness through incorporating new research in daily teaching.

To evaluate a teacher who has had little or no coaching or supervision can serve only as a diagnostic baseline from which to measure future growth. That growth will occur as a result of 1) motivation to be a growing professional, 2) opportunities to learn procedures for instructional effectiveness, 3) coaching and supervision to enable one to become an increasingly skillful professional, 4) informed self help in that becoming. Evaluation by itself reveals only existing strengths and weakness. It neither enhances the one nor remediates the other.

Consequently, the final evaluation of a teacher is a small although extremely important part of a year's program of staff development, coaching, supervision, and evaluation. Evaluation measures the success of the teacher's and supervisor's efforts. Those efforts and their results are the most important part of the process. It is easier and financially more defensible to develop and cultivate professional effectiveness than it is to remove someone without it.

What is Effective Teaching?
You could hear as many answers to this question as there are teachers in

the world. You would get the same response to the question, "What is an effective meal?" Some would focus on their favorite foods, some on the setting and eating companions, some on the way the food was prepared, some on the service. All would agree, however, that an effective meal, day after day not just one occurrence, should contain those nutrients that promote energy and health and should be served in a way that people would consume those nutrients. Coffee and donuts as a regular diet would not qualify. Broiled chicken, a baked potato, and a crisp salad put in a blender and served in a bowl also would not qualify, despite the nutrients.

It is the same in education. Fascinating lessons in which the students participate, are interested but learn nothing, constitute the "junk foods" of education. If the objective is to get a sick, apathetic child to eat *anything,* serve anything. If the objective is to convince students that school is not a bore, do anything. But don't sedate yourself into thinking that, while necessary at that moment, either behavior constitutes good nutrition in health or learning.

Effective teaching has three essential elements (nutrients) about which the teacher must make *decisions:* content, learning behavior and teaching behavior. Note, no one can tell a teacher exactly what to do. We can tell teachers only what they must *know and think about* before the decision is made about what to do with *these* students in *this* situation.

Decisions in Teaching
1. Content

The general area of what to teach is decided by the legislature, school boards, curriculum guides and parents. Within this dictated arena, teachers must decide what to teach each group of students tomorrow morning.

The first decision in effective teaching is based on diagnosis of what each student now knows and is next ready to learn. In the past, this content decision has been made on the basis of astrology. A student's age may still (unfortunately) determine much of his/her learning expectations and experiences.

Instead of using astrology, educators now know they must use psychology which establishes much (not all) learning as incremental. Simpler concepts must be learned before more complex concepts are possible. Simpler skills must be accomplished before complex skills become attainable. Consequently, content decisions must be based on what a student now knows, or can do, and what next learning is indicated by that accomplishment. Effective teaching requires adequate knowledge of content being taught, plus the ability to do a content analysis in order to determine which simpler skills or learnings must be acquired in order to achieve more complex ones. Based on that task analysis, learnings must be sequenced for teaching and learners need to be diagnosed to determine their entry behavior in that sequence.

There is a second dimension to a teacher's content decision. What, within this content, has the most transfer (not just practical) value? Is one preparing students for "trivial pursuits" of names and dates or for a life of creativity, informed problem solving and satisfying decision making? Selection of the most important specifics, concepts, generalizations and processes is an essential part of the content decision.

2. Learning Behaviors

There is no one best way of learning for every student at all times in every situation. In each situation, the learning behavior should enable the student who puts forth effort to be successful. Teacher or student needs to decide whether reading the material is more *or* less appropriate than watching a film or listening to the teacher. Would "hands on" *or* observation be more facilitating, initially, for *these* students in *this* learning? Would examining and interpreting diagrams be a more effective beginning behavior *or* should the student experiment with creating his/her own diagrams? There is no one best way to learn for all students in all content areas!

The professional question becomes, "What input learning behavior will be most facilitating to the accomplishment of this objective for these learners?" If the objective is, "The learner will participate productively in a discussion," are they watching a good discussion and having productive behaviors labeled, or are they determining ways to make a discussion more productive? Observing and labeling would be more appropriate for students with little or unproductive experience in discussions, while determining more productive ways could be appropriate for students who are refining high level skills. If the objective is, "The learner will explain the causes of the American Revolution," are they hearing the information from the teacher, reading a section from a textbook on American History, or reading primary documents from both English and Colonial writers? Listening would be more appropriate for students with low reading skills because information is their first priority. Reading the textbook would be appropriate for students who need to become more skilled in selecting and summarizing information from printed materials. Comparing sources would be appropriate for students who are ready to consider conflicting perspectives and synthesize (create) a position that is built on their own evaluations but takes into account both perspectives.

A second aspect of learning behavior is focused on the question: "What output behavior must students manifest to validate achievement of the intended learning? This is the basis for the behavioral element of an instructional objective. What *perceivable* evidence is the student presenting so the teacher validates that learning has occurred? Gone are the days when a teacher "taught" and hoped the students learned, appreciated, understood, or *really* understood. Now, we seek objective, valid evidence that learning has occurred. Can the student *demonstrate* critical thinking, *make* satisfying decisions, *factor* quadratic equations, *write* a persuasive essay, *identify* the subject and predicate, read the selection and *answer* questions, *take turns*, *raise hands* before speaking, *argue both sides* of a question, *be considerate* of others? What perceivable student behavior will substantiate an answer of "yes!"?

3. Teaching Behavior

The third category of teaching decisions is focused on what a teacher does to increase the probability that each student learns. This involves deliberate utilization of principles of learning that research has verified will affect a student's motivation to learn, the rate and degree of that learning, and the retention and appropriate transfer of that learning to a situation which requires critical thinking, problem solving, creativity, and responsible, productive decision making.

The psychological generalizations from which teachers make decisions in these three categories (content, learning behavior, and teaching behavior) apply regardless of age, ethnicity, content, learning style, method of teaching, learning objective, or instructional organization. Those generalizations provide a pharmacy of alternatives from which a teacher selects to create a teaching/learning prescription which is implemented in classroom practice.

Professional skills for those who have the responsibility for coaching, supervising, or evaluating teachers are 1) ability to articulate what constitutes effective teaching, 2) ability to make informed judgments about when certain techniques and principles are or are not appropriate, 3) ability to script tape an episode of teaching then analyze that tape as a diagnosis of professional skills, plus 4) communication skills which result in a growth evoking conference.

This book will not present the first two essentials. This book will focus on the skills necessary for conducting that conference. It is presumed that before attempting to coach or supervise the observer knows the psychological principles that undergird effective teaching and can make informed judgements about what has been observed. This book will focus on those skills necessary for collecting information from an episode of teaching, analyzing that information, then preparing for and conducting a growth evoking instructional conference.

PROFESSIONALS GROW THROUGH STAFF DEVELOPMENT, SUPERVISION, AND EVALUATION APPRAISAL

Education, as medicine, is a decision making, action performance profession based on cognition. Cognition includes intuition; that highly operant but inarticulate knowledge which has the potential for eventually becoming articulated and, therefore, transmittable to others. Because both education and medicine deal with the complexity of humans, there are no absolutes. Consequently, both professions are relativistic and situational because it is impossible to control all the variables including that elusive variable of "human will," "mind," "spirit," or whatever you choose to call it.

An additional hallmark of both professions is that the finest professional this year will not be the finest professional in years hence unless that person continues to grow both personally and in the artistic incorporation of new knowledge into daily practice. While it is assumed that professionals in education acknowledge the responsibility for their own growth, the probability of that growth occurring is enhanced by planned, continuing staff development, coaching, supervision, and evaluative appraisal. Each of these activities has certain features in common. Each, however, contributes a different accelerant to professional gowth.

Staff Development

Staff development has as its purpose the steady escalation of increasingly effective teaching decisions and increasingly artistic and effective implementation of those decisions in practice. Staff development programs should supply research based propositional knowledge ("declarative knowledge") in cognitive psychology terms). Staff development also should assist in the translation of those psychological and educational propositions into procedural knowledge, the action pattern behavior of "how to do it," as well as into conditional knowledge, "when?" and "why, *then*, to do it?" An example of propositional knowledge is the propelling effect on students' learning of the teacher's use of an example from students' own lives which involves the students' long term and working memories. Another example of propositional knowledge would be the six critical attributes of an effective example. Then, staff development needs to contribute to a professional's procedural and conditional knowledge *with guided practice* in generating examples that qualify on all six attributes, plus practice in determining how and when the teacher should generate those examples and when to move to student generated examples. Neither action is right nor wrong in every situation.

Staff development may be conducted in large groups, small groups, or with an individual. Usually, it is more efficient to present propositions in larger groups (staff meetings or district meetings), refine procedures and conditions in smaller groups (department or grade level), and custom tailor to specific teaching situations with the individual involved. An effective staff development program enables teachers to anticipate and prepare for what might happen in the classroom to reflect afterwards on what did happen, to develop productive alternatives when indicated, and continually to add to their repertoire of skills. Research based theory becomes the springboard for these professional activities.

One of the most important "innovations" of the last quarter of this century is the realization, by Boards of Education and the public, that staff development should be a continuing budget item in every school district. Knowledge of cause-effect relationships in human learning is escalating at such a rate it is no longer possible to "keep up" with an occasional, voluntary, inservice meeting. Routing staff meetings plus inservice days are the only way educators can keep pace with knowledge and incorporate that knowledge in performance behavior.

Peer Coaching

Peer coaching can assist in staff development providing peers 1) are knowledgeable in the theory that undergirds practice, 2) have seen excellent examples of that theory in practice, 3) have worked on incorporating that theory in *their own* practice, 4) have had guidance and coaching in the skills necessary for observation of appropriateness and artistry, not mere presence of absence, of a teaching or learning behavior, and 5) have developed the skills of growth evoking communication of their perceptions to another professional. Merely freeing one teacher to observe another without adequate preparation is the most costly expenditure of staff development funds and, while it has the virtue of being the first time many have had the opportunity to watch another teach, it's potentially inefficient, individualized, questionable "instruction."

Many school districts are maximizing the gain from peer coaching by videotaping a teacher's lesson with that teacher's permission, sending students from several classes, with supervision, to an educational film or extended recess period and giving 5 to 10 teachers the opportunity to view the videotape, then observe and/or participate in peer coaching. Observational learning, watching another teacher practice, is one of our most powerful and most neglected modes of professional learning. Prior training for this activity should have occurred routinely in staff meetings where an anonymous teacher's lesson is observed and analyzed. The anonymity of the teacher removes from the analysis the emotional barriers of "one of us." Videotapes have the additional asset of "stop, replay, and look again" when needed.

Supervision

Prior staff development builds a foundation for effective coaching and supervision which has enhancing teaching excellence as its primary purpose. Coaching and supervision assist in the translation of knowledge gained from staff development into skilled professional practice. Coaching, supervision, and evaluative appraisal require the same skills of the observer but the purpose of the observation is completely different. *Neither purpose can be achieved by use of a check list! There is nothing that an excellent teacher always does or never does!* The observer is not looking for presence or absence of any behavior but is looking for evidence to support the appropriateness or inappropriateness of *that* behavior for *these* students in *this* lesson. To support the observation, a script tape (a running anecdotal record of what was actually said or done, not categorical summaries, must be made to be used as a data source for the subsequent instructional conference. The script tape becomes the diagnostic instrument from which teaching performance is reinforced, fine tuned, or remediated in subsequent professional communication between teacher and observer. The difference between supervision and peer coaching is that a supervisor has the *assigned* responsibility for productively affecting the performance of the teacher. The procedures and outcomes of supervision and skillful peer coaching can be exactly the same.

Coaching and supervision have two foci. One is the integrity of *what* is being taught: the content or process in the curricular area which is the intended learning outcome. The other focus is on the effectiveness and artistry of what the teacher is *doing* to teach that content or process and what the students are *doing* to learn it and to demonstrate they have learned: the pedagogy or science or instruction being employed by the teacher. Neither content nor pedagogy is more important. Both are needed to insure excellence. It does no good to teach exquisitely that which is not correct or worth learning. Conversely, superb educational outcomes are to no avail if they are not achieved. Consequently, coaching and supervision must focus on both content and pedagogy. The content supervisor must have discipline specific information and facility with task analysis, curricular sequence, and objectives (with high transfer potential), which are worthy of a student's time and effort. An excellent coach or supervisor in one discipline will have difficulty supervising *content* in a discipline in which s/he has little experience.

A coach or supervisor with expertise in pedagogy can supervise *teaching effectiveness* in any content area. While it is highly desirable that a supervisor or evaluator possess competency in both content and pedagogy, that is easier to achieve in elementary school and a more difficult feat with the complexity of content in high school. However, it is also less likely that

9

high school problems in teaching are content errors, therefore, it is essential that the high school coach, supervisor or evaluator possess appraisal excellence in pedagogy as that is invariant across all content areas.

Evaluation

Evaluative appraisal has as its objective the assignment, with substantiating data, of the professional to a category. The categories may be "satisfactory" or "not satisfactory" or they can range through any number of categories from "unacceptable" to "outstanding." Evaluative appraisal is employed when a decision must be made for employment, promotion, or salary increase. While the recommendation may be summarized by a quantified summary check list ("most of the time," "seldom"), the data to support that summary must exist in the form of many script tapes or video tapes plus instructional conferences which cover a period of time adequate to validate that the teacher's performance is consistent in that category, not just a "one time" valiant effort or catastrophe.

A valid final evaluation is supported by staff development (opportunity to learn), coaching and supervision (assistance in that learning), growth (demonstration of having taken advantage of opportunity and assistance), and final outcome (evidence of growth and enhanced, current, professional performance as a result of all the above).

Staff development, coaching, supervision, and evaluative appraisal all require that the person responsible for supplying those professional services use all the learning principles and techniques that have been taught in staff development and are expected of the teacher. It is so easy to say what should be done, so incredibly difficult to do it oneself. Evaluators have been lured into ineffectiveness by crash courses of a few days or check lists which mask the difficult of promoting, inspiring, supervising, and evaluating professional performance.

It is the experience of these writers that it takes about two years of practice *with coaching* to equip a coach, supervisor, or evaluator with those skills essential to working in a growth enabling way with a teacher. Those skills are: knowledge of an ability to use cause/effect principles of human learning; ability to describe and coach several modes of teaching; ability to script tape an episode of teaching, analyze that tape, label teaching decision and behaviors which resulted in productive student behavior, and generate alternatives for those behaviors which were not as productive as they could be.

Accompanying this analytic skill, the coach, supervisor, or evaluator must have the *teaching* skills to design and implement a conference which incorporates all of the enabling behaviors expected of the teacher: an instructional objective, monitoring and modifying that objective when indicated, input from observer and/or teacher, checking for understanding, and providing for guided/monitored practice. Only then will "them as can, teach, and them as *can*, help others increase teaching excellence."

SCRIPT TAPING: AN ESSENTIAL TOOL

The fundamental purpose of all supervision is to accelerate the professional growth of those who are supervised. Essential to growth is the identification of three types of teaching-learning behaviors: those that 1) contribute to productive performance of teacher and student; 2) consume precious time, energy, and materials, but contribute little to productive performance; and 3) have potential to interfere with productive performance. Once these behaviors are identified, they can be strengthened, eliminated or remediated. Consequently, we need to engage in efficient and effective coaching and supervisory procedures which, given realistic time constraints, can be used to accomplish the objective of accelerating professional growth.

The easiest way to identify specific, productive or non productive behaviors is by observing them. Final scores, whether in sports, tests, or evaluations, indicate whether you have a winner or a loser, but only observation can yield the information necessary to change a loser to a winner or make the winner even more accomplished. To be useful, observation must be valid, objective, and recorded. A recorded observation enables observer and performer to "play back" the performance so that salient cause-effect relationships can be identified.

Video and audio taping would seem to be ideal for recording coaching or supervisory observations. Taping obviously eliminates any observer bias and the tape can be played back over and over again. On the other hand, cameras are too unwieldy to move around easily in a classroom; sound can be lost if an individual turns away from the microphone; and the cause-effect sequence could be misinterpreted if, for instance, the mike or camera focuses only on the teacher and not on students on the other side of the room. Electronic taping equipment also is expensive and requires locking up when not in use.

Eventually, all teachers should have several opportunities to view themselves on videotape with the option of erasing the tape or reviewing it with someone. At a point when it is agreeable to the teacher, videotapes shared with others can become an important source for discussion and professional development provided the viewers have developed sophistication in analyzing teaching and giving productive feedback.

Script taping is an easy and efficient alternative to electronic taping. It is the process of capturing with pen and pad what happened in a observed segment of teaching so that cause-effect relationships subsequently can be articulated and examined.

The observer then can plan a specific, meaningful, instructional communication based on objective, accurate descriptions from the script tape rather than vague platitudes or faulty memory. Skimming the anecdotal notes, the observer can pick up specific examples from actual performance to give meaning to the discussion. "When you said, 'Be ready to give an example of _____ ,' and then waited, all students were alerted to the possibility of being called on but were given time to formulate and refine their answers." This precision eliminates vague statements such as "You gave students enough thinking time." Regardless of the focus of the instructional conference, data that bring validity to the interchange are easily available from the script tape.

The following is a sample of a script tape as recorded by an observer:

"Open p.43 I'm ask ver hd? Use mark find ans whn fnd sho me w/ sig who has lots pep. Every had mark on rt ans. Who can't see Mr. Sleeper (wrong ans) that rt if asked who see but can't see. Now just rt."

From this script the human recorder can play back:

"Open your book to page 43. I'm going to ask some very hard question. Use your marker to find the answer, show me you're ready with the signal (thumb up). Who had lots of pep? Everyone had the marker on the right answer. Who can't see Mr. Sleeper? (A girl gave a wrong answer.) That would be right if I asked who can see Mr. Sleeper, but I asked who can't see Mr. Sleeper? (Same child responds correctly.) Now you're just right!"

From analysis of this script tape, the observer can verify that the teacher was monitoring each student's information location skills by having students answer every question with a marker. Also, the teacher is to be commended for dignifying the student's incorrect answer (That would be right if I asked who *can* see Mr. Sleeper") and giving a prompt ("I asked who *can't* see Mr. Sleeper") to help the student answer correctly, thereby giving the student a success experience rather than "being wrong."

The purpose of a script tape is not to have a "court reporter" quality record of everything that is said or done, but to record enough to enable the observer to accurately "play back" the teaching episode. This record reveals teaching behaviors that had high probability of causing subsequent student learning or lack of it.

Meaning, in terms of teaching behaviors which had high probability of causing learning, becomes more probable in instructional conferences as a result of focusing on specific examples from actual teaching-learning performance. Meaning is the relationship between what is being learned and what a person already knows or has experienced. A teacher's understanding of the psychological generalizations undergirding effective instruction is increased when examples from the teacher's lesson are used to connect teaching behaviors to principles of learning.

The specificity of examples from a script tape also ensures that both observer and teacher are focused on the same instance of a particular teaching behavior in the lesson as they discuss its effect on students' learning. Without the specificity, the observer may be talking about one part of a lesson while the teacher assumes they are discussing another part. This miscommunication often has been verified in supervision workshops by a third person stopping the conference after an observer's non-specific reference and having each participant indicate the part of the lesson being discussed. Two different parts are an all too common occurrence. Use of specific quotes from the script tape can more nearly guarantee meaning as well as a common reference point because it identifies a particular part of the lesson so there is no misunderstanding of the teacher's and/or student's action being discussed.

Advantages of Script Taping

Script taping is a highly productive but the least expensive tool of the observer. It effectively produces growth-evoking records because:

1. It requires only paper and pencil.

2. It has extraordinary flexibility. The writer can focus quickly and monitor two or more areas simultaneously. Quick sweeps of the observer's eyes can pick up activities and responses from all parts of the room.

3. It provides easily accessible, temporally accurate accounts of what occurred from which cause-effect relationships can be observed or inferred.

4. It is unbiased and accurate when done correctly. Recorded by an inexperienced or unsophisticated observer, script tapes can be biased if the record shows only what the observer thought was important or worth recording.

5. It can be "played back" anywhere because, from the written record, the observer becomes the playback instrument. The fidelity of the reproduction, as with all recording, depends on the sensitivity of the recording instrument and the reproduction capacity of the playback instrument. A trained observer can produce high-quality performance in both recording and playback.

6. The optical scanning of the human eye and the dexterity of the hand in turning a page are the only time consumed in locating the part needed for discussion in the conference. Skilled observers often quickly "margin mark" salient parts when recording them, making their locations easy. All parts of the lesson are almost immediately accessible, something which is not possible with audio or video tape.

7. The cost of storage is only the price of a folder and file space. Frequently, only summary notes and recommendations are kept and the script tape is given to the teacher.

Script taping should become a required proficiency for any educator who has responsibility for improving the performance of another. It should be an essential element in pre-service training, coaching, supervision, and administration, and is a constant element in effective supervisory performance.

Script Taping Skills*

When an observer first learns script taping, there is excruciating interference from the traditional practice of only watching the lesson. Formerly, some people were taught that it was a mortal sin to write during an observation as it distressed the teacher. In the past this was true because the observer merely sat and smiled as long as instruction was going well. When there was concerned demeanor and writing on the part of the observer, it indicated that something was wrong and the teacher predictably became anxious.

Consequently, the beginning script tape not only feels s/he is missing important visual aspects of the lesson but that recording also has potential for generating teacher distress, something all of us wish to avoid. To resolve the first concern, the skilled script taper has learned when it is more important to look up and when to write. Eventually both are done at high speed. Script taping is a psychomotor skill like learning to drive. First responses are hesitating and awkward. Eventually one learns when to look in the side mirror, rear view mirror, at the street signs, at adjacent cars while at the same time never losing sight of the road and cars ahead as well as oncoming traffic.

It is interesting, and reassuring, to find that if observers see a video taped lesson with no sound or hear a video taped lesson with no picture, the latter gives much more information as to the quality of the lesson. Skilled drivers learn when to look where. Skilled observers learn whether, at any moment, looking or recording is more important. For example, should the teacher make a reinforcing or a scathing comment, the student's subsequent demeanor is important to observe and record or remember.

To reduce the problem of generating teacher distress, teachers should have prior experience in staff meetings with someone script taping videotapes of anonymous teachers, then reading back what occurred and demonstrating the benefits of script taping to subsequent discussion.

As in every psychomotor skill, continuing practice is important. Many educators learn to script tape then don't use the skill for a period of time only to learn that they have lost their "touch" and have to start over again. We recommend that beginners, or observers who have infrequent opportunities to script tape lessons, maintain and enhance their skills by script tap-

---

*"Script Taping Lessons" a half hour videotape is available from Special Purpose Films, 416 Rio del Mar, Aptos, CA 95003

16

ing a minute or two of television each evening. This will not ruin the newscast or show, but will develop and maintain the automaticity of a psychomotor skill that will deteriorate without practice.

Learning script taping should incorporate the same principles of effective practice that are enabling to automating any psychomotor skill: massed practice for fast learning, distributed practice for automaticity and retention.

For initial learning, practice in script taping should be conducted by using a videotape for recording one to five minutes of teaching. While it seems to be more difficult to script tape from a videotape than from "live" instruction, the videotape has the advantage of replay to verify the accuracy of capturing "what occurred" on the observer's paper. Script taping several short, 2-10 minute teaching episodes, then reading them back during an initial practice period., followed by similar practice periods during subsequent days will develop functional skill in script taping a lesson. An additional minute or two of practice each evening over several weeks, while watching TV will result in a very durable skill. Using that skill several times a week as the diagnostic device used for planning and conducting instructional conferences develops stable competence in script taping.

The only real problem is that beginners have to overcome their negative transfer from the ease of "just watching" to the rigor of recording objective data of what happened. It's hard for beginners to believe that the new skill can be learned in about two hours with motivated practice plus enduring the initial pain from change. During practice, observers should experiment with a variety of techniques so the develop their own most effective way of recording lessons.

Some tips that will help develop speed, accuracy, and comfort in script taping are:

1. Write in the middle 3/4 of the page leaving margins for labels and notes.

2. Develop a set of your own abbreviations which stimulate recall of words; vg = "very good," hp = "help", b & g = "boys and girls." Each observer develops an individual "brief hand" system which is functional for playback.

3. Record mostly nouns and verbs, your memory will fill in the connectors. For example, if the teacher says "You will learn how to estimate answers," you can play that back from "you ln est ans."

"Take out your English books and open to page 96" could be recorded as "Tk bk p. 96".

"Be thinking of the three most important events in the story" could be recorded "Be th 3 imp in story."

"Write a one paragraph summary of the events in the story" is recorded as "Wr. 1 sum events story."

4. If you get lost or too far behind, make a double line (=) and pick up the current actions. You will never get everything but neither will a video camera.

5. Some observers need a mark to separate what the teacher said or did from what the students said or did. Other observers don't need those markers. Indenting students' responses can supply a marker. Identifying with a straight line "l" as a symbol of a "T" for teacher and a squiggle for the "S" for students' responses can also provide an assist if you wish one.

6. Be careful that you don't fall into the trap of writing labels ("concern," "reinforcement") in the margins while recording. Labeling behaviors will distract you from recording subsequent actions and you may miss something important. One can't help metacognating on the artistry (or the opposite) of a teacher while recording, but formal labeling and analysis of the script tape will come later. Done concurrently it will take neutral energy that is needed for accurate recording. The best stance is that of an high fidelity recording machine.

Observers frequently wish they knew shorthand. Those who do usually record too much. A verbatim record is not needed, only enough to play back the essence of what teacher and student did or said.

7. Use parentheses to bracket non-verbal aciton. "Teacher moved over to John's desk and glared at him" could be recorded as (T-J desk glare).

8. Don't attempt to record what the teacher or students are reading. The selection can be secured if needed. The same is true of material on the board unless it needs to be discussed in the conference. You might record "Parts of plants" and "Plants make their own food through photosynthesis" to help the teacher develop the parallel structure of "Parts of plants" and "Functions of plants."

9. If the student answers the teacher's question correctly, record the question and draw a line (----). If the answer is incorrect, record the answer. You will need the incorrect answer to help the teacher learn to rephrase the question or develop ways of prompting the correct answer from the same student.

10. Prior or subsequent to the observation, identify your script tape by the name of the teacher, date, subject, time, etc.

11. Some observers find it helpful to diagram the classroom before the lesson begins—particularly the teacher's and students' positions. If you don't know students' names, you can always locate them after the lesson. The diagram might help you recall areas where students were working productively/ non-productively, couldn't see, were easily distracted, etc. Diagramming is done only if it seems relevant. It is not a routine procedure.

12. The best position from which to observe is one where you can see the teacher, the students, and the board/screen. Try a side near the front. Do not sit where you might become a distractor to the class. You may need to sit wherever you find an empty place.

13. At times, it may be necessary just to observe how students are working, how one particular student is reacting, or just rest your hand. If you to do this, indicate with double lines (=) on your tape that the lesson continued while you were not script taping. This may help you remember something which occurred while you were not recording.

14. You may wish periodically to record the time to indicate the length of different sections of the lesson. Again, this is *not* a routine procedure but is done only if it seems relevant to the lesson.

15. When describing non-verbal behavior, record what the student(s) *did*. "Johnny stared out the window" is a record while "Johnny looked bored" is an interpretation.

16. Do not become involved in the lesson. If the students approach you with questions, explain that they need to seek help elsewhere. Your job is to script tape what is happening during the lesson. (Students should already know this)

Do not try to learn what the students are learning no matter how tempting is that learning. Your job is recording. You can learn the content later if you wish.

To summarize, the ability to script tape is an *essential,* enabling behavior for a coach or supervisor. It can be learned in about two hours and automated by short, frequent practice periods.

LET'S ELIMINATE THAT PRE-OBSERVATION CONFERENCE

The pre-observation conference emerged a quarter of a century ago when observers did not possess current skills in observing and analyzing a lesson. Consequently, it became accepted as "standard practice" and continued when, frequently, it no longer is necessary for an effective observation/conference process which enhances teaching effectiveness.

In the past, supervisors made infrequent classroom visits and were not trained in instructional or curriculum theory. Also, current research in cause-effect relationships between teaching and learning was not available.

Availability of practical, research based instructional theory, plus training in observation/conference skills, plus ongoing practice in using them, eliminates the need to routinely include a pre-observation conference for every observation. Effective supervisors visit classrooms frequently for short informal or formal observations rather than for the outdated practice of only once or twice a year to complete an evaluation form.

Teaching skills that accelerate learning, peer coaching, and the observation/conference process are becoming increasingly routine topics of discussion for administrative training and staff development activities as well as for faculty meetings. As a result, common vocabulary, professional knowledge, and expectations are developed. Changing patterns of more frequent classroom observations and communication about the skills of teaching eliminate the need for a routine pre-observation conference.

Staff meetings to discuss the observation/conference procedure are essential in a situation which involves a change from previous "once or twice a year" procedures. Teachers need to view several videotapes of unknown teachers and hear an analysis from a script tape so they understand that the process is analytical, not critical. This should reassure those teachers who lack confidence in the observer's ability to know what is "going on". Further reassurance occurs each time they are observed and receive growth evoking feedback.

Occasionally, a pre-conference may be the best way to build rapport with a particular teacher or to deal with questions that might not be asked in a group meeting.

When students are having unexpected difficulty or when a teacher is working with unfamiliar content, a *planning* conference before the lesson can be helpful. It enables the observer to assist with professional tasks such as content analysis, diagnosis, lesson design, grouping, and follow up activities. These professional skills should have been introduced and practiced at previous staff meetings so they can be custom tailored and collaboratively applied to the ensuing lesson.

Today, with our knowledge of cause-effect relationships between teaching and learning, plus the now articulated functions of increasing teaching effectiveness through formative evaluation, we are ready to consider discarding the time consuming activity of the pre-observation conference which in most cases has outlived its usefulness.

Elimination of the pre-observation conference is supported by the following assumptions:

1. *Teachers should know from the beginning of the year that the purpose of observation is to promote constantly escalating instructional effectiveness.* An observer's stance is analytical, not critical. Inservice or staff meetings where cause-effect relationships in teaching and learning are discussed, films of teaching are analyzed with productive teaching behaviors identified, labeled, and the research which would support them is cited, provide a more efficient and effective introduction to observation then can be accomplished in a pre-observational conference.

2. *Trust and rapport result from what happens in the post observational conference.* When a teacher finds that the observer understands the tremendous complexity of successful teaching, seeks the teacher's reasons for actions rather than proceeding on unfounded assumptions, appreciates and identifies productive teacher skills, refrains from imposing the observer's own style on the teacher and enables that teacher to continue to grow in teaching effectiveness, that observer will be welcomed back to that teacher's classroom.

No amount of skill in building rapport before the observation will compensate for an unsuccessful post conference. Therefore, time is better spent after an observation in building the belief that observation and feedback are facilitating to the development of increased teaching excellence. Trust and commitment are outcome variables, not something with which you start.

3. *An observation requires interpretation of each part of a lesson in relation to proceeding and subsequent parts, each behavior in terms of prior and subsequent behaviors.* Therefore, while the teacher and observer may be interested in the development or polishing of a particular skill or technique, the observer's focus must also include all other aspects of a teacher's performance. Viewed in isolation, no technique can be interpreted as productive or destructive. *There are no absolutes in teaching.* Consequently, while there may be a brief, advance agreement to focus particularly on and discuss in depth a certain skill, that cannot be done in isolation from all else that occurs. There also exists the danger that when a teacher knows that the observer is watching for a certain technique, that technique will be used to excess. Consequently, the observer will see or hear a lot of what possibly shouldn't be there.

4. *The pre-observation conference can build bias in both teacher and observer.* Having already told the observer what was going to happen often causes the teacher to feel s/he should continue to proceed in that direction even when data emerging from students indicate that changes should be made. A typical comment by teachers is, "I realized when I got into the lesson that many students had forgotten from last week, but I told the principal that I was going to work with mixed franctions so I went ahead with it."

Bias also can be created in the mind of the observer. Schema research has shown that anticipating what is going to happen can result in "seeing it happen" to the exclusion of what really is happening. The author suspects that observers previously depended on the pre-observation conference for a "crutch" to make up for their lack of training in determining and capturing in script tapes what really is happening in teaching-learning episodes. Acquiring the skills necessary to effective observation and interpretation can eliminate the need for such a "crutch."

5. *The time required for the pre-observation conference can reduce by one third the time available for observations and conferences..* Three observations and conferences can be conducted in the same amount of time required for two when the pre-observation conference is eliminated. Increasing the time available for coaching and supervisory assistance is an important achievement when it can be accomplished by eliminating an unnecessary procedure.

A *planning conference* is not considered to be a pre-observation conference. A planning conference is one in which observer and teacher collaborate in the design of a lesson which the teacher subsequently teaches, but responsibility for successful learning outcomes is jointly shared with the observer. Planning conferences are excellent opportunities for the teacher to experience the stimulation of team planning. The observer will experience responsibility for the "it ain't all that easy" results: a responsibility teachers experience daily in planning, teaching, and evaluating countless lessons.

The interaction of professionals in terms of clinical practice with particular students and specific content is a growth promoting activity for both observer and teacher which is long overdue in education. In the past, platitudes, vague generalizations, and admonitions have dominated the plans for and the results from observation of teachers. Now, with current observational and analytic skills, we can focus on specific cause-effect relationships in teaching and learning. Through commonly shared experiences, coaching for increasingly effective and artistic teaching can become a reality.

Let's use the time of the pre-observation conference, a routine practice no longer needed, to focus our energies on becoming increasingly skilled and productive with what we now know about observation, subsequent analysis and instructional conferences to accelerate teaching excellence.

THE COACHING OR SUPERVISORY CONFERENCE:
A COMMUNICATIVE INTERACTION FOR INCREASING
INSTRUCTIONAL EFFECTIVENESS

With a feeling of dread, many teachers, principals, and supervisors face that encounter labeled "the coaching/supervisory conference" which is suspected as being an evaluation conference. To eliminate the discomfort, valuable time is consumed by mutually laudatory, social interaction. "You're a fine teacher. Your lesson was outstanding in every category. Tell me about your summer vacation plans." "Thank you, you're a wonderful help. We're thinking of a motor trip to Canada."

You will recognize a situation in which you may have had a participatory role, either as a teacher, coach, principal, or supervisor.

Why is this potentially productive situation frequently sterile? Why aren't more educational benefits reaped from precious and costly conference time, often taking place before and after school when other tasks need doing? The answer is the same as the answer to the question, "Why didn't we land on the moon earlier?"

"We didn't know how to do it successfully."

This is not to deny that many coaches and supervisors intuitively have been doing an effective job of conferencing with teachers. Intuition, however, is an addition to not a substitute for professional competence. We now have the knowledge, and the professional vocabulary needed to transmit that knowledge, to develop competence in producing productive results from instructional conferencing. Potentially positive educational outcomes become probable as a result of the coach's or supervisor's instructional excellence.

Scrutiny of the many difference purposes and outcomes of that "catch all" category of coaching or supervisory conferences has revealed five important generalizations.

1. Coaching and supervisory conferences have three funcltions. The most important function is promotion of a teacher's professional growth in effective instruction: the business of the school. By increasing effectiveness and artistry in instruction, student learning is accelerated. A conference designed to improve instructional excellence has an objective: "The teacher will subsequently demonstrate increased instructional effectiveness and artistry."

A second function of a conference is provision of objective evidence rather than subjective impressions of that teacher's professional growth from previous inservice, observations, and conferences in subsequent performance. Ranking a teacher on a continuum of excellence, however, is no part of coaching or supervisory conferences.

A third function is to encourage teachers to seek continuing professional growth as a result of feedback from observations and conferences.

2. A coaching or supervisory conference, as a lesson, should have a major objective. In a conference, most of the time and communication should be directed to one major objective. This is not to say that there may not be other related objectives, but no objective antithetical to the primary purpose should be included. Making a weak teacher feel that, with increased effort, successful teaching is possible and in the same conference attempting to convince him/her that (s)he should choose a different occupation, could both be valid objectives but not in the same conference. Convincing an inexperienced teacher that (s)he is improving while identifying a major deficit are antithetical objectives.

3. The same principles of learning apply to teachers as apply to students. If, in the conference, the coach or supervisor uses learning principles appropriately, the teacher's learning will be increased. If learning principles are abused or ignored, teacher growth is less probable. Unless the supervisor or coach is aware of those principles and skilled in their use with adults, (s)he is apt to violate the very principles the teacher is being asked to learn and use. For example, one author and a principal observed a teacher work with a group of students in an extremely negative manner, criticizing, pointing out errors, never commending correct responses or productive behavior. In the subsequent principal-teacher conference, the principal opened with, "Do you realize Mrs. _____ That you never said one positive thing in that whole lesson? All you did was emphasize what was wrong—." The conference continued in the same vein with the principal completely unaware that she was modeling the very behavior she was attempting to change in the teacher.

4. Teaching is a performance behavior and can best be enhanced through analysis of that performance. In order to secure the information essential to a successful instructional conference, the supervisor must have observed a segment of teaching. The entire lesson need not be observed. (In the same way, a sports team can be improved only by analyzing players'·performance. Frequently what was observed in only a few plays will determine the focus of the next practice.) Observation time can vary from a few minutes to a half-hour. The writers' experience is that a 10-20 minute observation yields at least an hour of potential conference material. The observer must possess the skill of analyzing what is seen and be able to interpret behaviors observed in terms of those which promoted learning, those which used precious time and energy yet contributed little to learning, and those which used precious time and energy yet contributed little to learning, and those which, albeit unintentionally, actually interfered with learning. Then, that interpretation must be supported by objective data from a script tape of that teaching episode and from research based knowledge of instruction. The ability to script tape and to analyze an episode of teaching is a learned skill which, only recently, has been made predictably achievable by those who invest the time to acquire it.

5. Analysis of performance is essential to professional growth. The professional skill of analyzing instruction from a script tape is a far cry from former useless global platitudes of "loves children," "dedicated," "committed," "nice voice and manner," which in the past have obscured instructional strengths and deficits. Current platitudes include "too much teacher talk," "more hands on activities," "more high level questions," or "discovery learning is best," any of which may or may not be appropriate in a given situation. With the ability to script tape and analyze an observed episode of instruction as a "given" (would it were "given," it results only from learning effort plus rigorous, *coached* practice), the observer needs to make an initial diagnostic judgment as to which of five possible discussions should become the primary purpose of the coaching or supervisory conference. In the following descriptions, isolation of each discussion is only for the purpose of clarity. Discussions are labeled on the basis of whether identification of the part of the lesson being discussed is initiated by the observer or by the teacher. Conference discussions are not mutually exclusive, but each will generate different feelings and potential learnings on the part of the teacher. The artist in instructional conferencing will "mix and match" as appropriate to teacher and situation.

It is unfortunate that in their initial development these discussions were given letters of the alphabet for quick identification, unmindful of the fact that "A" "B" "C" "D" already had the meaning of grades for educators. Such meanings were not intended! They should have been labeled differently but now the original labels are is such widespread use that to change would only increase confusion.

Type A Instructional Conference Discussion

Purpose: To identify, label and explain the teacher's effective instructional behaviors, citing from the script tape what the teacher did that had high probability of resulting in what students did and giving the reasons for that behavior's effectiveness. The teacher then knows 1) what (s)he did, 2) why it worked, and 3) the generalization which causes him/her to use it or not use it in the future.

Objective: At the end of the conference (not in some nebulous future) the teacher will label his/her teaching decisions and behaviors that promoted learning and state reasons why, in this situation, they were effective.

To achieve this objective, the observer selects and labels those aspects of instruction that were effective so those decisions and behaviors are brought to the conscious awareness of the teacher who then has an opportunity to learn research based reasons for their effectiveness and the learning situations in which their future use is indicated.

Example: "When you walked to John's desk when he wasn't listening, he stopped looking out of the window and seemed to be paying attention. You were raising his level of concern. Research has indicated that people are more obedient when the authority figure is close. That's what happens to us when we see the police car in the rear view mirror. Then, your using John's name in an example about his being a good ball player not only built his self-esteem and caused him to listen, but bonded his interest in athletics with your lesson on sentence patterns so his positive feelings about athletics could "rub off" on grammar. You were causing interest in self and athletics to transfer to sentence patterns. You used three excellent instructional techniques. Physical closeness, use of the student's name in a meaningful example, and pairing the student's interest with academic content."

A sophisticated teacher, may be asked to supply the reasons for the decision. "When you moved to John's desk and talked about his being an excellent ball player, he immediately tuned in to the lesson. Do you know why that worked so well?" (The observer needs to be able to supply the generalization if the teacher cannot.)

With a Type A discussion, the teacher is given the opportunity to change what might have been intuitive behavior to purposeful instruction. Knowing why something worked, enables the teacher to make more deliberate professional decisions in the future. As a result, that teacher will value competent and supportive coaching or supervision.

In the conference, the observer must rely on professional judgment to determine whether to explain why a teaching behavior was effective or whether, through questions, to encourage teacher's self analysis.

Sample statements which identify successful practice:

"You were disciplining with dignity when you used Mary's name in that example about earning money. You made her look good but also alerted her to the need for

28

paying attention. Use of a student's name causes that student to listen. I suspect she knew you were doing it on purpose to get her to stop talking to her friend. She paid attention after that."

"Your change of objective was certainly effective. What alerted you to the fact that a change was needed?"

"Rephrasing your question enabled Tom to give the correct answer. What were you thinking when that occurred?"

"When you _____, students did _____. What principle of learning were you successfully using?"

For a first conference, or with apprehensive or defensive teachers, Type A discussions may be the sole objective of a productive instructional conference. The teacher's effective behaviors will be brought to a conscious level, so that by learning why and under what conditions they are effective, those behaviors can be used deliberately and appropriately in the future. Also, because there are not the typically anticipated negative overtones in the conference (what did I do wrong?), the teacher is more apt to welcome, engage in and request subsequent conferences.

Type B Instructional Conference Discussion

Purpose: To stimulate the development of a repertoire of effective teaching responses rather than the teacher's being limited to a few, frequently used.

Objective: The teacher, in collaboration with the observer, will generate alternatives to behaviors which were effective in the observed lesson but might be less effective or ineffective in future situations, as well as identify the conditions which suggest use of those alternatives in the future.

All of us tend to become habitual in our responses and, as a result, we may close off the development of a repertoire of new responses from which we can deliberately select the one which, in our judgment, holds the greatest promise in a specific situation. Teachers can become "set" in their patterns of presentation, discipline, homework, or practice and lose adaptability in their teaching. Type B Conference discussions are designed to break this encapsulation and create new options.

Example: "Standing by Bill's desk and using his name in a complimentary example was effective. With most students that will work. What are some things you might try if it didn't work?"

With a Type B Conference discussion, teachers are encouraged to gener-

29

ate alternatives which fit their particular style. At times, the observer might augment those alternatives by suggesting additional strategies so teachers have the opportunity to consider options which they may not have known about or considered. Observers, however, should avoid "what I would do" statements. Alternatives should be tailored to the teacher's personality and style as well as to the subject matter and the students.

Sample statements which increase a teacher's repertoire of skill:

"It really worked when you used Mary's name. Most of the time that will remind a student to listen. Let's develop some things you might do in the few cases where use of a student's name doesn't work."

"Your reinforcing Tom for his excellent thinking made him swell with pride and contribute more ideas. Most of the time we reinforce excellent thinking. Under what circumstances might you not reinforce a perceptive statement from a student?"

"Your use of the film certainly made the experience vivid for the students. How might you accomplish that intensity when no film is available?" (The observer needs to be prepared to make realistic suggestions.)

"Your examples were effective in connecting the new word with what the students already knew. If they hadn't learned so quickly and you needed additional examples, what might they be?"

Note that Type A and B discussions focus only on effective teaching; something singularly neglected in many previous conferences. Professional growth with A and B discussions results from the teacher knowing what made an action effective and from identifying and considering other potentially effective techniques along with conditions under which their use is or is not indicated in future situations.

Type C Instructional Conference Discussion

Purpose:	To encourage teachers to 1) do self analysis to identify those parts of a teaching episode with which they were, or were not, satisfied so that, 2) in collaboration with the observer, satisfying outcomes are enhanced in the future or 3) strategies are developed for reducing or eliminating unsatisfying outcomes.
Objective:	The teacher will identify the reasons for satisfactory outcomes and develop potential solutions to unsatisfactory aspects of the lesson.
Example:	Teacher: "The students were really interested in the lesson because I related it to them, however, I assumed they would remember the older material. I was disappointed to see how much of it they had forgotten." Observer: "It's not unusual that we assume students remember and

they don't. What might be done to anticipate and deal with that situation?"

While the teacher is given the first opportunity to suggest solutions, it is the obligation of the observer to also pose possible solutions (or to acknowledge that (s)he can't think of any). Instructional conferencing is not a spectator sport.

Example: "Sometimes a quick verbal or signaled check to see if students remember the process needed will not only help them recall it, but alert you if they don't. You also might do one example together on the chalkboard. That can serve as a warm-up and a reminder before you move on to new material. Other possibilities might be, 'Think of the steps in the process, raise your hand when you're ready to say them' or 'Be ready to summarize what you already know about _____.' If they've forgotten, you can reteach right then, when it's needed."

Sample statements which help a teacher analyze a lesson and identify the cause of student behavior which the teacher did or did not want:

"You're a very sophisticated teacher. How would you analyze that lesson?"

"What parts of the lesson went just the way you hoped they would? Are there any parts you would modify?"

Was there anything in that lesson you hadn't anticipated?"

"Were there any surprises in the lesson?" "Do you have any clues as to what triggered the giggling?" (in response to a teacher's concern).

"If you taught that lesson to a new group tomorrow, what parts would you be sure to repeat? Is there anything you would change?"

"What advice would you give a teacher who was going to teach that same content?"

"Help me know what answers you wanted from the students and let's figure out ways to get them." (in response to a teacher's concern about incorrect answers).

In a Type C discussion, the observer is active in helping the teacher become increasingly specific in identifying cause-effect relationships between teaching and learning, giving that teaching behavior the appropriate label and the generalization which supports its use in future situations. Because of these intellectual demands on the teacher in a Type C discussion and the fact that the observer may have to discuss a part of the lesson not anticipated when planning the conference, professional sophistication is necessary for both participants.

Note that with Type A, B, and C Conference discussions, not one single negative note has been introduced by the observer, yet each conference has tremendous potential for teacher growth.

Type D Instructional Conference Discussion

Purpose: To identify and label those aspects of teaching about which the observer has questions and which may not have been evident to the teacher. Should it be indicated, teacher and/or observer identify behaviors which might substitute for behaviors determined to be not as effective as desired.

Objective: The teacher will supply the reason for the questioned behavior or select, from alternatives, a teaching behavior which is potentially more productive.

It is important to note that this is the most commonly perceived objective of an instructional conference, yet it is only *one* of five possibilities for conferences that promote teacher growth. It is the only one that has potential, *but not the necessity,* for injecting a negative note in supervisory communication. When done skillfully, it is perceived by the teacher as helpful, not critical. When done poorly, the results are always disappointing and usually disastrous.

Example: Sometimes it's appropriate to have a student work on the board while others watch. When Blanche was doing the long division problem, the others couldn't see because she was standing in front of it. It took her so long that the class stopped watching and started talking. One way to avoid this is to have several students at the board working while the rest do the problem on paper and you circulate and give help to those whom you predict will need it. Another way is for you or a student to start a problem, then pass the chalk to another student who does a short amount and passes the chalk to another student. It's more like a game and keeps the group alert and following the process. You also can use this as a warm up activity or when they need a change of pace. However, at the beginning when they are working to understand the problem, it's better for you to demonstrate the process, labeling what you are thinking and doing so everyone can see and hear.

Type D discussions can be professionally stimulating. It is a positive experience to have perplexing instructional situations become understandable through analysis and interpretation by observer and teacher. One of the authors had the experience of having an incomprehensible (to her) lack of teaching success explained by an observer to be the result of an inadvertent teaching miscue at a critical point in the lesson. Finding out what caused the trouble was the only information needed to eliminate the problem. With a Type D discussion the observer has major, and sometimes the sole responsibility for identifying cause-effect relationships between teaching and learning, and for generating alternative teaching behaviors which might be more productive.

Type D discussions can be growth evoking only if they are delivered by an observer who has sensitivity to teacher and situation, knows learning principles, knows the process of teaching, and who has been trained to bridge the gap between theory and practice. Again, we should emphasize that this analytic skill can be learned by most educators who are willing to invest the effort and time. It takes approximately 60 hours to achieve beginning knowledge. Much more time is required to transfer that knowledge into judgment and wisdom.

Sample statements which encourage a teacher to reflect on a part about which the observer has questions:

"You had reasons for _____. Will you help me know what they are?" (Learn teacher's rationale.)

"Were you aware that _____?" or "Did you notice _____?" (Teacher awareness.)

"How does this incident relate to students' previous behavior? Is it typical? Is there a class rule or procedure that would handle it?" (determining context of incident.)

"You obviously did not want students to shout out answers. Let's develop some way to alert them to the expectation that they raise their hands." (Generate solutions.)

"The students were having difficulty with _____. Let's task analyze your objective to discover where they need help." (Diagnostic assistance.)

"The students by their lack of responses to your questions and suggestions, expressed lack of involvement, but for the life of me I can't think of ways of making it interesting. Let's both work on it and see if we can come up with something." (Diagnostic assistance.)

"Our school district policy prohibits the use of candy as a motivator. Let's develop some alternate ways to start them working that are comfortable for you." (Alternate solutions.)

"I can certainly understand why you blew up. I'd have been tempted to do the same thing. Let's look at some strategies which might avert that situation in the future and ways to deal with it when, in spite of your efforts, it occurs. (Alternate strategies.)

Rarely should a teacher experience only D discussion. However, when Type A,C, and C Conference Discussions produce little or no instructional improvement, it is a Type D discussion that communicates the data which confirm teaching performance as unsatisfactory; analytic and research based data yielded by sophisticated observation which will, if eventually necessary, hold up in court.

Type X Instructional Conference Discussion

Purpose: To promote continuing growth of excellent teachers.

Objective: The teacher will select next steps in enhancing his/her own professional excellence.

We have learned to challenge gifted students in order to encourage their continuing growth, but often our gifted teachers are left to provide their own stimulation or to become bored and atrophy. Countless principals have remarked, "I don't have to worry about _____, (s)he's an excellent teacher." By not contributing to such teachers' continuing growth, coaches and supervisors are neglecting those teachers who are education's more powerful resource. A Type X (for excellent!) discussion is designed to encourage growth beyond that which will occur as a result of only observation feedback.

A Type X conference results from several previous conferences in which the teacher consistently and skillfully analyzes his/her own lessons and needs little feedback from an observer. The quality of teaching is consistently effective so new, more advanced professional skills are ready to be acquired.

Examples: "You consistently make artistic and effective decisions in teaching. Would you be willing to put a similar lesson on videotape so we can use it to help new teachers?" (Analyzing one's own teaching and providing inservice for others.)

"Your ability to draw out shy students is remarkable. Will you go over your lesson with me to help develop written generalizations others can use to know when to stretch students and when to back off?" (Identifying and articulating reasons for professional behaviors.)

"You have the skills to pilot this new program so we can identify its strengths and weaknesses before we consider adoption for the whole school." (Developing and demonstrating new curriculum.)

"Your skills are such that others should be learning from

you. Would you be willing to take a student teacher? You will grow from explaining why you do what you do, and the student teacher will have the advantage of not only learning about effective teaching, but seeing it modeled daily." (Supervising beginning teachers.)

The reader may be raising the question, "Isn't teaching excellent enough? Why should we be asking for more?" The question is the same as, "Why don't we just let the gifted learner do an excellent job at grade level? Why do we stretch thinking and performance? The answer to both questions is: Growth is invigorating and self-actualizing. We do students and teachers a disservice if we do not permit, encourage, and demand that growth. Artistry in supervision exists in the timing, designing, and supporting of professional growth activities so they are welcomed and become satisfying rather than resented as "one more thing."

Sample statements which encourage an excellent teacher to continue growing:

"You have made an art of teaching. What will be your next direction of growth?"

"Using excellent teaching techniques has become second nature to you. What new skills are you interested in acquiring?"

"Your teaching is excellent. Video tapes of your technique and artistry would be very useful in training new teachers. Let's make several this year so you can select the ones you are willing to let us use.

"Would you be willing to conduct a staff meeting to share your knowledge about making math meaningful?" Asking a question implies you are willing to accept "No" as an answer. Usually, a choice by the teacher is appropriate. Sometimes the teacher needs to be encouraged in growth without the "temptation" of a choice.

"Either next year or the one after that you should change grade levels so you broaden your experience and continue to develop professional excellence. You decide when you want to do it."

"You have the ability to be a _____. Let's arrange some experiences to prepare you for that assignment."

Sometimes it is difficult to develop "next steps" for the outstanding teacher, but the teacher's identification of effective teaching actions, labeling the cues which suggested each behavior, then collaboration in writing that material for other's use has the growth evoking potential of bringing professional decisions to a conscious level of articulation for sophisticated analysis and transmission to others.

For the gifted teacher who has just achieved a new competence and has earned a respite, if a conference is required a Type C Discussion with the teacher assuming the responsibility for identifying effective teaching actions and labeling the cues which suggested each behavior has growth evoking potential and will meet the district requirement.

The five types of instructional conference discussions are not mutually exclusive, and the sophisticated observer is encouraged to "mix and match." A,B,C, and X conference discussions are totally positive and D has the potential for being positive or negative depending on the purpose or the conferencing skills of the observer. No conference will be successful unless the observer possesses the professional skills of sensitivity to teacher and to situation: checking the teacher's reasons for what happened, analyzing and labeling instruction in terms of cause-effect relationships, and generating solutions to instructional problems.

Beyond analytic skills, there exist communication skills:* those teaching skills that enable the observer to achieve the objective of an instructional conference. No instructional conference will be successful unless the observer utilizes and models those same cause-effect relationships which are so effective in teacher-student interaction.

It is not important that observer or teacher be able to categorize conference interaction specifically as A,B,C,D, or X. What is important is that the exchange of information results in satisfying and enhanced instructional effectiveness. As teachers become more aware of and comfortable with the professional exchange of ideas in an instructional conference, they will assume increasing responsibility for the productivity of these exchanges.

At the end of the year, the evaluative conference should be a summation of what has been discussed and the growth which resulted from the year's many instructional conferences. Information given and conclusions reached in an evaluative conference should come as no surprise to the teacher because the evidence to support conclusions has been made available and labeled in previous instructional conferences. As a result, the evaluative conference has high probability for being perceived as fair, just, and supportable by objective evidence rather than subjective opinion. A summative evaluation conference is the culmination to the year's diagnostic, prescriptive, collaborative work with coaches, supervisors, and administrators who assume shared responsibility with the teacher for continuous professional growth.

This growth will occur more rapidly when the teacher's effort to improve is rewarded, and any gaps or deficiencies are accepted as areas of next growth rather than a teacher being penalized because s/he doesn't im-

---

*Parent-Teacher Conferencing, *TIP Publications, P.O. Box 514, El Segundo, CA 90245*

mediately become the perfect model of the ideal educator. When coaches and supervisors work with teachers as teachers are expected to work with students, education will become a more successful, growth evoking profession.

PLANNING, CONDUCTING, AND EVALUATING CONFERENCES

All instructional conferences have "increased excellence in future teaching" as their goal. The teacher will never teach that same lesson to these same students again. Consequently, the purpose of the conference is not to compliment the teacher or repair that lesson but to use that lesson as a data source to reinforce and extend effective teaching or to remediate less effective teaching so, in either case, positive transfer of professional skills to that teacher's future lessons will become more probable. Observers must have skills to:

Observe and Script Tape the Lesson

It is assumed 1) that an observation will precede any instructional conference (unless teacher and observer are only planning for a subsequent lesson) and 2) that a script tape (running anecdotal record of what teacher and students said and did) will be made during the observation to be used as the primary data source for the conference.

Using a checklist to determine whether a teacher did or did not do something is an unproductive means for recording data to be used in an instructional conference because it is not a temporal record of cause-effect relationships or of the context in which the behavior occurred. Presence or absence of any teaching behavior is not the issue. The question is whether the behavior observed was appropriate or inappropriate for those students in that situation at that time.

Analyze the Script Tape

As soon as possible after the observation, the observer should reread the script tape, filling in from memory any abbreviations or unclearly recorded passages. The longer the time between script taping and reviewing of the tape; the less accurate and detailed will be the memory.

Using the script tape as data, the observer identifies the teacher's instructional objective, then analyzes the script tape in terms of that objective, interpreting the cause-effect relationship between what the teacher did and the perceived (not predicted!) results with students. The purpose of analyzing the script tape is to select potential discussion topics for the conference. Significant teacher and student behaviors should be labeled in the margins of the script tape to mark those sections which have potential relevance for the conference. Identification can be done by marks (?,!,*,---) or colored pen. Sections identified should be labeled with the professional term that will be used to describe and communicate learning concepts and generalizations in the conference ("anticipatory set", "massed practice," "extinction," "meaning," "transfer," etc.). Labeling builds a common vocabulary which can be used to discuss productive or questioned instructional strategies and techniques more effectively because those labels will have the same meaning for teacher and observer. The part of the script tape that will illustrate and support that label or generalization should be marked so it is readily located.

Examples

Script Tape:	"Sup did 10 prob all c ex 1 mistake wh fast wk% assig done corret."
Translation:	"Suppose you did 10 problems and you got all of them correct except one where you made a mistake because you were working too fast. What percentage of your assignment have you have done correctly?"
Label:	Meaning
Script Tape:	"Say self how expl mg. invariant. Ready when I call. Min to think."
Translation:	"Say to yourself how you would explain the meaning of 'invariant' and be ready to give your explanation when I call on you. I'll give you a minute to think."
Label:	Convert participation, Raising concern
Script Tape:	"Very percept ans. U took time consider E & C pt. of view.
Translation:	"That was a very perceptive answer. You took the time to consider England's and the Colonists' point of view."
Label:	Knowledge of Results, Positive reinforcement
Script Tape:	"Wh caused prob (S yell)"
Translation:	"Who caused the problem? Students yell answers."
Label:	Set, Expectations
Script Tape:	"Bill wh ans 5 (wrong) who help B."
Translation:	"Bill, what is the answer to no. 5?" Bill gave the wrong answer and teacher asked, "Who can help Bill?"
Label:	Concern, Dignify Error

Note that teacher behaviors frequently have more than one label as they may serve several functions. It is not important that the observer think of every possible label but select the label and function that would provide the most helpful insights for that teacher's planning and performance in a future, similar situation.

From that labeling, the observer generates two categories of potential discussion topics. The observer labels and groups evidence of 1) behaviors that were perceived as enabling to learning, and 2) behaviors about which the observer has questions. Both categories need marked evidence in the script tape to support their discussion in the conference. Many observers find it helpful to create a summary sheet listing behaviors which occurred throughout the lesson which are evidence of use or abuse of a specific learning principle. Selection of which behaviors to address in the conference is made from those lists. Remember the observer cannot determine that behaviors were "wrong" until the teacher's reasons have been identified. Those reasons could validate the behavior as appropriate.

A very common "trap" for observers is to project themselves into the lesson and conclude that the teacher was talking too fast because they couldn't keep up (but the students in that class could), that the teacher didn't explain enough (but the students understood), that the teacher was too hard on a student (but that student responded productively and was successful).

Another typical observer error is to make assumptions from false absolutes. "The teacher should have moved around the room to keep the students alert through proximity" (but all the students were focused and participating). "The teacher should have told the students the objective" (but the students' behaviors indicated they knew the objective and demonstrated that they had achieved it). "the teacher should have elicited the answer from the students" (when the students gave evidence of not having knowledge or experience as a basis for their "discovery"). "Too much teacher talk" (when it was effective input). "No visual aids" (when non were needed).

A problem can arise when observers use a list of potentially productive teacher behaviors as a "prompt" of what they should "see" in an observation. A skilled observer is not looking for presence or absence of any teaching behavior (a check list mentality). Instead, the observer is looking for evidence of the appropriateness and artistry of what the teacher is doing. It seems to be impossible to reiterate too many times that there are no absolutes in teaching. There is no teaching behavior that should occur in every lesson or should not occur in any lesson except abuse of a student.

It may be useful to cluster parts of the script tape which have the same label for subsequent conference discussion. Clustering behaviors enables the observer to cite many instances of a productive (or questioned) behavior. For example, under "level of concern," the following excerpts from the script tape would be marked.

"I will be collecting your work at the end of the period."

Walking around the class while the students did their assignment.

"I will be calling on several of you to share your ideas."

41

"This is one we have not tried yet so you may not be sure what to do at first."

From the script tape, teaching decisions and actions are analyzed by the observer to identify cause-effect relationships and to determine the conditions under which similar decisions could be effective in the future. For decisions that were not as effective as intended, theory based, *practical and specific* alternatives need to be developed.

Identify and label any non-typical, effective decision or behavior which occurred only once or seldom in the lesson. Frequently this is intuitive behavior so the teacher needs to be alerted to that behavior, learn the psychological generalization that supports its effectiveness, and identify the conditions under which that same behavior would be appropriate in the future. If the teacher can not subsequently state in his/her own words the conditions under which that same generalization would or would not be appropriate to use the probability of productive transfer to future teaching is very low.

Identify *patterns*, not just one instance of less effective teacher or student behavior. Usually, one instance of not enough "wait time," a blurted out answer, an inappropriate rhetorical question, a lack of specific feedback is not all that important but observers tend to "pounce" on such instances. This can be interpreted by the teacher as "not picking." Only sophisticated teachers welcome being alerted to their occasional "slips." An analogy would be the way a coach works with beginners as contrasted with highly skilled athletes who wish to refine and polish every aspect of performance.

Prioritize Discussion Topics for the Conference

From the summary sheet of potential discussion topics of both enabling and/or questioned behaviors generated from interpreting the script tape, the observer must prioritize discussion of behaviors that are estimated to have the greatest potential for growth of *this* teacher at *this* point in time. The temptation is to "do everything" in one conference. Resist that temptation! All of us can internalize and polish only a few behaviors at a time. For some teachers, reassurance that they are doing some things well is the most growth evoking message at this time. At another time, suggestions for developing new skills becomes stimulating and exciting. Occasionally. "These are the areas where you must improve. Where would you like to begin?" is the message necessary for growth.

The first items of priority are the concerns of the teacher: the discrepancy between what the teacher hoped would happen and what did happen. Little else can be accomplished unless those concerns are discussed, understood and handled. This does *not* mean you begin every conference with, "How did you feel about your lesson?" It does mean that *whenever* a teacher's concern surfaces it usually is attended to before proceeding to other matters.

If there were problems of inappropriate student behaviors that interfered with learning, those become the primary objective of the conference. Was the teacher *aware* of those behaviors and does the teacher see them as inappropriate? Very little can be accomplished when students are not in order, but sometimes what is considered inappropriate by the observer can be perceived differently by the teacher. If so, introducing the discussion of that behavior becomes more difficult.

Try to determine what triggered the unproductive behavior. Was it teacher, student or situation? Plan a workable (practical!) remedial plan that is possible for *that* teacher to implement with *that* student in *that* situation. Also plan how you will teach/assist/support the teacher in the implementation. Anticipate, also, how you will follow up to determine if the plan was successful and, if it requires modifications, how those will be determined and effective.

If teacher concern or interfering student behavior problems are not an issue which must be discussed, the observer needs to determine a primary purpose for the conference. Is it to identify effective teaching decisions and behaviors, to develop alternatives for future situations where those strategies might not work (increase the teacher's pharmacy of alternatives), to encourage the teacher to engage in self analysis, to develop alternatives to behaviors that were not successful or to stretch effective teachers to new heights of professionalism, or a combination of appropriate for that teacher in the time available?

Your primary purpose may need to be modified as information emerging during the conference indicates a different direction would be more productive. Remember in your conference to include strategies that encourage positive transfer to understanding and/or skills developed in the conference to future teaching situations.

The question of how to determine priority of discussion topics must be answered in terms of teacher, situation, and observer. Questions to ask are:

1. Are there areas about which the teacher previously has expressed interest or concern? In that case there will be a "built in" readiness for discussion and growth. These interests and concerns should be relevant to the teacher's performance in planning and teaching, not some esoteric or philosophical issue. The latter, while important, should be discussed at a future time, not after an observation.

2. Are these inappropriate or illegal behaviors that must be corrected?

3. Are there "trends" in teacher and/or student behaviors, or was what was observed an isolated instance? If the instance was a productive behavior, it probably should be brought to the teacher's attention so it will occur again deliberately and appropriately. If there was only one instance of a non-productive behavior, unless it is dangerous or illegal it probably should be ignored.

4. Which decisions or behaviors are most generalizable to future content and situations? Remember, the conference is not for the purpose of complimenting the teacher or fixing that lesson, but is to encourage transfer of productive skills to future lessons.

5. What learning, in the observer's best judgment, is possible for the teacher to achieve in terms of personality, ability, time, resources, and other constraints in this conference?

Thoughtful consideration of these questions will help the observer prioritize the data from the script tape. As in every lesson, priorities may change on the basis of information emerging during the conference.

Determine the Major Objective for the Conference

A conference is an individualized lesson and must include those same psychological elements which are expected in teachers' lessons: motivation, rate and degree, retention and transfer which increase the probability of accomplishment. The objective is a launching pad for designing a conference. While there may be more than one objective in a conference, a primary objective has the highest priority. That priority may change as a result of emerging information during the conference. Prior to the conference the objective guides the conference planning.

All conference objectives are focused on transfer of skills to future teaching. The teacher is never again going to teach that lesson to those students. The conference objective is not simply to identify what was productive in that lesson or to "fix" what wasn't. The objective is, "Through use of information about a lesson the teacher will become consistently, deliberately, and increasingly successful in future lessons."

As in every lesson, the *objective* of a conference is its anticipated outcome in terms of the teacher's responses during and at the end of the conference, not how the observer will make more probable those outcomes. The latter is the focus of planning the conference which may involve direct teaching by the observer, or problem solving through interaction or self analysis and discovery by the teacher. Some sample objectives are:

Objective: The teacher will recall and state labels of behaviors discussed ("raising level of concern," "maximizing learner participation") and describe conditions which suggest the use of those techniques in future lessons.

Possible teacher response: "When there is one right answer, I will beam the question to the entire group, to raise concern, give thinking time and get a signalled response from every student. When an elaborated verbal answer is sought I can use the same procedure, but call on a student who is anticipated to have a correct answer."

Objective: The teacher will select from self generated and observer suggested alternatives, those which will best fit his/her style of teaching and the students involved.

Possible teacher response: "I'd feel most comfortable having students jot down a brief outline so I know they are able to identify main ideas and supporting details."

Objective: Teacher and observer will plan tomorrow's lesson based on a task analysis developed together.

Possible teacher response: "Tomorrow, I'll begin with _____ then check by _____."

Objective: The teacher will select from alternatives an area for subsequent growth.

Possible teacher response: "I'd really like to become more comfortable with cooperative learning."

Objective: The teacher will analyze the lesson identifying parts that worked out as anticipated and parts which might be changed to accelerate learning.

Possible teacher response: "The parts that went well were _____. What I hadn't anticipated was _____."

Plan the Conference

Planning a conference to achieve the selected objective(s) involves four steps:
1. Determine the order that information will be considered in the discussion. The order may be changed on the basis of teacher interest or response during the conference.
2. Select and mark in the script tape those parts that will be needed to initiate discussions or validate information being presented.
3. Plan the introduction of a particular area or focus by creating an introductory question or statement.
4. Anticipate and plan for details that may facilitate or interfere with the teacher's thoughtful consideration of the information being discussed.
5. Develop a beginning and predicted ending for the conference.

Sequence the Discussion Topics

Keeping the primary objective in mind, plan the order of the topics to be discussed. While something initiated by the teacher may cause you to modify that order, it is wise to have a planned sequence in mind so important discussion is not neglected because time ran out.

When both reinforcing comments and suggestions for change are included in a conference, the observer should have determined the order on the basis of predicting results with *that* teacher not the "always start with something good" platitude. Last position in any sequence is a powerful one and if you wish the teacher to remember and transfer his/her productive behaviors into future teaching, it may be wise to end the conference with them. On the other hand, if the teacher is apprehensive, beginning by learning about one's productive behavior is reassuring. Conferencing, as teaching, is decision making. There is no one best pattern.

Select and mark relevant parts of the script tape. The second aspect of preparation is to mark your script tape in a way that the sections you wish to "play back" to the teacher are readily available. Don't bore the teacher by reading the whole script tape ("and then you—and then you—.") The teacher knows the sequence of the lesson. Going straight through a script tape should occur only when accuracy and inclusiveness of recording is being checked with another script tape of the same lesson.

Work only from the parts you have selected as important and develop those behaviors into generalizations with the conditions under which their future use is or is not appropriate. If the teacher raises a question about a certain part of the lesson, take time to find it in your script tape. Don't try to work from memory. This is the reason you need to script tape the entire observation, not just the parts you see as important. A different part of the lesson may be more important to the teacher.

Support your comments with data from the script tape so the teacher knows the part of the lesson to which you are referring. Always being aware of and responding to the teacher's questions and concerns, make your suggestions become generalizations useful in the future. Then determine how, during the conference, you will check for the teacher's understanding of the use of that generalizaiton in *similar* situations which the teacher may encounter. For example, "In your lesson when you beamed your question to the class, 'What, in your opinion, was the boy's most helpful behavior? There is no one right answer.' That caused all students to think and be ready with an opinion. It was important for you to state 'there is no one right answer. Do you know why?"

Create a statement or question to introduce each area of focus. Some initiating statements and questions are:

"You certainly know how to make math meaningful to students. Beginning your class with TV commercials on interest rates offered by banks and translating that into logarithms riveted students' attention on how to determine where they would get the most for their money." (Type A comment.)

"Your example of students earning money resulted in a lot of student comments and increased the alertness of the class. Do you know why it worked so well and what we call that principle of learning?" (Type A comment.)

"You obviously did not want students yelling out comments. Do you know why that happened?" (Type D comment.)

"It took a lot of your time and energy to quiet the class and get them ready to work. Let's look at some ways we could eliminate most of the unnecessary conversation." (Type D comment.)

"You're a very perceptive teacher. What parts of the lesson went just the way you had planned and what do you think caused that to happen?" (Type C comment.)

"Let's list the all skills in solving those kinds of problems and develop some alternative ways to teach them to a faster or to a slower group." (Type B comment.)

One of the most complex skills for observers to acquire is the ability to ask a question without implying that something was amiss. Typically, we are questioned only when something is wrong. It helps to precede the question with an indication that the teacher's action was productive, "Your rephrasing of the question was surely effective. What caused you to do it?"

If the teacher's action was not productive, questions are more difficult to phrase so they don't become value judgements or accusations and imply, "Why in the world would you do that?" An observer needs to develop phrases such as "Take me through your thinking when—." "What were you responding to when—." "Help me know the reason for—."

When the observer asks, "yes-no" questions they may become "think stoppers" rather than "think starters." For example:

"Is it OK for kids to sharpen their pencils whenever they need to?" results in a "yes-no" answer. "Why do you think Tom sharpened his pencil during the lesson?" stimulates a lot more information for interpreting the episode. "What procedures have students learned to take care of their needs, such as sharpening pencils, during the lesson?" elicits a discussion of rules and how they were taught. "Is it typical for Tom to sharpen his pencil during the lesson?" reveals the circumstances.

"Do you think your examples were meaningful" usually is better addressed by "What alternatives did you consider when you selected your examples?" or "How did you decide which examples to use?"

Beware of confrontive questions, "Why did you do that?" "What should you have done? "What in the world were you thinking of when you _____." In our society, a question frequently implies something is wrong." Why did you _____?" suggests you shouldn't have done it.

Think of your reaction should someone ask "Why did you wear that outfit?"

We wish teachers constantly to question and refine their teaching behaviors. To encourage this introspection and to eliminate the confrontive nature inherent in questions we might use one of two techniques such as:

a. Label the teacher's behavior as appropriate and then ask the question, "Your anticipatory set certainly sparked interest. What caused you to select it?" or "Landing like a ton of bricks on Mary and Jim straightened them up. What let you know this was not a time for being nice?"

b. Initiate contemplation by labeling your own uncertainty. "I couldn't decide whether it would have helped to _____ or whether it would have deflected attention. What do you think?" or "Often it is difficult to decide whether to continue prompting a student or to move on to someone else for the answer. What helped you decide?"

In your planning, try to anticipate the responses of the teacher. If there is a possibility that the teacher might become defensive or negative, try to think of a way to avoid this before it happens. If it should happen, determine some ways you might most productively deal with defensiveness when it occurs. Anticipation and preparation can divert or dilute a potentially destructive interaction.

Careful attention to details (that may be perceived as insignificant to an inexperienced observer) will result in a much more satisfying conference for both participants. These details include initiating statements that are non threatening, working from a teacher's strengths, describing behavior rather than making judgments, caution with questions or emotionally loaded words, and developing alternatives in advance.

Practice enabling statements: those which increase the probability that a teacher will "hear what you mean" and grow professionally. As a result, they feel you are really seeking reasons for their decisions which means you respect their ability to make informed professional decisions. "Tell me what you were thinking when you —." "Help me to understand what happened when—." "I'm sure you had a reason but I don't know what it was." "It worked beautifully. If it doesn't work at a future time you might try—." "There is a potential booby trap here that the strength of your teaching got you through. You need to watch out for—."

Avoid giving suggestions as questions. "Might you have tried, used, done?" needs to become, "Something you might try—." "Could you have —? is more honestly expressed as, "You could have." A genuine query is acceptable. Suggestions in the form of questions are not.

Develop ways to encourage the teacher to analyze and generate increasingly effective behaviors so self analysis becomes more routine after every lesson. Don't be afraid to give information, however, when it is requested or needed. Remember a sophisticated observer who is only observing and recording can often perceive more than a teacher who is having to generate high speed responses in terms of what students are saying or doing which often necessitate modifications of original plans: to "catch it coming down and run with it."

Avoid "loaded" words such as: "problem," "trouble," "disinterested" "bored." They may cause a teacher to feel inadequate and to become defensive. ("You had a problem when the students all called out answers.") Use "situation," "episode" or better, simply read what happened from your script tape. "You asked, 'What should we serve at the party?' and students started calling out answers. That is probably not what you wanted. Let's develop some ways to avoid it in the future." "When you asked—, the students didn't know the answer," is better addressed by, "When you asked—, no one raised a hand."

Avoid making assumptions, "The students were confused when—." From your script tape use specific accounts of what actually happened. "When you asked—, several students gave incorrect answers."

Beware of the use of "I" in the conference. ("I liked," "I was impressed by," "I noticed"). "*You*" has more potential to build the teacher's self concept. ("Your lesson was impressive." You used excellent judgment when you—." "You really thought on your feet as you—," "When you—it caused students to—.") Occasionally it helps to tape record your conference to discover whether you have the "I,I,I" habit, and also to hear how you "come across."

One of the most ubiquitous words in teaching is "I". "*I* want you to run to (look at, underline, do, consider, be ready to, line up, turn in)." "*I* like the way—." "Now, the next thing *I* have planned—" "*I* am going to—." We have become an "I,I,I'ing" profession.

You is the power word which builds self esteem. Consider the difference between "I am going to have you—" and "Now you are ready to—." "You" places power and confidence in the student. "I" maintains teacher control. (Yes, in the past, teachers were told to make "I" statements, but we've learned a lot since then. In the past, steak was a staple in a reducing diet, but we've also learned better than that).

An especially seductive use of "I" is a statement of approval. "I like the way you're listening (working, raising hands, lining up, writing). That implies, "You're pleasing me and when you don't, I won't like you." It also suggests that it is the students' job to please the teacher (And it is not!).

"You" builds self esteem. "You look great in that outfit. You certainly have good taste in clothes," gives a very different message from, "I like your outfit." "You did an excellent job of using descriptive words in your story. The reader could really hear and see what you meant," is infinitely more powerful than, "I was impressed by your use of descriptive words."

When *is* the use of "I" appropriate? When you are giving information about yourself rather than labeling why someone is competent, it is accurate to say, "I like your outfit. It is my favorite color." You'll build more self esteem and feelings of competence, however, if you say, "That color certainly compliments your eyes and makes you look vibrant. It also happens to be my favorite color," or "You did a great job with your surprise ending in the story. Most people never would have guessed it. In fact, I was completely off base."

The elimination of most (not all) "I" statements in an instructional conference also adds to the power of an observer's feedback. Throw away your, "I was impressed by—," "I liked the way you—," "I noticed that—." Replace these "I's" with, "You were effective when—," "You successfully—," "You captured students' interest by—." "You increased the probability of their remembering when you—."

A valid use of "I" in a conference conveys information about the observer. "I was perplex by—." "I don't know the answer to.—." "I was wondering if—." These statements give the teacher information about something that was occurring in the observer's mind.

It is not a mortal sin to use "I". It's simply a habit pattern that we know is not as effective as using "you". Audiotape yourself or have an observer tally how many "I's" you're using in teaching or in conferencing. (One conferencer used twenty-six "I's" in a twenty-munute conference—far more than he realized). Once you bring the use of "I" to a conscious level (most people have said it so many times they're not even aware of it), you can monitor your "I's" and change most of them to "you's".

Focusing your eyes (and ears) on your "I's" will help you begin to use the more productive "You" in a conference statement:

Work from a teacher's strength to a problem area if there is one. Plan questions that will elicit the teacher's reasons for what occurred before you make a judgment about it. "You've done an excellent job of teaching students to raise their hands and wait to be acknowledged. Some times you ignored Mary's blurted out responses and other times you accepted them as answers to your questions. Was there a difference in the two situations?" When you hear the teacher's reasoning behind actions, you may be impressed by the "custom tailoring" to differing sets of circumstances. If there was no difference, simply inconsistency in the teacher's behavior, it usually will be discovered as s/he hears the script tape and considers the answer to your question.

"The cafeteria manager really appreciates your getting the students there on time. Dismissing them by groups will make it easier for them to leave in good order. You might ask a question about the lesson they have just finished, give everyone time to think of the answer, call on a student and dismiss that section of the room. Three questions should get them all out in order and place an important learning in last position where it is more apt to be remembered."

"You did an excellent job of thinking through the directions students needed to have. If you give those directions *before* you pass out the materials, students will be more apt to hear them because they're not tempted to look through the materials."

"Your materials are always ready when you start the lesson. When you are interrupted, as you were today before you'd gathered your materials, give the students something to think about or do before you take care of the interruption. In that way they will be using the time productively instead of talking to each other and you'll have time to collect your materials."

Should a teacher not agree that modifications need to be made, avoid a confrontation in this conference and later develop strategies to handle the situation in the next conference.

The observer, *in preparation for the conference,* has the responsibility for developing several alternatives to less effective teacher or student behaviors. If the lesson wasn't interesting, what *specifically* could be done to make it more interesting? General admonitions or platitudes are useless. "Your lesson should be more related to the students so they are interested in learning," needs to become, "It's hard to make parts of speech interesting. Usually it helps to use students' names and interests such as 'Mark put the tape *in* the video player, *under* the video, *away* from the video.'" If the observer can't suggest something specific (and practical in terms of teacher time and energy), to make the lesson related to students don't expect the teacher to generate solutions. Also, make sure you communicate, "There are several ways of doing it, such as —," and suggest several, not just one way, or it becomes an order or the "best" way, rather than a repertoire of possible alternatives.

Even when the teacher's decisions were effective and the observer is extending that teacher's repertoire of skills in Type B communication, usually several alternatives should be presented. When only one is presented, it can be interpreted by the teacher as a "better" one. Suggesting several possibilities encourages the teacher to make different decisions for different students and situations.

Should a teacher reject your suggestions, find out why. If possible, agree with and support any part of the teacher's reason you feel is valid. If you agree with even a part of the teacher's rationale, s/he is more likely to believe that you understand the situation. Consequently, s/he may listen to and try suggested alternatives which are reasonable and possible for that teacher. "You are absolutely right that it is not possible to have exactly the correct level of difficulty for every student in all subjects every day. Let's plan some ways to adjust the level of difficulty for that group of five so they can be more successful."

Plan the Beginning of the Conference

The time and place of the conference should have been determined before or immediately after the observation, taking into account the logistics of working without interruption, in reasonable comfort, and in whoever's "turf" is more enabling to collaboration and accomplishment of the objective.

Beginning statements immediately bring the purpose of the conference into focus and the discussion can proceed with maximum utilization of the time available. Beware of wasting time on "small talk." It consumes precious moments and can be used to avert the more demanding process pf professional growth.

"Your outfit is gorgeous—where did you get it?" can devour time in discussion of styles, discount stores, or the way centain materials hold up.

"You look great. I need to schedule a conference with you to help me find clothes, but right now let's look at your excellent teaching techniques" compliments the teacher but clearly indicates that "small talk" is not appropriate at this time.

"I heard you have a new puppy. How are things going with that new family member?" can elicit a fascinating discussion of the dog's purchase, up bringing, problems with fleas, food, and destruction. All of this is great to establish common interests, sympathy, and friendship *at another time.* Don't let yourself or the teacher use it as a diversion technique to reduce the exacting demands of interactive professional growth.

"I'm dying to hear about your new puppy, but now is your time for us to focus on your lesson. I hope we'll have time after that for me to hear about Fido. If not, I want to hear about him at lunch."

"Shouldn't colleagues discuss areas of common interest not related to school?" you ask. Of course! But socializing should be *deliberately* provided for at lunch, before or after school, during coffee breaks, at parties, before meetings, and in chance encounters. That potentially powerful time for professional interaction about a lesson should not be consumed by important, but *not* appropriate then, personal matters.

Again, there are no absolutes. If discussion of outfits or puppies, in the observer's opinion, is the better part of valor, do it but also schedule a subsequent time devoted to professional growth.

Starting off with "what went well and why," usually will get teachers' attention and make them comfortable in the conference situation.

Some opening statements might be:

"Your lesson modeled some very good examples of teaching that facilitated learning. Let's look at the ways you checked for understanding to determine why they were so effective."

"Do you recall some of the things that you did to facilitate students' learning? Why do you think they worked so well?"

"Your lesson was well planned, were there any student responses that surprised you?"

Plan an anticipated conclusion of the conference. To compliment your beginning, plan for an ending which ties all the discussion together. You, or the teacher, may summarize or plan next steps. Beware of the "Spanish Inquisition," "Now summarize what we have discussed," places the teacher in a "frantically remembering" rather than a contemplative position. "We've discussed so many things. While I'm making some notes to help me remember, think about those things which have been most relevant to you" gives the teacher time to review the discussion and assign significance to certain aspects. "Help me to know which parts of the conference were most relevant to your concerns, so I can improve my skills" places the teacher in an advisory position—always flattering to the advisor. "So I know I have been comprehensible, tell me what you think I am suggesting for your next area of growth," checks the teacher's understanding of the communication while placing the responsibility of its success on the observer. Your plan for the summary should indicate teacher and/or observer reiterating the most important points and remaking them necessary. Avoid a summary that becomes a final exam. Determine whether those points will be recorded, how and by whom.

Build an enabling bridge into the next observation and conference. "I learned a great deal from observing your teaching. I'm looking forward to the next observation." or "It will be a learning experience for me to see how you develop these ideas." "Let me know how well our ideas work and whether we need to rethink them or develop some new ones."

Your anticipated ending may change on your perception of the teacher and the way the conference progresses. When, in your best judgement, a productive amount has been accomplished, conclude the conference. Better to stop with one or two techniques which have been developed into a plan, than supply a long list of all possibilities. Should the teacher ask, "Was there anything else you saw?" fight off the desire to tell everything you know or to "nit pick" something that really wasn't that important. You'll wind up with a shallow laundry list of possibilities and very little being learned in enough depth for appropriate use in the future. Also consider what the teacher is really asking by his/her question. Is it, "What else is wrong?" "Did you see some other things I did well? I need to hear them." "This is so painful, let's move on to something else." Or is it a genuine request of "This is great and I would like to get as much as I can!" The observer needs and advanced degree in wizardry to decipher some messages but the more sensitivity we develop to what the teacher is asking, the more our accuracy increases. Solace yourself, however, with the observation that even the "experts" occasiosnally misjudge and push when they shouldn't and don't push when they should.

Conferences usually should be concluded on the "up beat" with reiteration, by teacher or observer, of the teacher's professional skills and/or next focus growth in instructional excellence. If the content of the conference has been negative (and on rare occasions it must be) the conference is concluded by a clear statement of what is expected plus a "vote of confidence" that the teacher has the ability to achieve that growth and that the observer is committed to provide any information, support, and encouragement requested and/or needed to achieve that growth. "I know you were disappointed in that lesson. Few of us maintain consistently excellent teaching. With the strategies we've discussed in our conference, tomorrow's lesson should go much better. Let me know how it works out."

Conducting the Conference

A conference addresses the most volatile and sensitive issue in education, that of professional competence. Beginning with the first "view" of the teacher, adjustments may need to be made in the conference plan. (This is similar to the teacher's "sensing" the class as the students enter the door and making "on your feet" adjustments if they seem to be necessary.) The only exception to this is for the teacher who has learned diversion tactics. "Oh I am so ashamed of that lesson it was a disaster!" which lures the observer into "Oh, it wasn't that bad," when it was! or "I know you're going to tell me what a mess that was," to get you to say it wasn't - and it was!

Another trap to avoid, is being caught in the hall with, "How was my lesson?" This is designed to make it impossible for you to do anything but say "just fine" or "great" even when it wasn't and then a conference is anticlimactic. It's impossible to engage in any constructive discussion in a hall encounter. Handle such an encounter by, "I learned a lot" or "I found the students' responses really caused me to think," or "You opened a whole new area of thinking for me." followed by, "let's discuss it at _____ , when we have time to really think about it together."

All through the conference the observer needs to "read" the teacher's verbal and nonverbal responses. "Monitor and adjust" is just as important in a conference as it is in a lesson.

In a conference, two essential skills are:

1. **Be a good listener:** This is an incredibly difficult skill when you have to process what you hear, combine it with what you have planned and make productive adjustments which take both your objective and the teacher's responses into account.

    Check the accuracy of what you think you heard by using a variety of responses such as "Do you mean _____?" "Is your concern _____?" "Am I understanding you when _____?" Beware of the platitudinous, "I hear you saying _____." Unfortunately, we find a productive phrase, over use it and end up by giving a message to teachers that we are using a "mirroring technique" or some other "in thing" on them.

    Also, *make yourself wait* until the teacher has finished what s/he wants to say before you "jump in." Use wait time after asking a question or making a suggestion. If the teacher doesn't respond immediately, give the teacher time to think or process what you are saying.

2. **Dignify a teacher's potentially erroneous response.** This can be done by: a) supplying a situation where that action would have been correct, b) prompting the teacher to generate a more productive response, and c) checking the teacher's understanding of the conditions under which that response has high probability of being productive.

    "I don't blame you for blowing your top at Jane. When nothing else has worked, sometimes that will shock a student into doing the assignment. When we come on like gang busters, it gives a student the message we are really fed up and expect different behavior. Because Jane was in front of her friends, she had to act defiant not to lose face although I had the feeling she really was sorry. Can you think of a way you might have let her know 'that's enough' without her needing to show her friends she didn't care?" (The observer is modeling a way of dignifying the teacher's error in the way the teacher is expected to correct Jane's error but preserve her dignity).

    Typically, the teacher will suggest calling Jane to one side so her friends don't observe her with the problem thereby eliminating her need to show defiance in order to maintain status with her peers. Then the observer can add any additional information relevant to "disciplining with dignity."

To also maintain the teacher's dignity, it's reassuring to acknowledge at times we've all responded in the same way and to reiterate how difficult it is to respond professionally instead of personally, but "discipline with dignity" is the professionally productive response.

Another example might be the error of a teacher moving ahead without checking that students understood the material essential to the next learning or, even worse, when there was evidence the students didn't understand.

"You certainly are sensitive to the fact that these students are expected to be able to write an introductory paragraph and I commend your eagerness to get them to that point. Let's look at the skills they need to have in order to accomplish it." This statement needs to be followed by a collaborative task analysis which includes generating a provocative introductory sentence, generating sentences which indicate the substance and limits of the body of the writing and developing a concluding sentence which stimulates the reader to eagerly read the rest of the composition.

Remember, you are not "fixing" that lesson, you are teaching for appropriate transfer to all future lessons as a teacher has practice in and sees the value of task analyzing a skill in order to make sure that students have an opportunity to learn all the component parts before they are asked to put them together in a complex product. Then you and the teacher need to identify ways of checking that each part is understood and can be done so the teacher transfers appropriate assessment behaviors on which s/he bases the decision to move on, to give more practice or to go back and reteach.

Subsequent observations will inform you of your success or the necessity of your going back and reteaching. Remember the same learning principles apply to you as a coach as apply to the teacher working with students.

Analyze the Conference

In the same way that teachers need to introspect after a lesson, the conferencer needs to reconsider the sequence and success of a conference. Conferences are like lessons in that the better they are planned, the more productive they are apt to be. However, as in all teaching, things seldom proceed exactly as anticipated.

Video taping a conference (as in teaching) is an invaluable way to view (alone or with a skilled observer) interpret and reconsider decisions made "on one's feet (seat)" during the conference. Taking into account that hindsight always has more information than foresight, look back over your decisions and what you did to implement them. Don't punish yourself for errors; that is destructive. We all make errors. Devise ways that have greater probability for averting them in the future. That is productive and growth evoking.

The burden of achievement rests primarily on the teaching skills of the observer. If the conference is not successful, the observer, as the person responsible, must consider ways in which it might become more successful rather than retreating into the seductive excuse of "the teacher wouldn't listen" "was impossible," "was defensive," "doesn't want to hear it." We are professionals because we have skills to address (not always successfully) those problems. We expect teachers to exert professional energy to affect indifferent, disinterested, unmotivated learners. We should expect the same of ourselves in a conference.

Address these questions:

What in that conference seemed to be enabling to that teacher's growth? Why?

What would cue me to use it in the future?

What did not come out as I hoped? Is there any change I could have made before or during the conference that would have yielded more productive results?

What had I better remind myself of and include or delete in the future so the productivity of my conference increases?

An excellent technique to stimulate conferencers' growth is periodically to secure *anonymous* evaluations of conferences which have been conducted over a period of time. *Anonymity is essential.* There are few people who trust one another enough to be completely honest, particularly if one person has the power to affect the future of the other. Occasionally, an observer has built enough trust in a teacher to elicit honest feedback but it is rare. Valid feedback is more often secured from anonymous responses to the questions:

What did I do that was helpful and you wish me to increase feedback of that nature?

What happened in the conference that was not growth evoking for you and what might. I do that would be more productive?

What did I not do that you wish I would have done in our conference?

Such open ended questions invite suggestion that have high potential for increasing conferencing skills: a goal that is just as important for the observer as enhancing teaching excellence is for the teacher.

In the same way that continuing professional growth is necessary for teachers, observers must take advantage of every opportunity to grow in observation, analysis and conferencing skills.

TEACHERS' SUGGESTIONS FOR EFFECTIVE CONFERENCES

These guidelines reflect suggestions made by teachers who have been conferenced during Clinical Supervision II workshops taught at UCLA for several years. They represent comments from a cross-section of teachers: novice to expert, experienced teacher and student teacher. They are simply suggestions, not mandates.

Teacher's Goal: My goal for a conference is that I want to be able to look forward to another conference with that observer because I have found I will learn and grow, and it will be a rewarding experience.

Start and end with positive comments.
- It creates a feeling which facilitates my becoming productively involved in the conference.

Limit the amount of information you include in the conference.
- I need to be able to develop an understanding of the information presented and be able to remember it.
- The more information presented the less likely I will process it and/or retain it.
- Limit the number of effective decisions discussed in detail to two or three.
- Limit the discussion of less effective decisions to one (or maybe two if they are not too involved).

Expect me to be a participant who contributes in the conference. Some ways are:
- Make sure I understand what you're saying (check for understanding).
- Find out how this lesson fits into a sequence of lessons (task analysis).
- Find out why I decided what to teach (curriculum).
- Find out how I determined the content was appropriate (diagnosis).
- Ask what I thought went particularly well in the lesson (analysis).
- Ask if I had any surprises, things I didn't anticipate happening, in the lesson.

Ask for my concerns and be ready to help with them by offering alternatives which have potential for success with these students in future lessons.

Determine if I was aware of situations and why I made the decision(s) you question before you label it as a problem.
- You may find out the reason for the decision was a sound one.
- Have practical alternatives which are possible for me.

Monitor and adjust in the conference just as you expect me to monitor and adjust as I teach.
- If I don't understand something, clarify before going on. If I do under-

stand, don't continue when it's not necessary. Be flexible; if I identify an area you want to deal with later, deal with it when I bring it up. Remember, the conference is for me, not you.

Select important (as opposed to insignificant) areas to focus on in the conference.

- Select instances where a behavior was a pattern rather than one occurrence.
  (When all but one incorrect answer was dignified, don't identify that one instance as a problem.)
- Help me make generalizations which will transfer to other lessons rather than a specific for only this lesson. (Focus on question-asking techniques rather than redoing only one questions. Use that question as an example.)

Suggest alternatives to decisions which worked with these students but might not work with other students, if you think I will need them.

- "These students stayed focused while you wrote on the board. Let's develop some ways to work with students who couldn't stay focused."
- Push me to come up with alternatives, but make sure you also suggest some.

Be prepared with alternatives when you have identified a concern or question.

- If you don't have an alternative, either don't identify the concern or say you don't have any solution but you are willing to work with me to develop some.

Use specific examples from the lesson.

- "You did an effective job of dignifying Johnny's incorrect response when he aswered 45. You said, 'You're thinking of the answer to 9 x 5. I asked for 9 x 6."

Briefly summarize, sometimes in writing, at the end of the conference so I will remember the important points we discussed and decisions (if any) we reached.

- This is not a typed summary of the conference, but a list which we developed together during the conference.

Limit the length of the conference to from 10 — 30 minutes.

I want to be stretched, but I expect you to assist, not just ask questions or tell me. Help me develop new insights and techniques, Know when to apply them, and to continue to grow professionally.

WALK-THRU SUPERVISION

Do you have five minutes between classes or appointments? Twenty minutes because someone canceled? A half hour you could set aside each week? Do you go to classrooms to deliver messages, lunches, a book, to check on that leak, or to see if the new bookcase is the one that was ordered?

You can realize "double indemnity" from those odds and ends of time and from your administrative chores if you couple them with walk-thru supervision.

Walk-thru supervision is the short division form of traditional supervision. Walk-thrus are designed to augment, not to replace formal supervision in order to increase teaching excellence. The validity of frequent sampling is widely acknowledged in statistics. The same validity can be achieved by frequent, sampling observations of the quality of teaching. Objective data can be generated easily by walk-thrus.

Walk-thru observation is defined as a very short (15 seconds to 5 minutes) stay in a classroom, observing what the teacher and students are doing. Usually the observer is script taping so memory does not play tricks or specifics are not lost.

Walk-thru supervision involves:

1. collection of classroom instructional data thru script taping a 15 seconds to five minute observation;
2. on the spot or later analysis of the script tape for cause-effect relationships between teaching and learning; and
3. on the basis of the script tape recording of what actually happened (not broad generalizations or vague impressions), informal feedback to the teacher that labels and reinforces effective teaching, or remediates teaching that was not as effective as it might be.

You don't have to hear the whole concerto to tell whether Perleman is playing or the boy next door is practicing. You don't have to watch the entire play to determine that the actors are professionals or high school amateurs. You don't have to witness the entire game to determine that the play you observed was executed skillfully. In the same way you do not have to see an entire lesson to appraise the effectiveness of the segment that was observed.

Lest you are feeling, "but our contract requires that we observe an entire lesson," be reminded that walk-thru supervision does not replace formal observations but augments them and validates whether the "official visit" revealed the professional quality typical of that teacher or that, this time, the quality was exceptional in either a positive or negative direction. Walk-thrus also lesson a teacher's apprehension or feeling of unfairness associated with that one fateful observation where, in spite of the best preparation and intentions, kids will be kids, materials get mislaid, projectors chew up film, or Susie throws up. Incidentally, the way a teacher deals with these emergencies is an excellent measure of the quality of teaching.

To implement a productive program of walk-thru supervision, the principal or supervisor needs to possess the same skills that are needed for regular coaching and supervision.

Once teachers experience the "playback" potential of a walk-thru and see that it, too, can yield objective feedback which accelerates professional growth, their desire to "see themselves" thru walk-thru supervision increases.

Feedback to teachers. Walk-thru supervision achieves, at a very low time cost, the frequent coaching which is essential but has been missing from so many inservice programs. In the same way that a skilled coach can reinforce and/or improve blocking, kicking, and pivoting after a brief observation, the observer can reinforce and/or improve teaching effectiveness. Obviously, if something is seriously amiss (severe classroom management problems, discipline that destroys dignity, inability to design an effective lesson), a longer observation and conference time is required. When remediation is provided for the teacher, subsequent walk-thru supervision will reveal whether it was effective.

Remember that walk-thru observation is a "fast form" of supervision which can be achieved for *after* "slower" forms are learned, practiced, and internalized by the observer. Walk-thrus are not a short cut to achieving supervisory effectiveness, but a high speed performance skill based on "slow speed" excellence. Sometimes this is a non-threatening positive way of introducing an observer's positive feedback to the teacher. sometimes teachers need first to experience a regular observation and conference before they feel comfortable with a "quick" look. As with an educational decisions, which type of supervision to do initially depends on teacher and situation.

Let's look at some real examples of script tapes from walk-thru observation and the subsequent feedback they enabled the principal to generate:

Script tape (2 minutes):
82)275 round 80 80)250 (show 3)8)25, show where put 3, yes or n.
Next show sign, rt. Sue multiply 8 x 3 = 24. So all know, do 83 x 3.
Now do here, excellent.

Translation: The teacher was teaching trial divisors. (You don't have to know the objective in advance, you can deduce it from the teaching). She gave instructions to round-off the 82 to 80 and the 257 to 250 and then to simplify the problem to 8/25. She asked students to show with their fingers how many 8's in 25. Students showed 3. Then she had students say "yes" or "no" as she pointed to places in the quotient where she would put the 3. She then asked all students to make a sign with their fingers for the next operation in the division problem (+,-,x,-). All signaled x. The teacher asked Sue to dictate the multiplication while the teacher recorded it on the board. Sue multiplied 3 x 8. The teacher responded to this error with "So all of us see what Sue is doing, let's do it first this way," and wrote 82 x 3. Sue did it correctly. Then the teacher asked her to do the same thing in the division problem. She multiplied correctly.

Feedback given to Teacher (3 minutes)

Observer: "When you had all students signal responses instead of calling on only one you caused them all to think and you found out who knew and who didn't. When Sue said 8 x 3 = 24, do you know why she multiplied only the 8 instead of the 82? (The teacher shakes head.) You had just asked, 'How many 8's in 25?'"

Teacher: "Oh, is that why she did it? I couldn't figure out why she was making that mistake."

Observer: "You did productive thinking on your feet when you changed the problem to the typical multiplication form which was familiar to Sue. After she had done that correctly, many teachers would have transposed her answer to the division problem. You had the wisdom to have her do it again correctly in the division problem. Whenever a student is confused, if possible, reduce the complexity to something she does know, then help the student transfer that learning to the more difficult situation. Usually, this is much better than moving to another student, leaving the first student with a sense of failure from being wrong."

Teacher: "I didn't realize I was doing that. Now I'll watch myself for it."

Quite a dividend from a total of less than five minutes of supervisory time!

Not all walk-thrus are so positive.

Script tape (one minute):

Mat 3 pl. Book here, pencils there, paper over there. So no T jam, ex-

cuse gr. Boys first books, g paper.

Translation: "The material is in three places. The books are there, pencils there, and paper over there. So we don't have a traffic jam at one place, I'll excuse groups to different places to get your materials. The boys are excused first to get your books. Girls, you are excused to get paper."

Feedback to Teacher (30 seconds while students were getting materials):

Observer: "You're doing excellent planning to send groups to different places so you don't have a traffic jam with resultant discipline problems. In this day and age you can't separate boys and girls, much less excuse the boys first. We'll all be accused of promoting sexism. How else might you excuse the groups

Teacher: "Oh my gosh, I never thought of that. I could have excused them by those having birthdays from January to June, or by colors, or by names beginning with certain letters or sounds. I'm glad you called that to my attention."

Result: Increased insight (and public relations) from 1½ minutes of walk-thru supervision.

Here is a third example.

Script tape (3 seconds):

Tom 1st sent. comma Yes or n? Rt. Betty 2 comma. What no comma. Rt. Paul #3.

Translation: "Tom, does the first sentence require a comma? Yes or no? (Tom replies 'yes') Right. Betty, what about number 2? (Betty says 'comma.) *What?* says the teacher. Betty quickly changes to "no comma.' Right, says the teacher. Paul do #3."

Feedback (3 minutes):

Observer: "It's important that every student consider and try to answer every question. In that way every student practices determining whether each sentence needs a comma. You can achieve this by, 'Look at number one, be ready to signal whether it needs a comma. I'll give you a few seconds to think. When I say 'show me,' make a comma with one finger if the sentence needs a comma, a zero using both hands if it doesn't need a comma. Don't do anything if you don't know.' You'll need to teach your class to give signals and to demonstrate for them the ways to do so. When each member of a class signals, you have an immediate diagnosis of who knows and who doesn't without having to correct a stack of papers. If you are concerned about 'plagiarizing, have students close their eyes and show you. It's easy to identify those students who need to 'take a little peek.' After students signal, you or a student usually needs to say why a comma or no comma is needed. Because there are only two choices, a lucky guess can make someone right. When you explain why the comma is or is not needed, the lucky and unlucky guessers receive the information that will help them in the future. Now, so I know that what I've said make sense to you, tell me what you think I am recommending."

Teacher: "You want me to have kids signal a comma or no comma and when tell me why. But what if it's an answer different from a comma?"

Observer: "You're reminding me that we haven't had an inservice staff meeting on signaled responses. I should have scheduled one before now. We'll do it at our next meeting. In the next few days will you jot down some of the questions you might ask your class? We'll use them as our launching pad to work out ways to get responses from every student in order to achieve maximum responding with minimal paper correcting."

Three and a half minutes of walk-thru supervision provided impetus for a staff meeting that could dramatically reduce the time teachers spend correcting papers, yet increase the immediacy of the teacher's checking what each student knows so clarification or remediation can be provided as soon as it is needed. When a teacher, later, does check their papers, there will be an increase of correct answers.

These three examples of walk-thru supervision illustrate the kind of feedback that reinforces effective teaching behaviors, remediates teaching behavior that could cause, albeit unintentionally, problems, and teaches new behaviors that would be more efficient and effective. Do you recognize the similarity of these brief feedback messages to the characteristics and generalizations of more formal conference discussions?

If serious problems are detected in walk-thrus, a longer observation is indicated to determine if the ineffective behavior is typical or if it was 'one of those days." In the former case an in-depth analysis and well-planned conference are indicated. In the latter case the observer can forget it.

The increase in teaching excellence which can be realized from walk-thru supervision is dependent on two factors: (1) the training of the observer in script taping, analyzing, and delivering growth-evoking rather than destructive feedback, plus (2) a systematic and carefully planned program of inservice so teachers gain knowledge of principles of learning and the research on which they are based, amplified by having seen those principles in action through films or videotapes of artistic teaching performance.

These two factors of observer's skill and teacher inservice provide the launching pad for escalating teaching excellence. While there never is, nor probably ever will be, the time required for adequate teacher coaching, walk-thru supervision provides systematic, frequent feedback to teachers: feedback which augments and makes more valid those longer observations and in-depth instructional conferences.

For the army of supervisors and principals who "wish they had more time for adequate supervision" (not for those who want an excuse to cover lack of supervisory skills), walk-thru supervision requires an investment of time to learn the skills but yields one of the most productive time solutions to the problem of enhancing excellence in teaching.

WORKING WITH THE RELUCTANT TEACHER

Sometimes, in spite of our most diligent and inspired efforts we encounter resistant teachers: the few reluctant dragons of education. They may be identified by any of the following responses to our coaching and supervision:

"Look, I've been doing this for years. I know what works and what doesn't"

"Yes, but that won't work with these students."

"You just don't understand this class (content, parent, situation)."

"But this class is different. The kids are unusually slow (difficult, behind, aggressive, bilingual, spoiled)."

"What works in math just won't work with my subject."

"I've already tried that. It didn't work."

"Well, the reason I need to do it this way is _____."

"If I only had a different book (less students, more time...) _____."

"I'm really surprised by your comments. I've always been rated superior before."

"You're absolutely right. I'll try it." But s/he never does.

"What's wrong with the old ways of doing it? These new fads are just a flash in the pan. Next year we'll be on to something else."

"You're destroying my creativity. Teaching is an art."

Sometimes just silence, waiting for this to get over, is our cue to a passive resister.

If this is your first year with coaching or supervision, hope for some incidental or observational learning by that teacher, but focus your major attention and effort on other teachers where the return will be greater. If you feel obligated to "move in," accept the fact that you have repeatedly tried a positive approach and it is getting you nowhere. Then examine the situation with the following in mind:

1. What is the estimated return from your investment of time and energy? Is it worth the effort? The answer to these questions involves the following:

   a. Is this teacher actually destructive to students or is there illegal behavior? If so, you have no choice. If you are being paid as an administrator or supervisor you must do something about it.

   b. If you are a coach and have no assigned responsibility for another's growth you have to decide whether to report failure to the administration or forget it.

   c. If the teacher's class is simply a waste of students' time you move on to the next questions.

2. How long will it be before this teacher retires? If it's a matter of 1-3

years, it's unlikely a change will come rapidly enough to be worth the time and energy: a pessimistic but realistic stance.

3. How much "clout" do you have? Can you bring it off with pressure or is it apt to blow you out of the water? How much clout does the teacher have? Can s/he turn the staff against you, or the central office or the school board? Does the teacher feel so politically secure s/he doesn't need to change? Can you affect this security?

4. How much support will you get from superiors? Will they back you or vanish into the mist? Martyrdom may be noble but it's better to live for a cause.

5. What will be the effects of your actions on others? Will they rally to the support of the "underdog" or will they remain your allies? (Teachers usually know when another teacher is not working productively but, like many of us, when they feel sorry for someone they tend to support that person even when they know better.) Can you emotionally and politically survive that situation if it occurs?

6. Can you live with yourself if you ignore poor teaching? Will it erode your self esteem or turn you into a "what's the use" place holder?

If your answers to these questions convince you that you should do something, develop carefully deliberated answers to the following questions. You diagnose teachers for the same reason you diagnose students. The results from that diagnosis tell you what will have the greatest probability of success.

1. Is the reluctant teacher's behavior a result of insecurity as a professional? Many people avoid trying new behavior because of fear of failure. Such people need a great deal of support and extensive coaching. Do you have the time and energy to deliver that assistance? If not, where can you secure that essential help? Don't expect miracles, plan for and secure necessary assistance.

2. Is the teacher's lack of competence a result of lack of skills (just don't know how), a fear of giving up the old, or the result of disbelief after having tried once and it didn't work?

3. Has the teacher simply retired on the job and needs stimulation or a "jolt"?

4. Is the teacher just waiting it out? "This too shall pass." Has this stance worked in the past with others who have eventually given up on that teacher? If so, you'll know it will take longer.

5. Is the teacher genuinely convinced of his/her effectiveness? What discrepant evidence will you present that has the possibility of changing that belief?

6. Does the teacher have "honest disbelief" of research based ideas? Is

s/he convinced that "Failure is good for students." "What is hard is good for you." "Kids should get what they deserve." "If they enjoy it, it's not learning." "Parents, public, central office, etc. won't approve of it?"

If you believe that it's important to change the teacher's instructional behaviors, you have the know how, time, strength and clout to do it, and you are convinced the results will be beneficial to students, school, yourself, and to the teacher, then plan your strategy.

Assist with, but insist on improvement with the following in mind. Knowing there are no absolutes in teaching, coaching, or supervising, or in any other aspect of teaching, when learning is not progressing, we do not continue to do the same thing. We should:

1. Analyze and prioritize behavioral changes. Clearly, if safety or legality is an issue, you must start with those behaviors. Otherwise, you and the teacher can start with a) the teacher's choice, b) something easily accomplished so success becomes a subsequent motivator, or c) the area where you feel you can best contribute to the teacher's growth.

2. Work from the teacher's strengths. There must be some even if there is tenacious resistance and conviction. "You have many strengths. Let's use them to resolve some of the situations which were not what you intended or wanted." Focus those strengths on the first steps in growth.

3. Make clear, in oral and written communication, the specific improvements to which that teacher's strengths need to be addressed. Lay your cards on the table. Don't be subtle and indirect, the teacher won't "get it." Change your "Might we consider some alternative student behaviors?" to "Let's list more appropriate student behaviors and plan techniques you will use to achieve these as soon as possible." Make all expectations explicit, reasonable, and articulated in oral and written language which defines specific, observable teaching behavior. Check the teacher's understanding of each expectation. "So I know we are together on this, tell me how you will make our new procedures clear to students and what you will do to increase the probability they will follow them."

4. Acknowledge the teacher's feelings and accept them (but not the teaching behavior!). "I know you don't completely agree, but these are the district's expectations for student behavior." "You're right, this is a busy time of year but this is too important to put off I'll help you get started."

5. *Make records* of your expectations and *all* interactions which are

69

designed to contribute to their achievement. Give the teacher a copy of your records. Determine if both of you need to sign it to signify knowledge of the communication.

6. Within reasonable expectations for growth, give the teacher choices about how and where to begin so commitment is more probable. Ask, "What do you need in the way of help in order to achieve this?" But make it clear, "Grow you must!"

7. Plan subsequent activities with that teacher so necessary guidance is provided. Observe lessons to see what worked and what didn't so your next steps become increasingly informed and effective. If you're not available for frequent help and monitoring, find someone who is. Don't expect admonitions without observations and accountability to change ingrained behavior.

8. If indicated, you or someone else demonstrate expected teaching behavior in that class so the teacher sees how it looks in practice and that it works with those students. If it doesn't, you have secured important information that will help you replan.

9. *Mass practice!* You don't expect one lesson to "cure" a remedial student. Don't expect one observation and conference to "cure" a reluctant teacher. Plan several, closely grouped planning sessions, observations, demonstrations, and conferences so you can validate results, or lack of them, from your effort. You may need other coaches or supervisors to assist with this plan. Make sure you communicate with them so you're not riding off in opposite directions.

10. If you arrange for the teacher to observe others, you or a sophisticated coach accompany him/her so teaching behavior is interpreted in terms of cause-effect on student learning. Otherwise, most observation is wasted time for a teacher who cannot or chooses not to "see."

11. With every interaction, note and reinforce growth but do not sedate the teacher into complacency. It is sensitive judgment as to when a teacher needs a respite from demand and when continued pressure is more growth evoking.

12. Knowing your time and energy are limited, work with only one or two reluctant teachers at a time. Spreading your energies will be ineffective and exhaust you. Let the others "rock along." Most of them have been that way for years. A few more months won't be all that important and if they see you "mean it" with others, they may be more amenable when you get to them. Don't "major" in reluctant teachers, working with excellent ones at the same time will renew your energy and revive your enthusiasm. Excellent teachers also are

entitled to stimulation for continuing growth.

13. When, in spite of your best efforts, no improvement is noted, a written summative evaluation, which is beyond coaching and supervision, is indicated. Knowing you have done your best helps you accept this final resolution.

Working with a reluctant teacher is never easy and, at times, it can seem impossible. Most teachers, however, want to do a good job and if they seem unwilling to try it's usually because of fear of failure. Most people would rather be seen as not trying rather than as unable to be successful.

There is no solution guaranteed for every situation. The suggestions in this chapter are merely that, not a recipe to follow. Remember, teaching always involves making decisions. Successful coaching and supervision of reluctant teachers will dramatically increase the probability that they can achieve their professional potential.

PEER COACHING OR "WATCHING SOMEONE TEACH"*

School districts have embraced peer coaching, a potentially powerful strategy for enhancing instructional excellence, without the preparation essential to that activity. As a result we have many teachers "watching someone teach" with both observer and teacher reaping only a small portion of the dividends possible from that activity.

Freeing one teacher to observe another is one of the most costly activities in a school budget. Sophisticated and skilled peer coaching is, no doubt, worth the time and money. "Watching someone teach" is not the same process. Learning from watching, and there is some learning from watching, can more productively and economically be accomplished by a group observing a videotape which can be stopped for discussion, replayed for clarification or emphasis, and preselected to accomplish a specified purpose.

Let's examine the differences between peer coaching and "watching someone teach."

The peer coach, as a result of 25-50 hours of training:

1) has learned the psychological generalizations which express cause-effect relationships between teaching and learning;

2) has identified instructional situations in which use of those generalizations would be appropriate or inappropriate. There are no absolutes in teaching which is a relativistic, situational profession. There is nothing a teacher should "always" or "never" do (except abuse a student);

3) can recognize appropriate or inappropriate use of teaching-learning behaviors in videotaped and live teaching;

4) can script tape (make a running anecdotal record) of an episode of teaching;

5) can analyze that tape to determine appropriate and artistic use of generalizations and principles which affect learning or abuse of those principles; and

6) in a subsequent discussion, can reinforce appropriate practice or can make growth evoking suggestions in terms of additional or different instructional behaviors which are possible for that teacher.

"Watching someone teach," in contrast, can become random feedback which ranges from, "I liked the way you _____," to "May I borrow that ditto master?" The difference is that an untrained observer cannot articulate a theory base, has not had experience in observing and analyzing artis-

---

*This chapter first appeared in N.A.S.S.P. Newsletter, May 1, 1988

tic, in contrast to pedestrian, practice, may not recognize and/or cannot articulate the conditions which would suggest a practice would be appropriate or inappropriate and, as a result, is capable of giving only minimally growth evoking feedback or may even be destructive when that feedback is based on false absolutes. Granted any observation of teaching is better than no observation: a condition that existed until recently for many teachers. Granted, also, that being observed causes all of us to "pull up our socks" and more seriously consider what we are doing and how we might do it better. Yet, to engage in a costly enterprise with such meager dividends is a questionable expenditure of education's less than sufficient resources of time and money. It would be better to label such activities as "peer practice" where both parties have acquired information or skills from inservice and are now watching each other "do it."

So how shall we reap the most dividends from the learning potential embodied in peer coaching?

First, we need to conduct inservice, preferably on released time. If that is not possible, inservice should be scheduled for faculty meetings, before school in the morning, after school in the afternoon, during lunch or planning periods. In those sessions, the staff learns cause-effect relationships between teaching and learning, and the conditions which suggest those relationships' use. These learnings are translated into reality as the staff views artistic application using pre-selected videotapes followed by coaching in lesson analysis and practice in giving growth evoking feedback.

Next, teachers are encouraged to make deliberate, informed use of learning principles in their own classrooms, guided and encouraged by skilled observers.

Finally, strong teachers are encouraged to videotape segments of their teaching, view those tapes privately, then make a decision as to whether to erase them or show them to a small group of peers for discussion. At this point peer coaching becomes really cost effective, for many participants can simultaneously grow professionally from interaction with the perceptions of colleagues. While this requires a considerable inservice preparation and modeling by sophisticated observers, eventually, this process of viewing, analyzing and giving growth evoking feedback can become a routine staff development activity with increased professional communication and growth as the result.

This process of group interaction becomes especially effective when a principal, who has learned instructional, observational, and conferencing skills, demonstrates that learning by videotaping him/herself teaching a group of students so teachers see that no one is perfect and that the principal is willing to participate in an learn from being coached as well as to "try it again" with subsequent videotapes to demonstrate that learning. Credibility and admiration are very predictable results and staff members become more willing to "follow the leader."

If it is financially feasible to hire substitutes, a good plan involves hiring several substitutes for the same day. This permits release of several teachers for the period necessary to watch, analyze with skilled leadership, and give feedback from a live or videotaped lesson. Then the substitutes are sent to release a second group of teachers who repeat the process. Then, a third and possibly fourth group has the experience. For each one day substitute's pay, three to four teachers reap the benefit of engaging in the activity of sophisticated peer coaching.

If substitutes are not possible, the same process can be achieved by using planning periods once or twice a month. If teachers do not have planning periods, an interesting film will accommodate several classes in whatever large space is available. While one professional supervises (an easy task with an interesting film) the other released teachers watch a live or videotaped lesson and increase their professional competence by practicing or observing peer coaching.

Two conditions are essential to productive peer coaching 1) staff development that results in teachers' possession of articulated skills in instruction, plus skills in analysis of teaching and delivering growth evoking feedback, and 2) an administrator who also is practicing those name skills with teachers and students and who uses whatever resources are available to maximize the gain in instructional effectiveness from that activity.

If those two conditions are not present, the authors predict that "teacher watching" will become one or more unproductive "knee jerk" response which will quickly disappear, to be replaced by the next "quick fix" in education.

STAFF MEETINGS THAT RESULT IN STAFF DEVELOPMENT*

Many staff meetings could be nominated as promising candidates for a contest in "worst teaching possible." They typify the stereotype of "giving information to people who aren't listening and who couldn't care less." One teacher wrote, "School is really hectic these days with some long, drawn out faculty meetings which have been pretty discouraging to have to sit through. When all you have is criticism for over an hour for several weeks you begin to wonder if you're doing anything right."

Staff meetings constitute a procedure, already in place, that has high potential for meeting a critical current need: systematically enabling teachers to learn, review, or extend the best in educational practice and incorporate those professional skills in daily teaching.

Every school district has contract agreements allowing time, each week or month, for a staff meeting. Needing to be changed, however, is the traditional focus of that meeting from administrative matters to sessions which increase professional knowledge and enhance performance.

To accomplish this metamorphosis, several things need to occur.

1) A staff development committee, chaired by the principal, diagnoses a staff's professional needs. This can be (and should be) done by the principal and teachers through 1) brief classroom observations, 2) by the committee through polling the staff, 3) representative interviews, and 4) committee consensus. District plans and needs become part of the planning data.

2) A long range staff development plan is developed and articulated with specific goals that have observable outcomes rather than vague, noble sounding platitudes. Those goals then are task analyzed into their enroute components with time and resources to accomplished each component specified and budgeted. It is always tempting to select a group of "information about" goals without including the essential follow through that holds professionals accountable for having assimilated that information, refined it in terms of their own teaching styles and assignments, then translated it into effective and, eventually, artistic practice. In this translation, the principal's supervision plus peer coaching will determine the quality and success of the program.

Another temptation is to move rapidly through a group of "in thing" foci, where there is no unifying strand in terms of a research based theory of effective teaching. Each meeting should be clearly related to and become a part of a professional tapestry not a patch work quilt of "what are we doing this week?"

---

*The original version of this chapter appeared in *Principal.*

Modifications in the articulated staff development plan are made on the basis of emerging wisdom, not ad hoc deflections. If it were not important enough to be in the original plan, it probably should not be included unless it will contribute to achieving the identified professional goals.

3. Each staff meeting becomes a "lesson" planned with the same precision and artistry expected of teachers in the classroom.** A staff meeting objective is specified in terms of precise content and perceivable teacher behaviors that validate achievement.

Examples might be:

- Teachers will practice dignifying student errors by indicating the question to which the incorrect answer belongs, supplying a prompt, and holding the student accountable for learning and remembering the correct answer.
- Teachers will list five behaviors expected of students, then develop plans for teaching, practicing and reinforcing those behaviors to automation.
- Teachers will task analyze an objective relevant to the age of their students and list components in an instructional sequence.

Once the meeting objective is specified, a "lesson plan" is developed which incorporates, as needed, elements of effective instruction. (Not all elements need to be in every meeting!)

The *Anticipatory set* should be developed before the meeting so teachers know expectations and prepare for the learning involved. This can be done by bulletin or by spoken communication. It is inexcusable for teachers to arrive with "what are we talking about today?" questions.

The *Objective* may or may not be articulated at the meeting. In a well developed meeting, the objective is obvious and there is no need for a "By the end of this meeting you will be able to _____" robotic ritual.

Input and modeling, when necessary, may be done by persons, a video or film, a publication *distributed in advance* or by an *informed* discussion. Videos are an excellent source for "how this procedure looks in *classroom practice.*"

Observational learning from a video or film is a powerful, non-threatening strategy which is not used enough. This does not mean showing a film or videotape with a "go thou and do "it" admonition. Films or tapes seldom should be shown in their entirety but should be stopped at key points, discussed, and parts replayed when indicated. In the same way, we stop to "digest," question, reexamine, and summarize printed material.

Checking for understanding, as in a lesson, should occur at several points during a staff meeting not just at the end. Checking may occur during dis-

---

**Plans for a staff meetings are described in *Prescription for Improved Instruction, Mastery Teaching* and *Aiding in Education.* TIP Publications, P.O. Box 514, El Segundo, CA 90245.

cussion or by questions. "Be ready to summarize what we have discussed so far" will cause most participants to reprocess and paraphrase the information or skill being presented. The expectation to summarize raises everyone's level of concern and listening becomes more focused. Judgments of teachers' understanding can also be inferred on the basis of volunteered or selected answers.

Guided practice may occur throughout the meeting or when participants verbally translate information into application for their own assignments. It also occurs during subsequent supervision and peer coaching.

Independent practice, done day after day in teaching, will produce automaticity, internalization and artistry. We have greatly underestimated the time necessary for this phase of professionalism. As a result teachers "do it for a while and then drop it." The learning principle of "distribute practice for long remembering" needs to become a consciously programmed part of any staff development program.

To reiterate, not all elements of an effective lesson need to be (or even should be) incorporated in every staff meeting. It may take several meetings to prepare teachers for guided practice. Some meetings may focus *only* on guided practice. The same principles of educational decision making apply to staff meetings as apply to classroom teaching.

With most meetings focused on staff development, the administrator may ask, "when does the routine business of the school get accomplished?"

Successful administrators have learned to handle day to day business through a weekly bulletin which lists special events, what is due, when, procedures for doing it, and informational announcements. If any activity was not planned and "bulletinized" in advance, it will have to wait until next week's bulletin. Last minute announcements will not be permitted to erode the meeting time needed for staff development. Under these circumstances, it's amazing how much better everyone's planning becomes. It's also amazing to find how much teaching time is salvaged from the blizzard of daily bulletins, ad hoc notes, unanticipated events, and public address announcements that plague teachers. Teachers can read and, when it is expected of them, become conscientious about and accountable for that reading as well as grateful for having information well thought out before it is presented. Emergencies, which require immediate action, occasionally occur but they should be conspicuous by their infrequency.

In summary, enough is now known about effective teaching to make it possible to escalate *every* teacher's competence. The time necessary to accomplish that continuing professional growth is partially provided in the weekly or monthly staff meeting. That time will be productive if a long range staff development plan is in place, with realistic time and resources budgeted to achieve it. As with all successful learning, the elements of effective instruction and the psychological principles that affect learning should become an integral part of those staff meetings and of the coaching and supervision that follow to insure incorporation of increased professional knowledge in daily practice.

Growing to greatness as an educator is never ending. Staff meetings can provide one of the nutrients.

TRANSLATING THE PROGRAM INTO REALITY

Assuming all of the necessary beginning school procedures, to a reasonable degree, not to perfection, have taken place at early staff or inservice meetings, now the task becomes translation of a professionally growth evoking coaching and supervision program into reality. This translation requires two ingredients. The first is a well planned staff development program collaboratively designed by all people affected so it has a research based, continuing focus where each professional skill or decision being learned relates to previous skills and leads to future competence. This is far cry from the "What will we focus on for this inservice meeting?" or "Whom can we get to speak?" ad hoc patchwork of most staff meetings. Even worse is the staff meeting with a focus on "administrivia" which would have been better handled by a bulletin that teachers could read at times optimal for them and then use as a continuing reminder.

The second essential ingredient for a successful coaching or supervision program is a principal committed to the notion that increasing instructional effectiveness is the first priority of the business of schooling and that his/her skill in staff development and supervision is the best predictor of meeting this priority. The principal also needs to take responsibility for and advantage of opportunities for continuing self renewal and professional growth thereby providing a model for the staff.

A principal practicing the same learning principles expected of the teachers in the classroom when that principal is working with discipline, meeting with parents, occasionally teaching students, and conducting conferences, sets the tone for professional excellence in the school. Granted, the principal has other important time demands. Granted, there is never enough time for adequate coaching and supervision. As the principal's skills develop, more can be accomplished in less time. (This also is true in the classroom.) Principals should set aside an absolute minimum of two hours a week (most principals can average much more) that are inviolate for walk-thru supervision and 10-20 minute classroom observations with subsequent brief conferences that yield increased instructional effectiveness. Those well spent hours guarantee dividends in reduction of student or parent problems, cafeteria or hall problems, and teacher concerns; a reduction that eventually yields additional time for staff development and supervision. Alerting parents to the school's program of escalating instructional effectiveness will not only elicit their support but the same principles can be learned at parent meetings for parenting effectiveness.

There may be a few, very few, times when those "inviolate," schedule coaching or supervision hours are consumed by emergencies. If this happens very often, something is amiss in administrative efficiency and organization.

Here we need to deal with the fallacious argument that the supervisor should not be the evaluator. The reasons given, which we consider invalid are 1) teachers will not reveal needs or weakness to someone who eventually will pass judgment on professional effectiveness, and 2) the evaluator will bias subsequent evaluation on the bias of previous problems whether or not they have been resolved.

Our argument against both of the statements is 1) weakness in teaching cannot be concealed from a competent evaluator, and 2) subsequent evaluation should be biased in favor of a teacher who has the maturity to accurately assess self and request help to remediate weakness. To argue the "yes but" position that not all evaluators are non-biased and competent is to argue that, because this may be the current state, it is all right for the biased and incompetent to evaluate teachers. Could there be a weaker professional position?

Time Line for Coaching, Supervision, and Evaluation

In the previous year or summer before the beginning of the program, a district or school staff development committee of representative staff members has been created to form and re-form the year's staff development plans. "Ownership" is currently the "in" word, but it is the authors' opinion that it is teachers' feeling of perceivable, resultant professional growth from observations and conferences that is usually more effective in selling the program and causing it to endure and flourish rather than, "It came from us!"

At the beginning of the year the staff development committee, with the principal, introduces the plan, explains its research basis, demonstrates its procedures, and responds to the staff's questions and concerns.

Given the two requirements of a continuing, planned staff development program and a principal who not only practices what is preached but models the acquisition of new skills as a growing professional, let's look at a possible time line for an effective coaching and supervision program.

During the first two weeks of school in the fall, the principal is highly visible in "walk-thrus" in classrooms. This habituates students and teachers to his/her presence and gives the principal valid diagnostic data of teaching skills that are already present and what next needs to be learned. It also has a reassuring effect on parents when they hear, "The principal was in our room today!"

Informal positive feedback from those brief observations reassures teachers that the principal is looking for what is right rather than what is wrong.

While the principal should have an agreed upon, tentative, school based staff development program in mind before school starts, diagnostic data from these beginning brief observations validate or begin to modify the plan.

After the second week, when beginning school adjustments are made and inevitable snarls unraveled, systematic growth evoking supervision can begin. It is advantageous to start with the most expert teachers. It takes little to stimulate them to continuing growth and the rest of the staff then bonds supervision to effectiveness rather than to remediation. Those teachers also are potential future coaches in the second year of the program. They, when trained, will augment, not replace, the principal's efforts.

When the principal's feedback conferences with those excellent teachers are helpful, the word spreads and the principal will wind up with more requests for coaching and observation than can be scheduled. It's tempting to work only with "those who want to learn." The teacher faces the same problem in a classroom. Like the teacher, the principal must subsequently provide learning opportunities for the less aggressive, or remedial, or reluctant staff learners. Giving them a choice of "this week, or would you rather wait until next week" makes it clear an observation will occur but leaves them in charge of when.

Should a teacher be in serious trouble, the principal or other competent help needs to be immediately available and observations of other teachers will have to wait. Working with a teaching problem as soon as it emerges saves hours of "mop up" time later. An exception to this generalization is the mediocre teacher who has stayed barely afloat for years. A week or two of help will not solve this situation so s/he is better left to limp along until the stronger staff members are "up and flying", thereby freeing the time necessary to accomplish the difficult feat of changing long practiced behavior.

After the initial six weeks to two months of coaching and supervision, which has been a combination of walk-thru and longer observations, the principal needs to take stock of what has been accomplished in transferring learning from staff development meetings, observations, and conferences into teaching performance behaviors. If reasonable results are not perceivable, modification is indicated.

By the beginning of the third month of school, coaching observations and conferences should have become a routine of concentrating on a manageable group of teachers for two to four weeks, then changing focus to a new group with only occasional visits to the first group to maintain quality practice and to stimulate new growth. Eventually, observations and conferences will rotate back to each group for additional massed (new learning) or distributed (older learning) practice.

The principal and staff need to judge when it is possible and desirable to free teachers, who have been trained to observe and to give feedback, to work with their colleagues while the principal takes that teacher's class (excellent for principals' modeling and growth). It is even more efficient in time for the principal or a teacher to take an assembly (films, programs, speakers) so several well trained teachers are freed to observe others. If the school has budgeted for it, substitutes are hired to free teachers for observations and conferences.

After a year or more of staff development activities, the most efficient and effective staff observational learning occurs when teachers videotape their own lessons, view them, then make the decision to erase the video or let colleagues view and discuss it in planning periods, during lunch, or after school. With many viewers, analysis and discussion to add insight about cause-effect, not to make judgments, can result in growth for the entire participating group, not just the teacher observed. The decision needs to be made about inclusion of paraprofessionals in these discussions. If they are included, acceleration of skills, a new respect for the complexity of teaching, and the desire for continuing staff development are highly probable outcomes.

Taping and group viewing usually will not occur during the first year of the program while professionals are learning cause-effect relationships and consciously practicing their appropriate implementation on a daily basis. If a staff development program is successfully mounted, effective teachers will routinely be scheduling growth evoking "viewings" of their teaching during the second year. Some teachers will volunteer lessons to be viewed by the entire staff for observational learning and discussion.

It is especially effective when the principal takes the lead in this growth process by videotaping him/herself teaching students and then analyzes that tape for the group while also inviting comments about situations where similar behaviors would be appropriate or inappropriate. Through this process, staff members will learn that there are no absolutes in teaching, no one is a perfect teacher, and all teaching is "never as good as you hoped or as bad as you feared."

Throughout the year additional information about teaching cycles through staff meetings to teach theory translated into practice; to observe videos to determine conditions in which certain principles of learning are appropriate in practice; to implement new knowledge in subsequent classroom practice; to conduct small group or individual coaching observations and conferences to reinforce or remediate practice; and to schedule group observations and discussions to refine, extend, and develop artistry in practice as well as in resolution of problems. The sequence of these activities is not a set one, but should be custom tailored to the needs of the staff.

In summary, the following elements will more nearly ensure an excellent staff development, coaching and supervision program.

1. Before the program begins, the principal should have received extensive instruction and coaching in principles of learning as they are evidenced in teaching, as well as in skills of script taping and analysis of lessons plus practice, *with coaching,* in the observation/ conference process.

2. In the year or summer preceding the program, a representative committee has considered options and developed a plan.

3. At the beginning of its implementation, the principal has explained the committee's plan to the entire staff and has modeled what s/he will be doing during the first two weeks of school. Staff members' questions, comments, and suggestions should be considered for further development of the plan.

With the preceding program in "full bloom", something not completely accomplished in the initial year, almost all staff members will move towards growth in professional competence. Collegial collaboration can become established as an important educational function in making professional decisions (rather than sharing dittos) and ongoing professional growth in curriculum and instruction will become an increasingly established procedure.

Two important additional foci included in this program for continuing professional growth will be 1) curricular competence in each discipline in terms of district articulated outcomes and 2) facility (artistry!) in communication with parents. Both foci also should be addressed in staff meetings, job alike seminars, and individual conferences. Those activities involve the very same principles as does effective teaching, but they are not included in this book.

EFFECTING A RECONCILIATION
BETWEEN COACHING, SUPERVISION, AND EVALUATION*

We take exception to the assertion that teacher evaluation is a high-cost, low-yield investment. Teaching has improved more in the last decade, since we have done research on teaching and teachers are being evaluated in terms of that research, than it had in the previous centuries. Granted, there always have been outstanding teachers, but their skills were usually intuitive, not consciously practiced. Granted, also, that more research has been available for determining effective teaching in the last decade than in previous centuries. We need look only at the contribution of criterion referenced testing to improvement of student performance to supply evidence that high yield is the result from application of research to the evaluation of students (teachers or principals).

We also acknowledge that many principals have not yet had the opportunity to learn how to coach, supervise, or evaluate a teacher: an indictment of our universities, some of whom still do an inadequate job of preparing principals for these professional responsibilities.

Another issue which, in most cases, is no longer relevant is the "fix or fire," "improve or remove" implication of previous formative and summative evaluation. We are way beyond those rudimentary notions. The outcome for coaching, supervision, and evaluation should be escalating teaching effectiveness. Summative evaluation becomes a check point at the end of the year when decisions need to be made about salary, assignment, promotion, or release. Expectations should vary for beginning and experienced teachers, but both must be certified as growing professionals, not merely "adequate" teachers. The process of gathering supporting, valid evidence for formative and summative evaluation is much the same. Observing, script taping, and analyzing constitute the diagnostic phase of both activities. Making plans for continuing professional growth or decisions about future status constitute the prescriptive phase. Formative, then summative evaluation must be a sequential process, not simultaneous or discrete. Final evaluation is a summation of and achieves validity from coaching and supervision. The decision to terminate must be based on evidence from many observations, throughout the year, that the individual has had the necessary help, but has not demonstrated the capacity and/or intention to grow professionally from that opportunity. Intent to grow usually is stimulated as a result of supervision by someone who has the power to make a final evalua-

---

*This chapter first appeared in *Journal of Personnel Evaluation in Education*, Vol. I, No. 3, Winter 1988. University of Connecticut Storrs.

tion and who has collected ongoing data to support final judgment. Of course, principals want to, and need to be supportive. They will feel so if they have been involved in helping, not just judging.

In a Los Angeles inner city school, the principal attempted to help a resistant teacher. Finally, in desperation, the principal issued an ultimatum that better professional skills would be demonstrated or the teacher would be released. Improvement began. By the end of the year, the principal rated the teacher as "better than average" and confessed. "I've always been ashamed of myself for losing my temper and threatening to fire you. What caused you to grow?" The teacher responded, "No one had ever explained professional growth to me that way before."

When there are two administrators, working together rather than separately on formative and summative evaluation should be the procedure. In that way stimulation and correction are built into both processes. To have no communication between the two is like concealing from your doctor all relevant health informaiton when you have your annual physical.

It is time we do some "marriage counseling" to avert the potential divorce of teacher evaluation from supervision and coaching. The two really are very compatible. With understanding of the role, purpose, and activities of each, professional techniques for escalating instructional effectiveness (and even bliss!), are possible to achieve. Those who believe otherwise seldom have had extensive experience in dealing with both processes in routine clinical school practice.

It is interesting that in no other enterprise do we consider helping people become more skilled, and determining that they have become more skilled, to be mutually exclusive enterprises. Typically, the teacher who works daily with a class believes no one else can evaluate them as fairly and accurately. Surely, teaching adults in graduate classes does not interfere with grading those same students. We would stipulate it contributes to a fair grade!

A coach who has worked with players usually can give a more accurate appraisal of their present skills and future potential than can a one time, skilled observer. Only in competition where the contestants are being compared and ranked in identical situations, are the judges different from trainers who could be biased in terms of their "one and only." Evaluators of teachers do not have a "one and only" who is competing against another's "one and only" in identical situations. Competence must be evaluated in terms of appropriateness and artistry of teaching decisions and behaviors in bewilderingly different situations. The athlete's high jump bar is not at different heights when it is supposed to be at six feet. The condition of the ice does not vary considerably from one skater to the other but classes and teaching situations do.

Teaching is an action performance behavior based on cognition. Information or skills can be acquired through inservice, coaching, self analysis, observation, or independent study. The "how" is less important than that artistic skill and accurate knowledge are acquired. Proficiency and artistry develop, as in all action performance behaviors, through practice with coaching. In education, we call the coaching process supervision or peer coaching or formative evaluation. All coaching requires that the coach possess and utilize the skills necessary to increase the effectiveness and/or artistry of another's performance (something not always true in current peer coaching). It does not require that the coach be able to perform better than the individual being coached. The diagnostic-prescriptive aspect of coaching which enhances or remediates professional performance through formative interactions has been missing from much previous supervision (hence, the name "snoopervision"). The primary purpose of supervision, coaching, or formative evaluation is to enhance performance. All employ the process of observation, script taping, and analysis of productive and, if they exist, less than productive behaviors. Teaching effectiveness and artistry are encouraged through a subsequent instructional conference.

Summative evaluation is a summation of the results from those same processes for the purpose of certification and/or assignment of a person to a category which can range from "inadequate" to "outstanding". Evaluators must have the skills necessary for making judgments about teaching performance which can be supported by reasonably objective data gathered from frequent formative observations and conferences. A defensible summative evaluation cannot be made after one observation or one conference.

Consequently, to validly supervise or evaluate teachers, one needs to be highly skilled in both formative and summative evaluation in order to determine whether the teacher's decisions and behaviors were appropriate (and artistic!) or are *becoming* increasingly appropriate for *these* students in *this* situation with this particular content being learned. The professional skills essential to engaging in supervision and evaluation also require formative supervision/coaching during the acquisition of those skills as well as require summative evaluation by a person qualified to certify their possession.

This is not to say that only a final evaluator contributes to professional growth. Both principals and teachers need all the help they can get to translate research about teaching and learning into effective and artistic classroom implementation. Principals welcome the augmentation which results from assistance of resource teachers, central office supervisors, and peer coaches to assist with, not replace, their own supervision. Daily assistance for a teacher who needs it usually is not possible for a principal, given other school responsibilities.

It is essential, however, for a principal to know the area on which a teacher's attempt to grow is focused and to be aware of the effort put forth and the progress being made so this information becomes an important consideration in the final summative evaluation. It is naive to believe that the teacher will reveal problems to a coach or supervisor and conceal them from an evaluator. Problems in performance behavior cannot be concealed. They are inevitably revealed to any sophisticated observer. Do you think the coach doesn't know who lacks skill in passing? The teacher doesn't know which students can't multiply? The observer doesn't know when a teacher has discipline problems, doesn't understand math concepts, asks only "yes/no" questions? To believe that a teacher must reveal a problem for a skilled observer to know it exists is naive thinking.

It is equally naive to assume the principal does not have the time for supervision when instruction is the first priority of school. Granted, none of us has all the time we need and we welcome and need additional help. Every principal can schedule a few hours, inviolate, each week to supervise (assist with) the development of escalating excellence and artistry in teaching. "Walk thru" supervision enables principals to visit four to six teachers in a half hour. Seldom should any observer's visit last more than ten to twenty minutes. The necessary feedback and coaching can follow at breaks, before and after school, in preparation periods, or in the classroom with the students on "autopilot." Frequently, "don't have time" means "don't know how," which is understandable, as skills of supervision often are not adequately acquired in administrative preparation.

Supervision is a process much more difficult than evaluation although the latter appears more formidable. Supervision requires diagnosis of what the teacher is next ready to learn, prescription for how best to acquire that knowledge or skill, plus monitoring the process of acquisition, acceleratiang or remediating the process is required, and assuming part of the responsibility for the teacher's professional growth.

Evaluation, while not easy, requires only a final assignment to a category with supporting objective evidence. To do either supervision or evaluation well, requires the same process: observing, script taping analyzing and interpreting the script tape, then holding a growth evoking conference with the teacher. Each, however, has the different purpose of "teaching" or "grading·" Teachers see a final evaluation as fair and just if it is based on many samples of their teaching, not on just one visit.

Principals feel secure in final evaluation when they have been involved in a teacher's growth throughout the year. "Summative" becomes truly a summing up of a year's effort and achievement in the demanding process of teaching. Evaluation should be an outcome which reflects the quality of supervision and teaching effort in the same way that grading students is the outcome that reflects their efforts and the quality of instruction.

Let's look at some actual situations which support the marriage of formative and summative evaluation.

1.   Teacher A is a nice "average" teacher. Students make routine progress in her class but are not very excited about school. Parents (and the custodian) don't complain, but never request that teacher. The supervisor works hard all year to try to get Teacher A to try some new ideas, to add a little spark to her class, but to no avail. At the end of the year, things are just the same as they were last year and the year before and the year before that.

Teacher B is a teacher who begins the year with considerable chaos. The room is disheveled, the students noisy, and teaching is inconsistent. The supervisor works hard and slowly things begin to improve. At the end of the year students are well behaved most, but not all of the time. The room is usually orderly, but exciting student activities sometimes leave it messy. Teacher B has tried and mastered most, but not all of the teaching techniques suggested.

An evaluator, unaware of what the supervisor has been striving to accomplish with both teachers makes a visit to each room. Which teacher do you think will receive a better evaluation? Which has demonstrated more potential for continuing growth and eventual excellence? How can the evaluator know that?

2.   An evaluator observed a class where one boy was drawing a motorcycle while the teacher was explaining a process. The evaluator marked the teacher down for not making the boy put the motorcycle away. He was unaware that the teacher had grown from "taking the student on" in a public display of "tug of war" from which there was no honorable retreat for either party, to ignoring behavior that was not disturbing to others and was well along the way to interesting the boy in the lesson. The evaluator, not having worked with the teacher, had no way of crediting the teacher with professional growth in a very difficult situation or knowing that the boy was behaving the best he ever had.

3.   One author (who has supervised and evaluated untold numbers of teachers) observing a mature teacher felt he left a lot to be desired. The principal, who had been supervising him all year, stated that he was an administrative transfer from another school where he had been permitted, by "average" evaluations, to continue with less than mediocre performance. The current principal had assisted with, but insisted on, improvement and the growth had been remarkable. School district personnel marveled at his improvement and predicted he would shortly attain better

than adequate performance. Would the author's one observation or the principal's year-long supervision be the more fair evaluation?

An important aspect of evaluating teachers is knowing what new skills they are learning, how eagerly they seek constructive appraisal, what and how hard they are willing to try in order to improve their performance and how much they have accomplished professionally this year. The person who coaches or supervises should be aware of these aspects which are predictors of continuing professional growth or stagnation. Evaluators without this data from many supervisory visits and conferences may not be cognizant of how well teachers have learned what they have had the opportunity to learn and how much supervisory effort it took to achieve these results.

It is interesting to note that in the Napa Project* where consultants supervised and principals evaluated, as soon as the consultants left, the teachers no longer continued with what they had learned but went back to their "old ways." Evidently, the teachers felt there were different expectations in supervision and evaluation. This provides provocative evidence that supervision and evaluation should be marriage partners, not divorced activities. Let's reunite them but, through inservice in both, build future compatibility.

---

*Journal of Elementary Education, February 1987

TRANSCRIPTS FOR PRACTICING ANALYSIS
AND DESIGNING CONFERENCES

Conferences, as lessons, should be designed with the particular learner in mind. First, read the transcript of the lesson. Then analyze the transcript to assess the teacher's strengths and the behaviors about which you have questions before you look at our analysis. Your analysis probably will not be exactly the same as ours because we observed the actual lesson so we have more information than is in the transcript.

Design your conference and have a colleague, who also has read the transcript, role play as validly as possible the teacher's reactions to your coaching. In your conference implement what you have learned about how to begin, how to design enabling statements or pose non threatening questions, and how to summarize and conclude the conference with positive feelings.

Get feedback from your role playing colleague so you build correction and artistry in your conference skills. Remember, a conference is a high speed performance behavior that requires a great deal of practice to translate knowledge into artistic action.

The first transcript, "Locating Information," is followed by four possible excerpts from sample conferences depending on whether the teacher is new, involved in a beginning staff development program, experienced with conferences, or very sophisticated in lesson analysis.

The second transcript and example of an (not *the*) appropriate conference is directed to a teacher who needs help.

The following transcripts an analysis are for you to practice analyzing and designing and appropriate conference.

Videotapes of lessons with analysis and conferences are available from: Special Purpose Films, 416 Rio del Mar, Aptos, CA 95003 (408) 688-6320.

TRANSCRIPT: LOCATING INFORMATION

T   Now, open your books to page 43. I'm going to be asking you some very hard questions. This time you are going to use your marker to find the answer to the question I ask. When you find the answer on your page, show me with your signal how you will be able to read the answer."

S   The students all put their thumbs up on the desk in front of them.

T   "Exactly right. Okay. You've got a thumb up. I'll know you're ready. Who has a lot of pep? (pause) "Brandon. In your loudest voice."

S   "Mr. Hopper has a lot of pep."

T   "Perfect. Everybody has his or her marker on exactly the right answer. Okay, listen to the next question. Who is not peppy?" (pause) "First person to find it put your thumb up." (pause) (The teacher touches Erica's arm to answer.)

S   "But Mr. _____ is not peppy."

T   "Perfect. Listen again. Who has his mat with him?" (pause) Who has his mat with him? (pause) (She touches Miguel to answer.)

S   "Mrs." (The teacher interrupts.)

T   "In your loudest voice."

S   "Mr. Sleeper has his mat with him."

T   "Perfect. Put your thumb up if you are a person who had your marker on the very last sentence on page 43." (The teacher looks around the group.) "And you'll know you were exactly right. Okay. Turn to page 44. (pause) Be ready to listen to my question. I might go a little faster this time. Who can see Mr. Hopper?" (pause) "Patrick."

S   "We can see…." (pauses)

T   "that" (The teacher tells the word.)

S   "that Mr. Hopper is…" (pauses)

T   "glad" (The teacher calls on a student who has her thumb up to indicate she can say the word.)

S   "glad if be"

T   "he" (The teacher corrects.)

S   "he can hop and hop and hop."

T   "Excellent. Can you go back to the word–put your marker on the word that gave you a little trouble. (pause) Can you read that word?"

S   "glad"

T	"Perfect. You got that. Okay. Move your marker overs to page 45. Listen to my question, "Who gets to the stump?" The teacher touches Morgan's arm indicating he should answer."
S	"Mr...." (The teacher interrupts.)
T	"Louder voice."
S	"Mr. Sleeper gets—gets to the stump."
T	"Put your thumb up if you agree. (The teacher looks around the group She touches Patrick's hand.) Do you agree or disagree? (to Patrick) (pause) Okay.

TRANSCRIPT ANALYSIS: LOCATING ANSWERS

Productive Behaviors
1. Combination set/obj./input/checking for quick, clear transition to a new segment of lesson
2. Concern–thumbs and markers–visible and accountable
3. Knowledge of Results
   "Ex. Rt" (th.up) (specific)
   "Perf." (ok ans. obvious)
   "Perf. ev. marker it place" (specific)
   "Perf." (corr. ans.)
4. St. thumbs up when hear error–Tr. control for amount of wait time, who will "help"
5. Dignify error–Patrick–"Word gave trouble"

Questioned Behaviors
1. Open books first direction ok with simple or routine directions—usually start and not hear directions.
2. "very hard questions" need jolt? what reactions?
3. Other phrases when you feel perfect becoming overused?
4. "Who can see Mr. Hopper" Patrick–long sent.–3 errors Reason for sent.? Choose Patrick?
5. Thumb up to disagree good for opinion or choice—may "put down" another student.

LOCATING INFORMATION: SAMPLE CONFERENCE I

For the teacher who is new to coaching and needs to hear only productive behaviors:

Objective: The teacher will have the opportunity to hear what techniques she used to lower the level of difficulty and how it influences motivation.

O   Karolynne, you did a super job of breaking a very complex task into very small steps. That was very important for these students. When you are working with students who have had so much difficulty learning to read and write you are very wise to carefully design the lesson so they are very certain of success. They must feel that if they try they will be successful so they will be motivated to keep trying. They continued to put effort into the task because you had them in a group where the objective allowed them all to move along at about the same pace. You also gave them enough time so each one could think of the words on the cards or find the sentence in the book rather than calling on the first one with the answer. You also provided just the right amount of help when they needed it such as when Erica said "is" instead of "as". You said, "Look at it very carefully. It would be..." and she said "as" even without the clue of "if this were an 'i.'" That is such an effective way to help because you are giving a student the opportunity to think it through for herself as much as possible.

One of the reasons your lesson was effective was because you helped those students be successful so they would continue to be motivated to put forth effort by breaking the learning into very small steps, giving them enough time to think and be ready to answer and by giving just enough help so they could correct their own mistakes rather than hearing a correct answer from someone else. These are all signs of effective planning and teaching.

None in this brief conference the teacher only listened. While interaction between observes and teacher is desirable, in this case the teacher was reassured that she was doing well and left feeling good about the conference.

97

LOCATING INFORMATION: SAMPLE CONFERENCE II

For the teacher who is new to the observation/conference process, but is participating in an on-going staff development program:

Objective: The teacher, having heard them from the observer, will recall techniques for maintaining an appropriate level of concern and state when those techniques would be appropriate in other lessons.

O   Karolynne, the students in your reading group were certainly focussed and involved in the lesson. You used several techniques to keep their level of concern at a very productive level. You have taught them to put a marker under a sentence in the book so you can easily see who has the correct answers to your question. When students are that visible to the teacher, they are more likely to put effort into doing the task correctly. Another way you maintained an appropriate level of concern was having the students grouped around the small table. Being so close to the teacher that you can reach out and touch them usually causes them to keep their minds on the activity. Techniques like these are particularly important when you are working with students who have had a hard time learning to read and have experienced so much frustration. (The teacher was taking notes and appeared interested in these ideas.)

    Are you aware of some of the other things you did that were so effective in maintaining that level of concern for your students?

T   I think so, but I'm not really sure. (A little tentative and hesitant.)

O   Most of the time you waited a few seconds after you asked a question before you called on someone rather than calling on the first person with the answer. You also reached over and touched Patrick's arm when he wasn't looking for the answer. Also you never let them know who was going to be called on next. All of these techniques let the students know you expect them to be ready with every answer even if they had just been called on.

    When would you use these same techniques in other subject areas when you have a larger group?

T   I guess any time I ask questions in social studies or math I should wait a few seconds to make sure everyone is thinking and ready to be called on.

O   You used a very important qualifier when you said, "everyone is thinking." When the student needs time to formulate a more complex answer, it would be important to provide that wait time. Can you think of a time when you want a very rapid answer from a student?

T   Oh, yes. When we are drilling on math facts, I want an immediate answer. I don't want them to have time to count on their fingers.

O   When you have given them time to understand math facts or learn what a word means in context and you are working on instant re-cognition you're right, you would not provide much wait time.

    As you are teaching lessons in the next few days, keep track of some of the times when you think students need that wait time for thinking and when they should have a very rapid response. You can help me develop examples for other teachers when we discuss that technique in our faculty meeting next week.

LOCATING INFORMATION: SAMPLE CONFERENCE III

For the secure teacher who is ready for dialogue instead of just listening:

Objective: The teacher will identify parts of the lesson which were effective and explain why they were effective and parts of the lesson that were less effective than she had hoped and select alternatives for improving those parts.

O   Karolynne, your students were very focussed and participated very well throughout that lesson. What were you doing that helped your students do such a good job of paying attention?

T   One thing I have found that works well is to make sure they know they are all responsible for answering every question so I usually show them a word card and wait a few seconds so they know I expect all of them to be ready to say the word.

O   It was very evident that that worked well in *these* students. Do you know why it worked so well?

T   I'm really not sure, but I remember hearing someone suggest it one time and I have continued to use it.

O   What you were doing was raising your students' level of concern to a very appropriate level so their energy was directed to the learning task rather than other things. That few seconds of "wait time" often causes students to feel accountable to participate and to learn. Are you aware of anything else you did to maintained that productive level of concern?

T   I hadn't thought of it that way before but I guess the markers would help too. They know if they are not getting the right answers we will keep working on it until they do.

O   That's true. You are holding them accountable for learning. You are also causing them to be very visible. They know that it is very easy for you to see if they have the correct sentence to answer the question. Being visible to an authority such as the teacher maintains a very productive level of concern when the student feels competent to do the task.

O   You have identified two very effective ways to maintain an appropriate level of concern to motivate students. When you make it clear they are accountable for learning, such as building in a few seconds of "wait time", or when they know they are very visible to a "significant other" such as the teacher, they are much more likely to be motivated to focus on the learning task. In that lesson you modeled two excellent teaching techniques.

LOCATING INFORMATION: SAMPLE CONFERENCE IV

For the teacher who is sophisticated, confident, and has had experience in labeling teaching behaviors:

Objective: The teacher will identify techniques for maintaining an appropriate level of concern and when those techniques would be appropriate in other lessons.

O   Karolynne, as usual, you planned a lesson that included many things that would help those students improve their reading skills. You continue to add new skills to your teaching as we work in our staff development program. What have you been working on that you felt worked out well in this lesson?

T   I think I am better at getting more of the students paying attention and participating more of the time. These students are so used to tuning out and not trying. They work with a very low level of concern. They couldn't care less about following in reading. I think they are doing better because I am asking questions of the whole group, then waiting till most of them indicate they have the answer and then calling on them in a very unpredictable order. Sometimes I call on the same student for two answers in a row. At first they were quite surprised but now they are used to it and are ready most of the time.

O   It isn't easy to keep students like these on their toes most of the time. You are certainly getting more productive learning time for them with the ideas you mentioned. Have you tried these same ideas in your larger groups?

T   Yes, but there is more time between the times the same student gets to answer so some of them begin to tune out in the larger groups.

O   The ways you had each student use a marker to find the answer to the question really kept them accountable and tuned in. It kept their level of concern at an appropriate level because they were accountable and very visible to you. Let's think of a way to adapt that technique to any of your total group lessons.

T   I'm not sure what you mean.

O   The way you have them use the marker is a group response that is like having all the students say the answer out loud when you hold up a sight word on a flash card and say, "Everybody" for a choral response. You could develop some similar signals that students in a large group could use. For instance, when you are working on the sequence of events in a story, you could give them 2 or 3 or 4 events and ask them to tell if the event is 1st, 2nd, or 3rd by holding up 1,

2, or 3 fingers. That way all the students would be answering instead of just one at a time for each question. Signaled or choral responses work best when there is just one right answer. Are there some other skills that you are working on where there is usually just one right answer?

T   I guess number facts with answers of 10 or less is the most obvious.

O   Yes. You are adding to the kinds of questions that could be answered with a number. There are other signals too such as using crossed fingers to show addition in a math problem or just the horizontal index finger to show subtraction when you are working mathematical problem solving strategies. (Observer models response on own fingers.)

T   I could use the same idea when I am giving them practice on sentences that end with a period or a question mark. They could show a period with a fist and a question mark with a crooked finger. (pause) Another time I could use a signal is when I am having the students listen for the different vowel sounds in a word such as "a" and "e". "They could show 3 fingers on one hand if they hear an "e" and 2 fingers pointed down with the other finger across for an "a" (Teacher models with fingers.)

O   You are really getting the idea of having students signal their answers so all the students are responsible for thinking and participating. Let's get together next week to develop lots of other examples of signalling that all our teachers might use.

TRANSCRIPT: SQUARE ROOT LESSON

Students come in with noise and disorder. Teacher is at door of room but does nothing to quiet them down. Teacher goes to front of room, waits and then pounds on desk and says in loud voice, "Boys and girls."

Student's become quiet and teacher says, "It took us a little longer to get quiet, but I wish to compliment you. It was better than this morning when we needed to go outside and come back in again, but it took you much too long to give your attention. Paul, go to the door and show us how to come in because you were one of the worst. (Paul goes to door and comes back in quietly). That's the way I want you to come in. He came in nicely, sat down, and paid attention. No more of this crazy business. I've had enough of it.

"OK, it's math time. (Students groan but teacher ignores it.) Yesterday we worked with decimal fractions. We'll do more on fractions tomorrow but today we'll learn about square root. Raise your hand if you've ever heard about square root. (No hands) Jill, put your pencil away. Thank you. I like the way you listened and did it right away. Who has ever heard square root? (No hands) What do you think square root means? Raise your hand if you know. (No hands) Raise your hand if you think you know. What do you think it means Peter?"

Peter (in tentative voice): "The root of a square?"

Teacher "That's pretty close. (The phone rings.) I'll be right back, I need to get the phone." (Students begin to talk loudly.) Teacher yells, "I need to hear, talk quietly!" (Students talk in loud voices.) Teachers yells, "I need to hear. Stay in your seats and whisper." (Students continue noisy talking.)

"OK, boys and girls. Close your books and put down your pencils. I don't know how many times I've had to tell you when I'm on the phone, you're to sit quietly and wait. That was the assistant principal and when she heard all that noice, what will she think of you? (Students yell out answers.) We just lost 15 minutes of recess. (Students fuss but teacher ignores them, they quiet down.)

"We started talking about square root. Peter told us it was the root of a square. Anyone else have an idea?"

Student: "Number in a square?"

Teacher: "Could be."

Student: "Grown square?"

Teacher: "We'll stop guessing. Will you pass these papers out? (Hands papers to several students.) When you get your paper it tells you in the top box what square root is. I'm going to call on someone to read it. (Much noice) If there are not enough papers, share them with the person next to you. Read the box at the top. It tells you what square root is. Mary, you've been very quiet, read it".

Mary: "Square root is that number which when multiplied by itself produces the given number."

Teacher: "Let's read it together. (Students yell it out together.) This is...(teacher stops until students become quiet). Thank you for quieting down. This is the square root sign. (Writes it on board.) It has a number inside. (Writes a 4.) This is the given number. What number multiplied by itself equals four? (Students yell out answers.) We have talked so many times about when you're ready to say something you raise your hand. Right, $2 \times 2 = 4$. I'll put the answer up here. (Writes it over problem.) Think of what would be the square root of 9. (Students yell out answers.) Three, good. You're really getting this. You'd never know you didn't know it before. What is the square root of 25. (Puts problem on board, and students yell answer.) You're getting this quickly but remember to raise your hands. This is a hard one. What is the square root of 64? (Students yell answer). I'm going to stop and wait. Debby, you had your hand up. Very good, eight.

"Look at your paper, Read the top box again, Larry. (Larry reads.) I'll give you time right now to do the ten problems at the top. (Students groan.) Quiet please, we're wasting so much time by talking out. We've already lost 15 minutes. When you finish you can do your book reports or your social studies. Your homework will be problems 11-20. (Students groan.) I'll just wait. (Students become quiet.) This is as quiet as I want it. What numbers will you do for homework? Raise your hands. (Students answer 1-10.) Right, no, that's what you do right now. (Students yell 11-20.) Don't help each other. Do it by yourself."

ANALYSIS OF TRANSCRIPT: SQUARE ROOT

Productive Behaviors

1. T is working on students' coming in.
2. T doesn't make big issue of groan over math.
3. T thanks S for following directions.
4. T acknowledges quiet student.
5. T can always quiet S.
6. T compliments S on learning.
7. T tells S what to do when finished.
8. T checks understanding of assignment.

Questioned Behaviors

1. T identifies Paul as "one of worst."
2. T focuses students on decimal fractions when focus is square root.
3. T has students guessing meaning of square root when she has evidence they don't know.
4. T hasn't planned for students' behavior when there is an interruption.
5. T punishes without warning.
6. T accepts answers without S raising hands then scolds them for it.

Possible Conference Objectives

1. The teacher and observer will develop several "sponge" activities which the students will begin as soon as they enter the room after each break. The teacher will select whether she or the observer will introduce this activity to the students and conduct their initial practice. A date will be set for the observer to return to observe how successful students are in a productive beginning after a break.
2. Teacher and observer will develop productive "desk work" that students can work on alone when the teacher is otherwise engaged and a signal for their doing it. Plans will be made for introducing these tasks to the students and giving them practice.
3. The teacher, with the observer, will make plans for becoming more consistent with accepting answers only when hands are raised, introducing the plan to students, and giving them practice.

The following objectives would be appropriate after the class has "settled down":

1. The teacher will identify situations where information is appropriately elicited from students and when the teacher should present information.
2. Teacher and observer will collaborate in designing lessons so the teacher becomes more proficient in all elements of teaching.

SAMPLE CONFERENCE: SQUARE ROOT

Objective: The teacher will design sponge activities and strategies for their use when students enter the room and at times of interruption.

O   Ruth, you have many teaching strengths. We are going to design ways you can use them to achieve the behavior you expect from that energetic group of students.

T   They are a very difficult group. Those boys are just rowdy.

O   Yet, one of your strengths is that you can get them quiet any time they see you mean it. A weaker teacher could not do that. Also you indicated you have been working on their coming in quietly and sitting down. Let's use your strengths to speed up that process.

Do you remember our staff meeting on sponge activities, those activities that sop up waiting time with practice of something already that needs to be more fluent or more easily recalled?

T   Sort of. It's kind of vague.

O   We talked about teaching students to look at the chalkboard as soon as they entered the room to see what they should immediately start doing. In this way they get needed practice and it also eliminates most of the discipline problems. What are some things that your group needs to practice?

T   They can always practice spelling.

O   That would be an excellent sponge at the beginning of a spelling or writing lesson. What could they practice that would focus them on math.

T   Well they could be guessing what square root means.

O That would focus them on your lesson but guessing encourages talking which you want to eliminate. You know from your lesson that they didn't know what square root means. Perhaps you could have them think about what number multiplied by itself equals 4, 9, 16, 25? That would get them settled, thinking, and focus them on your lesson rather than talking to each other. Let's think of other things you might do in math so every day they have something to do when they come in.

T We've been working on word problems. I could have them solve some.

O All students need practice with that. It involves more work on your part to write the problem on the board unless you write the number of a page of their math book. Sometimes just putting the problem on the board in numerals and having them make up a word problem to go with it is effective because it requires they really understand what they are doing in solving problems. For example, you might place 5 x 5 and 10 x 10 on the board with "Be ready with a word problem from your own life that would go with each of these." Eventually after students learned the routine you could write M.W.P. for "make a word problem" and the students would know what they were supposed to do. We want to make the least work possible for you. Then, when you start the class you could call on two or three students for their problems which would make math more meaningful for the others.

We've thought of two ideas, what else could they do so you have variety from which to choose?

T They can always work on number facts.

O How would you have them do that.

T They could test each other.

O That would be an excellent activity as soon as they were in charge of themselves. Right now they need to learn to work quietly by themselves. You might use a class period to dictate the times tables allowing just enough time between each fact for them to write the answer or make a line if they don't know it. Then they can make their individual flash cards for those combinations they don't know or need to speed up. They could start practicing those flash cards as soon as they come in. You also could use the cards when they are being dismissed by taking their practice cards and asking them one of the combinations.

Let's now look at how you might start this new procedure by teaching it to students.

T	I could tell them about it but I've done that before.
O	You're right. Telling isn't enough. New procedures have to be taught. After you explain it, they need to go out of the room, come in, look at what you have on the board and start to work. You used excellent reinforces in your lesson when you said "Thank you for getting quiet" and "You're really catching on fast." Give that same commendation to those who start right away on the sponge. If you're not quite sure of how to start the procedure, I'll be happy to come in, introduce it and take them through their first practice. However, I have complete confidence in your ability to do it well. You decide which you'd prefer.
T	I think I'd rather do it so the kids don't think I sent for the principal to settle them down.
O	You obviously don't need a principal for that. Those noisy boys stopped as soon as you clamped down. Start with a sponge each day in math. If you want to use one for every period, the students will learn it faster but it will be more work for you each period thinking of one. You already suggested they work on spelling for their language period. They might also have a library book in their desk so when you have an interruption, such as a phone, they know they take the book out and read if you haven't given them another sponge.

Incidentally, I apologize for that phone interruption. I'll need to remind people again they are not to phone when the class is in session unless it is a real emergency. Taking care of those phone interruptions will be my job.

Let's list your other strengths so you know they are very visible. We've talked about your positive comments and that you're working on better classroom behavior. If you consistently refuse to accept any answer that is shouted out the students will learn to raise their hands. You also gave them instructions for what to do when they finish and checked their understanding. Those good techniques will help as you teach them to come in the room quietly and get started. Are you comfortable with how you're going to start that tomorrow morning? |
T	Well, I'm going to think about it a little more.
O	Remember, I'll help in any way you wish. You might tell the class you're going to invite me in to see how well they take care of themselves and start to work. How soon should I come in to observe and praise them for their progress?
T	Oh, in about a week.

O   Great, I'll come in a week from today to congratulate them.

Note that the observer worked on only one new behavior for the teacher even though much remains to be done. A hint was made of lack of consistency in accepting blurted out answers. That can be worked on next. When the class is in order, the focus will be on designing a productive lesson.

Transcript: High School Economics Lesson

Teacher has on board: "Be ready to state the three functions of money."

T   I have this (dollar bill), plastic (credit card), jingly things (coins), and this (checkbook). How are they all the same?

S   Money

T   That's so perceptive of you (laughter). In our class we've been studying limited wants and resources which means we didn't have enough what?

S   Wants

T   Oh, we had plenty of those, but our resources were limited so we couldn't satisfy our wants because we didn't have enough money. We've studied supply and demand curves and the vertical axis represented...

S   Money

T   The dollar sign. We've studied equilibrium point, the average selling price. We've talked about things that dealt with money. Yesterday we learned what money is. Today we'll review the functions of money, the forms money takes in our society and the three kinds of money.

At the end, or during the lesson, I'll be asking you questions to make sure you've learned because you'll have a test on Thursday.

First, tell me the functions of money, let's see hands.

S   Medium of exchange.

T   That will be number 1 (holds up one finger)

S   Standard of value.

T   That will be 2 (two fingers).

S   Storage of value.

T   That will be 3 (three fingers). Doug here gets a pay check every week, a payment for goods or services. Let's see hand signals. What function would that be? (Students signal with fingers on chest.) Right, a medium of exchange.

George is going to buy a Porsche so he puts away part of his pay check every week, what functions would that be (student's signal). Right, a storage of value. This pair of shoes costs $30 and that pair

112

$35, what would that be? (Students signal.). Right, a standard of value.

Now, what makes this stuff (indicates bill coins, credit card) a good medium of exchange? (Writes on board, "Characteristics of money" and lists ADD PS under it). When we write a letter we can ADD a PS (points to letters on board).

Doug got his money and took it to Coynan's McDonalds to buy a hamburger but Coynan said, "We only take cows' ears here." So he went to Ann's Outpost to buy jeans and she said, "We only accept cows' ears." He went to Jeff's station for gas and Jeff said, "That will be 16 cows ears." What is the medium of exchange?

S   Cows' ears.

T   Why? (Students chorus, "Acceptable.") Yes, it's what we agree to use (writes "Acceptable" for first A on board).

Salt was used for money in dry climates. Steve here went over the hill and across the river with his salt to buy something in the next village and clumsy Steve fell into the river (class chuckles). What would happen to his salt? (Class says, "Dissolves.") So what does money need to be? (Class says, "Durable.") Teacher writes it after D on the chalkboard.

Cows have been used as a medium of exchange. Irving has a cow but he wants a loaf of bread from Kim's bakery. Nobody in his right mind would trade a whole cow for a loaf of bread. You can't cut off a part without destroying the cow so money must be (class says, "Divisible"). Yes, you need to buy little things (shows coins).

(Picks up dollar bill) I've given these away to players who played 50 innings and they put them in their pockets. Now, what if the medium of exchange was cows? (Students say, "Big pockets.") So you have to be able to carry it around so the P stands for (students say, "Portable," and teacher writes it by P on the board).

Supposed I am the high ruler and I say we're not going to use money any more, sand will be the medium of exchange. What would you do the minute school was out? (Students chorus, "Go to the beach.") That would not be a good medium of exchange because it's always there. You can't be able to get it that easily, you have to control the supply, so it must be (students chorus, "Scarce").

Look at these (points to characteristics on board). I'm going to erase them and you tell your neighbor the five characteristics of money (students tell neighbors).

Let me have your attention. This next part is easy: The four forms money takes in our society (lists C,C,C,C on board). What is this?

(Holds up credit card and students chorus, "Credit.") Yes, if you wanted to buy a new outfit for the dance and you had a credit card or could use your parents', you could pay for it with this. What's this? (Holds up coins, currency, and checkbook and students chorus, "Coins, Currency, and Checks," as teacher writes each word by the four C's.)

Has this been easy? (Students nod.) The next three are easy because they're short, but they're also hard because they're new ideas that most adults don't understand. You'll understand them because you always do a good job (writes "kinds of money" on board).

Yesterday we talked about barter. People used things of real value like cows. Salt was very valuable in dry climates, or precious things like gold (student says, "rocks"). No, rocks had no value, Susan. We call things of real value commodity money (writes "commodity" on board). It was used for 1000 years and was equal to the value in trade. This (showing dollar bill) was backed by value in gold or silver and it is called representational currency (writes "representational" on board) because it represented gold or silver. It was used because it was portable. In a sense it had real value.

Now, this is worthless (holds up bill). It costs about an eighth of a cent to print. Why do you suppose those baseball players are so dumb they took it for playing 50 innings and put it in their pockets? Because it is our medium of exchange. It is Fiat money (writes "Fiat" on board, students say, "Fiat," meaning car). Yes, if you've got enough of it, you could buy a car. Fiat means 'by law.' Your government said that we will accept this medium of exchange.

Let's check whether I have made this clear. Show me with hand signals.

Analysis of High School Economics Lesson

Promoted Learning
 1. Had sponge on board.
 2. Used forms of money as anticipatory set.
 3. Reviewed to bring previous learning to students' minds.
 4. Told students objective.
 5. Used students names in familiar examples.
 6. Used mnemonic devices.
 7. Used chalk board well.
 8. Had students signal.
 9. Students practice with neighbor.
10. Excellent feeling tone as evidenced by students participation and laughter without getting off target.

Questioned Behavior
1. Reason for learning was test.
2. Accepted choral answers without "think time."
3. Two student errors not dignified.
4. Didn't circulate to check on or assist when students were practicing with each other.

Possible Conference Objectives
1. The teacher will analyze her own lesson.
2. The teacher will state the generalizations undergirding productive behaviors, identified by the observer, and the conditions where future application is or is not appropriate.
3. The teacher will describe ways that increased diagnostic evidence for each student could be available.
4. The teacher will practice ways of dignifying an incorrect answer and eliciting a correct one from the same student.

Transcript: Pre-Algebra Lesson

The script tape was done by an observer who didn't know algebra. If there were mathematical errors (highly unlikely) they went unheeded. The pedagogical factors in the lesson are obvious to a sophisticated observer.

Teacher takes roll while students wait.

T What did you have trouble with?

S 18, 21, 24

Teacher writes those numbers on board and then works each problem on board for class.

#18: Area of rectangle 95 ft. x 1.5 ft.

#21: Wall 17 1/3 ft. x 12 ft. One gallon of paint covers 400 sq. ft. Is it enough paint for two coats?

#24: Trapezoid 5′ x 8′ with 2 slots 6′ x 2′. What is the surface area?

T You need to start with the formula because each time you write that formula it will help you remember it for the test. Now do pages 202 and 203. Skip problems that are multiples of three. Raise your hand if you need help.

Analysis of High School Pre-Algebra Lesson

Promoted Learning
1. T checked on problems that gave trouble and modeled them.

2. Problems had real life meaning.
3. T explained need for formula.
4. T offered help to those who needed it.
5. T reduced number of problems assigned.

Questioned Behavior
1. S had nothing to do while T took roll.
2. T did not give S similar problems after each problem was explained on board to check whether S now could do it.
3. T might have anticipated problems that would give trouble and prepared S before they did incorrect homework.

Possible Conference Objective
1. T will design sponge activities to be used while taking roll or during interruptions or other activities when S are not involved.
2. T will describe ways of immediately checking for understanding in tomorrow's lesson.
3. T will identify problem spots in future homework assignments and plan ways to make sure students can do that type of problem before assigning it.

Transcript: Junior High Vocabulary Lesson

The teacher was vibrant and enthusiastic. The 20 junior high school students were attentive. On the board was the following:

prior - adj.	rebuke - v.
prolong - v.	proficient - adj.
vent - v. n.	nurture - v.
perjury - n.	vigilant - adj.
presume - v.	prolong - v.

O Today we're going to learn the meaning of these words and write them in sentences. "Prior" is an adjective. It's something that happened exactly before what you're doing now. What did you do just prior to leaving your house this morning?

S Kiss mother. Fight sister. Pet dog. Eat breakfast. (Every student answered.)

T Put your thumb up if you understand what "prior" means. Good, you all understand "prior.". Who can guess what "prolong" means?

S You prolong life.

T You're right, you live longer. It means you expand something. Like you probably increase the life of a plant or you prolong a meal. What does that mean?

116

S	The plant grows taller. Your stomach gets bigger, you eat more.
T	It means you make the time longer. When you prolong something, you make it longer in time. Tell your neighbor something you prolong (students tell each other). Now, what did your neighbor tell you?
S	Prolong life. Prolong the length of a book. Prolong a meeting.
T	Right, suppose you wanted to leave and I prolong the meeting by saying I wanted to discuss something else, or if you prolonged a visit. What might happen?
S	You might miss an airplane.
T	Think of a sentence where you use "prolong." Thumbs up when you think of one.
S	I'm going to prolong my final draft to make it better.
T	You mean you're going to prolong the amount of time. Did you all hear him? Say it again (student does). Are there any questions? What do you think "vent" means?
S	Let air go through?
T	Did you hear Mimi? Say it again…Yes, we open a window to let air go through like the vent on an air conditioner. What if it's a verb like: We vent our anger by screaming and yelling where we let it out, or we may punch a pillow. What are the things you do when you're angry? Tell your neighbor (students tell each other). Did anyone have any fun ways?
S	Break things. Kick. Etc.
T	Remember, it's not anger, you can ventilate a room. Are there any questions? Let's go to our next word, "perjury." Has anyone heard that word? It means you don't tell the truth. Have you seen courts on TV? What does the witness do? He puts his hand on the Bible. What if he says something and it's not true?
S	He's telling a lie.
T	What if he doesn't know it's a lie? He has to do it on purpose. Why is it a serious crime? Why do you have to tell the truth in court? Why is it illegal to commit perjury? Let's look at the next word, "presume." Does anyone know a word that sounds like it?
S	Predict. Assume.
T	It means sort of know, take for granted. You don't literally know the facts, but you are quite sure it is true. For example, if I hear Tom's stomach growl, I presume he didn't eat breakfast. If there's a dance and you like to dance, I presume you'll go to the dance. Let's look at "rebuke." Your mother told you to be home at 9:00 and you don't get home until 10:00 and she says, "Shame on you. I told you you

	should be home by 9:00." Think of synonym for rebuke.
S	Scold. Remind. Shouting.
T	What do you get rebuked for?
S	Homework.
T	Let's look at the next word, "proficient." What does "pro-" mean? Do you have any ideas?
S	Ice skates. It means you can perform under pressure.
T	Very good. Think what you're proficient in.
S	Eating pizza. Fighting with my sister.
T	You're talking about things you do well. Let's look at the next word, "nurture." That means to love and care. Do you know of another word that means the same?
S	Cuddle. Love...
T	Yes, mothers nurture children. Some people nurture their talent so they're proficient in painting and drawing. Can you nurture a plant? How could you make it grow?
S	Talk to it. Play music. Water it.
T	Let's look at the last word, "vigilant." Have you seen vigilantes on TV in the New York subways?
S	Yeah, they wear white suits. They're looking for crimes.
T	It means be alert, look for, watch. What if a guard in the army went to sleep? Who are vigilant?
S	Lifeguards. Protects baby sisters.
T	Yes, I wrote "prolong" two times. Now make up sentences using each of these words. (Students do follow-up on writing sentences.)

Analysiss of Junior High Vocabulary Lesson

Productive Behaviors
1. Varied active participation of learners (signal, tell neighbor).
2. Most words translated into students' lives.
3. Wrong answers not demeaned.
4. Word was listed with part of speech.
5. Had students repeat rather than saying it for them.

Questioned Behaviors
1. Not getting or giving accurate definitions or examples of meanings.
2. Student participation inappropriate. "Thumbs up" does not validate understanding. "Tell your neighbor" should be used *after learning* and teacher should monitor answers.
3. Had students guess meaning when they had no information.

4. Student did not practice using word in sentence which was terminal objective.
5. No checking for understanding. Student said what they did to vent anger, or prior to coming to school, not what the word meant. Deflected student from meaning with their life experiences.
6. Didn't build in correction for guesses or errors.
7. Much "birdwalking" (vigilantes, vent anger).

Possible Conference Objectives
The teacher will:
1. Replan lesson using accurate meanings.
2. State when each type of student participation is appropriate: signal, tell neighbor, state or write in a sentence.
3. State the differences between students' experiences adding to or deflecting from meaning.
4. Develop techniques for introducing any new words including modeling them in "meaning bearing" sentences.
5. Develop techniques for presenting a word in several contexts so students can infer (*not* guess) meaning.

cook's kitchen reference

ONIONS

The complete guide to onions, garlic, shallots, spring
onions and chives, with over 45 great recipes

Brian Glover

LORENZ BOOKS

This edition is published by Lorenz Books

Lorenz Books is an imprint of Anness Publishing Ltd
Hermes House, 88–89 Blackfriars Road, London SE1 8HA
tel. 020 7401 2077; fax 020 7633 9499
www.lorenzbooks.com; info@anness.com
© Anness Publishing Ltd 2002, 2006

UK agent: The Manning Partnership Ltd, 6 The Old Dairy, Melcombe Road, Bath BA2 3LR;
tel. 01225 478444; fax 01225 478440; sales@manning-partnership.co.uk

UK distributor: Grantham Book Services Ltd, Isaac Newton Way, Alma Park Industrial Estate, Grantham, Lincs NG31 9SD;
tel. 01476 541080; fax 01476 541061; orders@gbs.tbs-ltd.co.uk

North American agent/distributor: National Book Network, 4501 Forbes Boulevard, Suite 200, Lanham, MD 20706;
tel. 301 459 3366; fax 301 429 5746; www.nbnbooks.com

Australian agent/distributor: Pan Macmillan Australia, Level 18, St Martins Tower, 31 Market St, Sydney, NSW 2000;
tel. 1300 135 113; fax 1300 135 103; customer.service@macmillan.com.au

New Zealand agent/distributor: David Bateman Ltd, 30 Tarndale Grove, Off Bush Road, Albany, Auckland;
tel. (09) 415 7664; fax (09) 415 8892

A CIP catalogue record for this book is available from the British Library.

Publisher: Joanna Lorenz   Designer: Isobel Gillan
Managing Editor: Linda Fraser   Photographer: William Lingwood
Project Editor: Jennifer Schofield Production Controller: Joanna King

Previously published as *Know Your Onions*

1 3 5 7 9 10 8 6 4 2

NOTES
Bracketed terms are intended for American readers. For all recipes, quantities are given in both
metric and imperial measures and, where appropriate, measures are also given in standard cups
and spoons. Follow one set, but not a mixture, because they are not interchangeable.

Standard spoon and cup measures are level. 1 tsp = 5ml, 1 tbsp = 15ml, 1 cup = 250ml/8fl oz
Australian standard tablespoons are 20ml. Australian readers should use 3 tsp in place of 1 tbsp
for measuring small quantities of gelatine, flour, salt etc.
Medium (US large) eggs are used unless otherwise stated.

Contents

INTRODUCTION

Members of the onion family have been cultivated ever since people started to form communities and grow their own food. Wild onions were gathered and eaten even before that. With a few exceptions, onions are now used in the cooking of almost every culture across the world. There is no country where this indispensable vegetable, in one form or another, is not now grown.

The evolution of the first, wild onions into the cultivated plants that we know today is not entirely clear. Many varieties, such as the common or garden onion, only seem to exist in their cultivated form and are not known to grow wild at all. There is a "missing link" in the development between the wild species of the plant and today's cultivated onions.

The mystery surrounding this transition suggests that the cultivation of onions occurred a very long time ago. People would seem to have perceived onions as good things to eat very early on in history, and onions are among the first plants to have been grown to add flavour to the human diet.

Onions belong to the allium family, which contains more than 300 species. Many of these different varieties are grown in gardens, some as ornamentals in flower borders, others as herbs and edible plants in vegetable patches. For a long time, botanists disagreed about whether the alliums belonged to the larger plant group of lilies (*Liliaceae*) or amaryllis (*Amaryllidaceae*), but now most place them in an order all of their own – the *Alliaceae*.

From the grower's point of view, alliums are very easy to identify. They form bulbs, or fleshy leaf bases; they have long, narrow, flat or tubular leaves, usually blue-green in colour; they have round, globular heads of flowers made up of many individual flowers; and all, to one degree or another, have the same unmistakably characteristic onion smell, especially when the bulb or leaves are damaged or broken.

pejorative associations have been made. They are forbidden to certain social groups and are sometimes considered taboo or to have evil powers. The effect of their odour on the breath and sweat has led them to be labelled as vulgar, and unacceptable in polite society.

The relationship of the onion family to people throughout history is marked by these contradictory attitudes. While onions and other alliums are revered and praised and popular in dishes around the world, they are also frowned upon and rejected by many cultures and social groups.

Left: Alliums are an important crop in France as its traditional cookery has always made very good use of these vegetables, especially onions and garlic.

The pungent onion smell is caused by the presence of allicins – chemicals that include volatile compounds of sulphur – which are released by the action of enzymes when any part of the plant is cut or bruised. It is these compounds that make the eyes water when an allium is chopped and which give onions that are used in cooking their characteristic flavour and bite.

The alliums' inescapable chemical signature has brought them to people's attention from the earliest times. Their smell and taste have made them into plants with an ancient and special place in the evolution of human culture.

From the earliest records, it appears that onions have always been regarded as important foodstuffs and imbued with symbolic and religious meaning: they were grown in the best fields and can be found in important tombs and paintings. However, along with this reverence and value, a number of

Opposite: Onions have been cultivated for thousands of years. Their distinctive blue-green leaves and round flower heads make them easy to recognize.

Right: Delicately flavoured bunching onions and green onions are popular in Vietnamese cooking, and can always be found in their food markets.

ONIONS AND OTHER ALLIUMS THROUGHOUT HISTORY

Whether praised or criticized, the onion family has attracted attention from the very earliest times. In different societies and at different periods in history, these vegetables have been bestowed with symbolic and spiritual meanings and have been considered vital in herbalistic and shamanistic medicine. The onion figures prominently in folklore, literature and even painting: few other vegetable families have such a value-laden history.

The actual origins of the onion are not known. However, they do seem to have been among the first families of plants to have been cultivated and selected. The recorded evidence suggests that onions were first cultivated over 5,000 years ago, around 3000 BC, in Asia Minor – the area of central Asia that now includes modern-day countries such as Iran, Pakistan and Afghanistan. These onions

would have been close relatives of the cultivated varieties that we are familiar with today.

Garlic probably began in this area too, and was then taken to Greece and on to Egypt. A type of garlic (*Allium sativum*) still grows wild in some parts of the Mediterranean, particularly on the island of Sicily. Shallots are also likely to have originated in central Asia and, according to food historian Alan Davidson, were known and used in India before they travelled to the Middle East.

Onions were also being cultivated in parts of China around 3000 BC. These would have been bunching onions (varieties of *Allium fistulosum*), rather than bulb onions. The Chinese also grew leeks, although these were a different variety from European leeks and derived from *Allium ramosum*.

At some point in the Han dynasty, dating 206 BC–AD 221, bulb onions (*Allium cepa*) and true garlic (*Allium sativa*) were introduced into China, probably from India. The bulb onion is still known as *hu-t'sung* or "foreign onion" in Chinese.

The cultivation of onions and garlic is mentioned in some of the early Vedic writings of ancient India. They are also noted in scribal records from Sumer (*c.*2400 BC), which record that the city governor's onions and cucumbers were grown in "the gods' best fields". The mentioning of the various alliums in these early texts shows that they were considered to be a most important crop.

Below: Onions and garlic have been an essential cooking ingredient in many countries, such as Brazil, for centuries.

ALLIUMS IN ANCIENT EGYPT

By the time of the ancient Egyptians, there is evidence that onions, garlic and leeks were being grown and consumed in huge quantities. Onions figure prominently in the decoration and hieroglyphics of one of the Egyptians' best-known legacies – the pyramids. They appear on the walls of the pyramids of Unas (*c.*2423 BC) and Pepi II (*c.*2200 BC) and onions were found in the eye sockets of the mummy of Rameses IV, who died in 1160 BC.

The Greek historian Herodotus, in 450 BC, reporting on his travels in Egypt, writes of inscriptions on the walls of the pyramids that show a breakdown

of the cost of building these great monuments. Among the items listed is an entry showing how much was spent on "black radish, red onions and garlic" for the labourers on the pyramid at Giza.

Centuries later, the 17th-century diarist John Evelyn remarks in his *Acetaria* (1699) on "How this noble bulb was deified in Egypt ... and that whilst they were building the pyramids, there was spent on this root ninety tun of gold among the workmen". When the labourers' onion and garlic ration was cut, they are believed to have gone on strike.

Below: Egyptian labourers working on the pyramids received rations of onions, garlic, leeks and beer. It was believed that all the alliums provided physical strength and prevented disease.

Right: Onions have been found in eye sockets, armpits and body cavities of ancient Egyptian mummies, which were stored in decorative cases. This may have been because onions acted as antiseptics or because they were believed to have supernatural powers.

Above and above right: Onions are commonly depicted in the wall paintings in Egyptian tombs. It is thought they acted both as symbols of eternal life and as food and medicine for the journey into the afterlife.

The significance of alliums to the ancient Egyptians seems to have been very complex. Onions were placed in tombs as food for the journey into the next life and as symbols of eternity because of the circle-within-a-circle structure of the bulb. Many paintings show onions as part of religious symbolism. They were also known as powerful antibiotics and antiseptics. Labourers were fed on onions, leeks and garlic, as these vegetables were believed to keep them fit and well for their manual work.

There is evidence also that the lingering smell of the onion in the body had great significance for the ancient Egyptians. The passage of the onion smell through the body was considered a sign of good health and fertility in women; although it was taboo for certain priests to eat or smell of onions.

The onion family was also popular with the Egyptians' neighbours, the Hebrews. In the Bible in Numbers XI:5, the Israelites led out into the desert by Moses complain about how hungry they are, and remember "the cucumbers, and the melons, and the leeks, and the onions and the garlic", which they used to enjoy in their captivity in Egypt.

The association of alliums with this part of the eastern Mediterranean remained strong for many centuries. For instance, in many European countries, the name for shallots (*Allium cepa*, Aggregatum Group) is derived from the ancient Palestinian port of Ascalon. This was reflected in their old Latin name (*Allium ascalonicum*) given by the Romans. No doubt Ascalon was the place from which shallots were first imported to Rome, and the name stuck.

Centuries later, the tree onion (*Allium cepa*, Proliferum Group), and the shallot-related potato onion, were still both called Egyptian onions by the English and French.

Below: Onions and other alliums are mentioned several times in the Bible. The most famous occasion is when the Israelites recall the pleasures of eating onions, leeks and garlic before their flight from Egypt (Numbers XI:5).

ALLIUMS IN GREEK AND ROMAN TIMES

The classical Greeks used alliums too. Hippocrates (*c*.400 BC), who is credited with founding modern medicine, notes that onions, garlic and leeks were grown in kitchen gardens or harvested from the wild. The food historian Alan Davidson points out that a section of market in Athens was called simply *ta skoroda*, meaning "the garlic", suggesting that the trade in alliums was an important feature of everyday Athenian life. The alliums even merit mention in Homer's great epic poem, the *Odyssey*.

Like the Egyptian pyramid builders, the Greeks believed in the onion's ability to promote health, virility and potency. Onions were used to prepare athletes for games, and competitors not only ate onions, but also rubbed onion juice over their bodies. Greek soldiers were fed on onions to develop a martial vigour, and it was said that the enemy always knew when the Greek army was advancing by the powerful smell of onions that preceded the arrival of the troops.

In Rome, bread and onions were the standard diet of the poor. Archaeologists excavating Pompeii have found onion-shaped cavities where onions were growing in gardens, just as the writer Pliny the Elder (AD 23–79) described in his *Historia Naturalis*.

Because onions played such a vital role in the diet of the poor in Rome, they were held in some contempt by sections of the wealthy elite. The priestesses of Cybele, for instance, refused entrance to their temple in Rome to anyone who smelt of garlic. The poet Horace considered the smell of garlic a mark of real vulgarity and called it "more poisonous than hemlock", and Juvenal mockingly writes of onions as "kitchen gods".

Leeks seem to have been universally popular at all levels of Roman society, which may well have been because they were milder and tainted the breath less. There are many leek recipes in Apicius' 1st-century *De Re Coquinaria*, a cook book intended for the literate middle classes. Apicius was a shadowy figure, and there may have been more than one person known as Apicius involved in the book over a considerable period of time. The recipes show a great love of leeks and, to a lesser extent, onions in a range of sophisticated dishes that include Beets with Leeks in Raisin Sauce,

Below: As with the Greeks, the Roman army was fed on onions and garlic, and took them on their invasions. They are credited with introducing garlic, onions and leeks to Britain, Germany and Gaul.

Above: The Roman emperor Nero was nicknamed porrophagus or "leek eater" because he ate so many of them in his belief that they helped his singing voice and oratory.

Peppercorn Leek Sauce and Quinces Stewed with Leeks. *De Re Coquinaria* contains few recipes for garlic, however, which suggests that garlic was less popular with middle-class Romans.

The Romans not only cultivated and cooked with alliums, but are thought to have been instrumental in taking these vegetables into all parts of Europe.

While Romans enjoyed eating onions and other alliums, they did not imbue them with the same significance as the ancient Egyptians and the Roman satirist Juvenal (*c*.AD 60–140) mocks the Egyptians' contradictory beliefs:

How Egypt has grown mad
  with superstition
She makes gods of demons as
  is well known
It is a deadly sin to eat an onion
But every clove of garlic has a
  holy power.
A pious country, and with fine
  houses
But every garden is overrun
  with gods.

ALLIUMS IN THE MIDDLE AGES

After the Romans' introduction of edible alliums to other parts of Europe, these vegetables soon became established as an important part of the European diet. They were popular in the Middle Ages, especially among the poor. Even before the introduction of cultivated varieties, it is certain that wild alliums, such as rocambole (*Allium scordoprasum*) and ramsons (*Allium ursinum*), would have been gathered and eaten. The English words leek and garlic come from the Anglo-Saxon word *leac,* meaning plant, and *garleac,* meaning spear-shaped plant. In Anglo-Saxon, the leek was known as *porleac* and the onion *ynioleac.* Onions get their name from the Latin *unio* via the French *oignon* and Anglo-Norman *union.*

Alliums became an important crop in medieval Britain, particularly leeks, which were one of the few vegetables to withstand a normal winter unprotected. In the *Forme of Cury* (*c.*1390), a cook book written for Richard II, a *salat* was made from *persel, sawge, grene garlec, chibolles* [Welsh onions]*, oynouns and leek* all dressed with oil and vinegar. And *porray* (from *porrum,* the Latin for leek) was a white soup made from leeks, almonds and rice.

The trade in alliums was important in medieval Europe. Onions from Brittany and garlic from Picardy are recorded as having been sold in London food markets as early as the 13th century.

By Chaucer's time, in the late 14th century, it is obvious that leeks were considered commonplace, everyday fare. He often uses the phrase "Not worth a leke" to suggest something that is entirely worthless.

Because they were so hardy, leeks could be grown in the coldest places and are associated particularly with Scotland and Wales, becoming, in Wales, a symbol for Celtic doughtiness and survival. Legend has it that the Welsh wore leeks, like feathers, in their caps, as a badge of identification during their victory over the Saxons in AD 640. It is probable that these would have been wild alliums – ramsons or rocamboles maybe – rather than the familiar modern-day leeks. But by Shakespeare's time, the Welsh wearing of leeks on their national day – St David's Day, March 1 – had clearly become well established. In the play *Henry V*, Pistol taunts Fluellen about his Welshness by promising to knock "his leek about his pate upon Saint Davy's day".

To this day, leeks still figure as a part of Welsh identity. They are an essential ingredient in cawl, a comforting soup or stew of lamb and leeks, which may be considered traditional Welsh soul food. Championship leek growing is still a major competitive hobby in many areas

B. nanīte c. īī. sĉ. f.i. z̄. melīus erco. moōīce acuītatīs.
Īunamentūm. tossīcīs. nocūmentūm. expūlsīue z cerebʒo.
ȳmouo nocūmentū. cūm accetoso et oleo.

Left: In medieval herbals and medicinal manuscripts, many members of the onion family were recognized to have curative and therapeutic properties.

Left: In Chaucer's The Canterbury Tales *the Summoner's vulgar character is shown by his love of garlic, onions and leeks.*

The ribald and lewd associations of onions and leeks started early in Britain. This Anglo-Saxon riddle dates from before the Norman conquest of 1066:

> *I stand erect and tall, well-rooted*
> *I stand proud in bed*
> *I am hairy below. Sometimes the*
>   *fair peasant's daughter ...*
> *... grips my body and holds me*
>   *hard ...*
> *I will bring tears to her eyes.*

Above: An illustration of garlic from Pierre Jean François Turpin's Flore Médicale *showing the bulb structure.*

of south Wales. Most people, however, have taken to wearing the less odorous daffodil on St David's Day.

Although onions were important in dietary and medicinal terms in medieval Europe, the Roman inhibitions and prejudices about how onions smell and the effect they have on an individual's moral character also prevailed.

Throughout the Middle Ages, alliums were associated with vulgarity. For the Egyptians and Greeks, the alliums were thought to promote strength, fertility and vigour, and it was only a short step until onions became associated, in ribald terms, with licentiousness and sexual prowess. In the 14th century, Chaucer's lecherous Summoner in *The Canterbury Tales* is described thus:

> *Wel loved he garleek, onions, and*
>   *eek lekes,*
> *And for to drinken strong wyun, reed*
>   *as blood.*

Similarly, in William Langland's *Piers the Plowman*, an allegorical poem dating from the 14th century, Gluttony is offered "a pound of garleek" as an inducement to step into the ale-house rather than go to church.

In France, the various members of the onion family were also associated with sexual potency. King Henry IV, for instance, was commonly reputed to have been baptized with garlic water, so prodigious was his sexual potency and so strong his breath.

Within late-medieval philosophy, edible bulbs, such as garlic and onions, were considered among the least noble of food plants. Existence was structured into a Great Chain of Being, a hierarchy which placed God at the top and inanimate objects, such as plants, at the bottom. All creation was ascribed a level in this hierarchical way of seeing the world and bulbs were placed at the very bottom.

THE ALLIUMS' FALL FROM GRACE

Despite their associations with the poor, vulgar and lecherous, onions, garlic and leeks continued to be popular in British cooking until the 17th century. Eating them uncooked, however, began to be frowned upon and was seen as a distinct social taboo, particularly for women and those who held social pretensions or aspirations.

Towards the end of the 17th century, there was a noticeable rise in the social prohibition against garlic, the most odorous of the alliums. The diarist John Evelyn, a great grower and eater of vegetables, wrote a treatise on salads as a preface to his *Acetaria* in 1699. Regarding "garlick" he writes: "we absolutely forbid it entrance into our salleting, by reason of its intolerable rankness, and that made it so detested of old … to be sure it is not for ladies' palates, nor those who court them".

Below: In some sections of society onions were considered as only fit for poor people as in this scene of humble living called Preparations for Lunch *by Bernard Lepicie.*

Above: Towards the end of the 17th century, alliums became unpopular in genteel society and tended to be associated with the poor and vulgar. Although onions were still used in cooking, they were rarely used as a main ingredient in their own right.

Throughout the following centuries, garlic features little in British cook books, and although onions continue to appear in countless dishes, they rarely figure as a main ingredient in their own right. In Hannah Glasse's *The Art of Cookery Made Plain & Easy* (1747) onions are pickled, stewed, "ragoo'd with cucumbers" and made into a pie. Garlic, however, is not included. Leeks are not mentioned at all by Glasse. As with onions and garlic, they had become associated purely with peasant food and thought unsuitable for the middle classes (at which audience most 18th- and 19th-century cook books were aimed). Isabella Beeton, the great

bastion of the 19th-century middle-class kitchen, sums up the doubtful regard in which leeks were held when she advocates boiling them really well or else "they will taint the breath".

Throughout Anglo-Saxon Europe and much of the United States, the social taboo surrounding the effect of onions and garlic on human breath and sweat lasted for almost three hundred years. Undoubtedly, onions, leeks and, to a lesser extent, garlic were still eaten, but to smell of them was considered socially impolite and a mark of low breeding. In countries outside Europe and the United States, similar social taboos were attached to the eating of onions and other alliums. For example, in Japan, to smell of onions or garlic has traditionally been perceived as being discourteous and has a great social stigma attached to it. Japan is still the one country in Asia that makes very little use of garlic in its cooking.

From the time of the earliest records, onions, and in particular garlic, have been accused of exciting sexual and libidinous desires: Egyptian priests were denied garlic precisely because they had to remain celibate. To this day Kashmiri Brahmans and Jains are forbidden from eating strong-tasting foods, in particular onions and garlic, because they are thought to heat the blood and have the ability to inflame carnal desire. Some Chinese Buddhists avoid the prohibited "five strong-smelling vegetables" for the same reasons.

The Hindu sacred texts place great emphasis on the idea that a man is what he eats and rules are given for the right foods. The three upper castes, Brahmans, Kshatryas and Vaisyas, should avoid onions and garlic in their diet. The Sanskrit poem, *Mahabharata*, suggests that onions and garlic should not be eaten by "honourable people".

Left: Garlic became very unpopular in countries such as Britain towards the end of the 17th century, but garlic and bay sellers such as this one were still able to eke out a living in France where garlic was not frowned upon to such a great extent.

THE REHABILITATION OF ALLIUMS

Some countries in northern Europe maintained their antipathy towards onions and garlic, but much depended on the general food culture of a society. In the 1580s, when the German ambassador of the Holy Roman Emperor visited the court of the Byzantine emperor Nicephoros II, his entourage was appalled by the food and the smell of garlic on the emperor's breath. For the northern Europeans, the great consumption of large quantities of vegetables, including onions and garlic, was little short of scandalous. In large parts of northern Europe, especially in comparatively rich countries such as Britain, Germany and the Netherlands, good food was synonymous with meat.

However, many cultures, typically those around the Mediterranean, never fell out of love with the onion family. It was for this reason that the vegetable-loving cultures of the Mediterranean region were for centuries looked down upon as gastronomically uncivilized.

In France, in particular, onions, garlic, leeks and shallots – in fact the whole allium tribe – remained extremely popular at almost every level of society. Brittany, a region well known in the 20th century for its bicycling onion sellers, and the west of France were particularly linked with cooking with onions and garlic.

The French trade in onions and garlic began early; onions from Brittany were exported to London as early as the 13th century. The trade continued until well into the 20th century, with onion sellers cycling around southern English towns selling their familiar strings of onions and garlic from their bicycles. Food writer Lindsay Bareham notes that the last of these onion sellers was still working in the mid-1990s.

Onions and garlic were, and still are, an intrinsic part of much French provincial and peasant cooking. Garlic festivals, such as the garlic and basil fair at Tours on St Anne's Day, July 26, occur throughout France, usually when the new season's crop has been harvested. Even when the alliums were at their most unpopular in Britain, in the 18th and 19th centuries, onions were still celebrated in France. As food historian John Ayto points out, the classic sauce, *sauce soubise*, was named after an 18th-century French general and courtier Charles de Rohan, Prince de Soubise, showing that aristocracy did not see any shame in being associated with onions.

In sophisticated Paris, onions had their ups and downs, but by the early 19th century they were actually thought quite *de rigueur* in polite society. The poet Shelley, writing of a trip to Paris, seems quite delightedly shocked at the

Above: In the early 19th century, Parisian society considered onions and garlic positively fashionable.

thought of the onions' fashionable status: "What do you think? Young women of rank eat – you will never guess what – garlick!"

In Spain, too, onions were consumed with gusto despite the fact that certain elements of society frowned upon the practice. An old Andalusian saying states that "*Olla sin cebolla, es baile sin tamborin* [a stew without onion is like a dance without music]". In Cataluña they celebrate the new crop of their local, large green spring onions (scallions) –

Onions in the United States

Columbus, and then the first pilgrims, took onions and garlic to North America, while the Spanish introduced them to Central and South America. But many varieties of wild onion, leek and garlic grew indigenously in North America and were used by native Americans in cooking and, especially, in medicine. Chicago was named after the Illinois Indian name for "the place which smells of onions". *Chicagoua* – the plant that gave Chicago its name – was probably a form of wild garlic or ramps (*Allium tricoccum*). This species and other wild onions, such as *Allium cernuum* and *Allium canadense,* still grow profusely throughout North America. Père Marquette, the French Jesuit explorer and missionary, who camped on the shores of Lake Michigan in 1670, wrote of being saved from starvation by eating the various kinds of wild onion and garlic that grew there. Later generations of Americans took these plants to their heart, and much onion breeding took place in the first decades of the 20th century. The emphasis was on producing sweet, early-summer-cropping onions, which have a high water and sugar content. There was also a move towards producing low-sulphur and hence less smelly onions.

calçots – with a special feast called *la calçotada*. It consists of green onions, grilled (broiled) over charcoal and served with salsa romesco, made from chillies, nuts and garlic.

Despite the popularity of alliums in such countries, these odorous vegetables were slow to return to favour in England. Onions, shallots, even leeks, but most especially garlic, remained fairly unpopular and became associated with "foreign food". Writing in 1861, in her hugely influential *Book of Household Management*, Isabella Beeton observes rather sniffily of garlic: "It was in greater repute with our

ancestors than it is with ourselves ... on the Continent, especially in Italy, it is much used, and the French consider it is an essential in many made dishes". Mrs Beeton gives only one dish that includes garlic – a Bengali recipe for hot mango chutney – highlighting the influence of Indian cooking on the English kitchen.

Why did the alliums stay so popular in some cultures but attract such great opprobrium in others? One answer may lie in the nature of cooking in different cultures. In northern Europe, especially England, and in North America, regional, peasant and rural cooking lost ground

Above: During World War II when onions were in short supply in Britain, leeks became even more important.

in the face of a growing move towards industrialization as people migrated to big cities in search of work. Alliums have always been associated with regional, peasant cooking. These traditions remained strong in all the Mediterranean countries and had a great influence on the middle-class cooking of the day. In Britain, cooking was effectively cut off from its rural and peasant roots and a "genteel" style of middle-class cooking – ironically influenced by notions of French *haute cuisine* – was adopted in its place.

By the late 20th century, the health benefits of the vegetable-based Mediterranean diet, including lots of onions and other alliums, was vaunted in Britain and the United States as a much healthier way of eating. This had always been the case in poorer areas of Europe, where onions have always remained a vital and much celebrated way of injecting flavour into the diet.

Left: French onion sellers, like this one depicted by Stanhope Alexander Forbes, were once a common sight in many English towns.

ALLIUMS OVER THE LAST HUNDRED YEARS

Apart from long-standing religious and social taboos, the history of the onion family over the last century or so has been one of gradual rehabilitation. In the United States and Australia, the massive influx of immigrants from garlic-loving cultures (Greek, Italian, Hispanic), has had an effect. In Britain, the growing love affair with Indian "curries", especially after World War II, was important, too.

Italian and Greek food, both heavily garlic- and onion-reliant, came into great vogue in the 1960s. Food writer Elizabeth David, whose books on Mediterranean and French cooking were published in the 1950s and '60s, had a huge impact on breaking down the social taboo against garlic.

There had been a few earlier voices. *The Gentle Art of Cookery* (1925), written by Miss Olga Hartley and Mrs C. F. Leyel, included a whole section solely on onions, including soups, stuffed onions and a recipe for an Alsatian *gâteau aux oignons*. Mrs Leyel was the founder of Culpeper's herbalist shops, head of the Society of Herbalists, and was obviously an adventurous cook and traveller. She includes garlic as one of the essential ingredients in her "Alchemist's

Storecupboard". In 1933, the cookery writer Ambrose Heath wrote his *Book of the Onion*: a whole book (albeit small) devoted to recipes containing onions as a major ingredient. But these were lonely voices.

As the century progressed, the old middle-class sanction against using (and hence smelling of) onions and garlic started to falter. By the 1960s

Below: Onions and bicycles have long been associated with each other because of the traditional French onion and garlic sellers who, even today, can be seen selling their produce.

onion-smelling breath or body odour became less of a problem than it may have been in previous centuries.

Nowadays, onions, garlic and leeks are celebrated as never before. Garlic and onion festivals are held in places as distant as the Isle of Wight in England, and Gilroy, California in the United States. New varieties of onion are constantly being developed and bred, providing a year-round supply. Some restaurants devote themselves to wholly garlic-based menus, introducing such unusual dishes as garlic ice cream. Thousands of websites on all members of the onion family have been launched.

Exciting discoveries are being made about the medicinal qualities of the alliums. Today, the onion family is perhaps more popular and considered more indispensable than at any other time in its long and complex history.

Above: Specialist growers selling many different kinds of garlic, shallots and onions are a familiar feature of French and Italian markets.

Right: These enormously long strings of garlic for sale at Korla market in the Kinjiang Province in China demonstrate the popularity and importance of this allium in Chinese cooking.

and '70s, using garlic in food became a mark of culinary sophistication and trendiness. The famous "garlic dinner", cooked by American chef Alice Waters in 1976 in her Berkeley restaurant Chez Panisse, launched a huge garlic revival in mainstream American food culture and was extremely influential in establishing the important Californian garlic-growing industry.

Whereas the taboo started in the 18th century as a middle-class attempt to mark themselves out from the lower classes, it was to be the middle classes themselves in the 20th century who started using garlic as a mark of their sophistication and extensive travel. No doubt, as the food writer Jane Grigson noted, standards of hygiene improved in the 20th century, and diets and digestion with them, so the issue of

MYTHS, FOLKLORE AND MEDICINE

Throughout their long history, all manner of special powers have been attributed to the onion family, especially to garlic, and many myths and taboos have built up around them. To some extent these have grown out of the alliums' potent medicinal properties.

ALLIUMS IN MYTH AND FOLKLORE

Priests, shamans and healers have used alliums throughout the ages, and it is inevitable that the onion family has been attributed mystical powers. The ancient Egyptians considered that the layered structure of the onion made it a symbol of eternity, and they were certainly aware of the onion's curative powers. For the Egyptians, the onion not only cured disease and gave vitality, it also replicated the cycle of life itself. As such, it was also a fertility symbol: used in tombs to grant souls a fertile afterlife; used to ascertain female fertility; and denied to priests who might be incited to lustful acts of procreation if they ate onions.

For the Greeks, too, alliums were bestowed with sacred significance and linked to the afterlife. Theophrastus records that garlic should be placed on the side of the road at crossroads as a gift to placate Hecate, goddess of the Underworld, and this practice was continued well into the 11th century AD when the Christian Church put a stop to it. In Homer's *Odyssey*, the power of an onion (probably *Allium moly*) allows Odysseus to enter the lair of Circe. A well-known creation myth of Turkish Muslims records that, when the devil was expelled from Paradise and fell to earth, garlic sprung up where his left foot landed and onions from where his right foot came to rest. An Indian legend concerning the origins of garlic tells that when King Rahu, lord of the demons, stole the elixir of life and was punished by the god Vishnu by being decapitated, garlic sprang from where his blood fell. To this day, the followers of Vishnu refuse to eat any alliums.

From ancient times, onions have always had something of a diabolic, other-worldly connection, but they also suggest the triumph of life over death.

Above: The many different members of the onion family, including garlic, leeks, shallots and chives, all contain allicins – compounds which are believed to have natural antibacterial and antifungal properties.

The devil in onions, present in their fiery bite and effect on the palate, was also thought to incite men to lust and carnal desires. Again and again during the Middle Ages, a connection is made between eating onions, drinking alcohol and sexual incontinence. Or, as Thomas Nashe put it in his book *The Unfortunate Traveller* (1594) "Garlic ... makes a man winke, drinke and stinke". This attitude towards the alliums persisted beyond the Middle Ages in cultures as disparate as Imperial China, caste-structured India and 19th-century Britain.

All these beliefs come into play in one of the best-known myths that surround the allium family – that of the vampire. This myth began in the 16th century in central and eastern Europe but culminates in Bram Stoker's late 19th-century classic, *Dracula*.

Above: In country districts, strings of garlic, such as these sold by a French garlic seller, were often hung on thresholds or on children's cradles to ward off evil spirits.

In the vampire myths, garlic wards off evil and protects potential victims against the undead. Traditionally, in Romania, garlic was used in amulets to protect against the evil eye. In Stoker's *Dracula*, the threshold, windows and hearth are all rubbed and strewn with garlic flowers to prevent Dracula from entering his victim's bed chamber. The hero is also offered garlic as a protective talisman by the peasants on his way to visit Dracula's castle.

In the 19th and 20th centuries, the story becomes a sexual allegory: virgins may protect themselves against male desire by using garlic – men do not like the objects of their desire to smell of garlic. Garlic's part in the Dracula myths brings together all the various qualities ascribed to the "stinking rose" through history. In this story we find garlic's other-worldly, dark associations; garlic's connection with sexuality and desire; garlic's quality as a life force in the face of death; and even its ability to fight off infection as a natural antibiotic.

THE ALLIUMS IN MEDICINE

Alliins, the chemical compounds that create allicins, which give all onions their characteristic smell, are also the source of their remarkable medicinal and curative qualities. Alliins are the thioallyl or sulphur compounds present in all alliums. These compounds are volatile, which means that they break down when any part of the plant is cut or bruised. When the cell walls are damaged and exposed to the air, the compounds are converted by enzyme action to diallyldisulphides or allicins – which work as effective antibacterial and antifungal agents. Of the everyday culinary alliums, garlic, with its naturally low water content, has the highest concentration of alliins (1–2 per cent) and hence the greatest medicinal value.

Throughout history the health-giving properties of all the alliums, especially garlic, have been recognized by many writers and many cultures, especially in folk-medicine and herbalism. Garlic was thought of so highly as a medicinal herb that Galen, the Greek medical codifier of the 2nd century AD, labelled it the

Above: The ancient Egyptian Eber Codex, The Book of the Dead, *suggests garlic as a remedy for a wide variety of medical problems.*

poor man's theriac, or cure-all. This passed into medieval English as the "poor man's treacle" (or treat-all), and for many centuries garlic was used to treat a great variety of complaints. As John Trevisa, the 13th-century writer, says, "it [garlic] is cleped tryacle of cherles among auctours in olde tyme".

Early medicinal uses

The earliest texts to mention the use of onions as medicine are the 5,000-year-old Ayurvedic texts from India. Garlic is mentioned as a useful treatment for digestive disorders, throat and bronchial complaints and even for typhoid. The Egyptian *Eber Codex, The Book of the Dead*, is a medical work of therapies and cures from around 1550 BC. Garlic is again mentioned here as useful for treating many complaints as diverse as headaches and the pains of childbirth. Throughout the classical and medieval period, writers again and again extol the curative properties of the alliums. The most common complaints mentioned include chest and bronchial problems

(Nero was not alone in thinking alliums improved the voice), worms, intestinal problems, bladder problems and lack of libido. They were also used to treat open wounds, to guard against infection from animal bites and to treat colds, headaches, haemorrhoids, sunburn and even leprosy.

The Greek Hippocrates (*c*.400 BC), the father of modern medicine, thought garlic good for wounds and toothache. Dioscorides, the Greek doctor who travelled with the Roman army (which was largely fed on onions, leeks and garlic) in the 1st century AD, notes its use against tapeworms and snake bites. He was also convinced that garlic could help clear the arteries and cure coughs. Pliny the Elder (AD 23–79) in his *Historia Naturalis* gives over 60 garlic remedies, including cures for bites by wild animals and low libido. This latter is a common theme in the use of garlic, and links in with the idea that all the onions excite the carnal appetites.

Right: An early illustration of garlic (Allium sativum) showing the flowers and the mature bulb.

Below: Hippocrates, the father of modern medicine, praised the healing powers of garlic and posited it as a cure for a great number of diverse ailments.

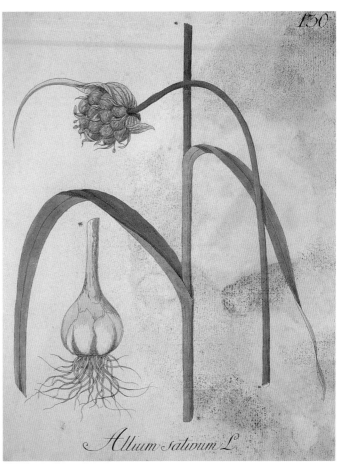

Allium sativum L.

Medieval medicine and beyond

These notions held by the Greeks survived well into the Middle Ages. The 14th-century French herbal *The Four Seasons of the House of Cerruti* claims that white onions help to bring forth milk in nursing mothers and promote virile semen in men, and the herbal also considers garlic to be an undoubted aphrodisiac. Food historian John Ayto quotes an observation from *Andrew Boorde's Dietary of Helthe* (1542), which claims that "onions do promote a man to veneryous [sexual] actes", much as the Roman writer Pliny had done centuries earlier.

Medical thought and practice was governed throughout the Middle Ages by the doctrine of the humours, which explained how humans interacted with the natural world. The humours were the four bodily fluids: blood, choler, melancholy and phlegm, which were thought to determine character and physical health. The four elements of fire, water, air and earth also had characteristic qualities: hot, moist, cold and dry respectively. All living things – plants, animals, human beings – were governed by one or more elements and displayed one, or a combination of, these qualities.

Onions were considered hot and moist and were thought to govern the blood, the humour of the sanguine personality. Garlic was considered hotter and drier and thought to be good for treating the cold and wet phlegmatic personality. In John Trevisa's 13th-century translation of *De Proprietatibus Rerum,* he says of garlic "if colerik men ete to moche therof it maketh the body to hoot ... and is cause of madnesse and of frenesye", but later he admits its use: "and garlek abateth the ache of guttes aboute the reynes [period pains] also". John Evelyn, in his *Acetaria* (1699), observed that garlic was "dry toward excess ... and more proper for our northern rustics, especially [those] living in uliginous and moist places. Whereas leeks are hot, and of vertue

prolifick ... the Welch, who eat them much, are observ'd to be very fruitful". In the doctrine of humours, a plant's fecundity is thought to reflect its good effect on human fertility.

Other cultures also developed systems of categorizing the natural world and hence food. In China, the alliums are yang in the yin-yang balance of properties. Yang foods are male, dry and hot so, during the T'ang Dynasty (AD 618–907), garlic was endorsed as good for heating the blood and as a tonic. The Iranian "Araqi" classification ranks garlic as one of the hottest foods.

The alliums, especially garlic, have repeatedly been mentioned for use as treatments for open wounds, bites by venomous snakes and wild animals and cleansing the blood. Trevisa writes in

Above: Nicholas Culpeper, the 17th-century apothecary, extolled the curative virtues of onions and other alliums in his popular herbal, The English Physician.

the 13th century that garlic has "many maner vertu yfounde ... to putte out venym and all venemous thinges". Thomas Tusser, the 16th-century writer of agricultural doggerel, says that "now leeks are in season, for pottage full good and spareth the milch-cow, and purgeth the blood". Nicholas Culpepper in his well-known 17th-century herbal remarks that onions "Provoke urine and women's courses, helps the biting of mad dogs and other venonmous creatures ... [it] kills the worms".

There is also evidence that, in pre-Colonial America, native Americans used roasted wild onions and honey to neutralize snakebites and to help heal open wounds. Even as late as World War I (1914–18) garlic was used by the British as an antiseptic on a large scale, as noted by Mrs Grieve in her *Modern Herbal* (1931). The garlic was pounded to express the juice, which was then applied on swabs to open wounds to help staunch bleeding and prevent the wound from becoming infected.

Left: This medieval illustration shows the harvesting and bunching of garlic, which was believed to be good for treating a phlegmatic personality.

Alliums as preventives

In general, onions and garlic have been considered to be preventives and act as a general tonic against both infection and infestation. They are mentioned as preventives in outbreaks of the plague, for instance, both in France and England. The alliums' prophylactic properties were often linked with their use as talismans to ward off disease, rather than as remedies to be imbibed or rubbed on the body.

The Egyptian *Eber Codex* advocates wearing garlic around the neck as a way of driving out tapeworms. Greek and Macedonian mothers hung garlic around their babies' necks or cradles to ward off disease. In ancient China, onions, garlic and bunching onions were considered part of the "five strong-smelling foods" (*wu han*) and were hung on red cords at the threshold to protect the household against disease. John Evelyn (1699) considered garlic "a

charm against all infection and poyson", even though he despised it in salads. Pre-colonial native Americans considered that wild onions worn around the neck protected the wearer from colds and bronchitis. Most famously, of course, a garland of garlic was supposed to guard the wearer against being attacked by a vampire. Even in garlic-phobic Japan, in the northern town of Tsukuba-Khinoya, there is an annual festival, which dates from the Heian period of more than 1,000 years ago, when garlic is hung at the entrance to the house to prevent disease crossing the threshold during the coming year.

Alliums in the modern diet

Many contemporary writers consider that the onion family, particularly garlic, should be an essential part of our diet. Alliums aid good digestion, maintain a balanced blood pressure and work as a general tonic to help stave off infection. Recent research seems to confirm most of the herbalist lore that has built up through the ages.

Left: With the growing interest in the healing potential of food, organically grown food, such as these leeks, is becoming more popular.

Below: Of all the members of the onion family, garlic, in particular, is renowned for its healing properties.

Above: Links have been made between garlic and cancer prevention, and experts agree that even a small amount every day will help strengthen the immune system.

There is evidence that garlic reduces blood pressure, helps lower LDL (low-density lipo-protein) cholesterol and may prevent the build-up of cholesterol within the arteries. Raw garlic has always been considered an effective antibiotic. There is evidence that although garlic is not so strong as modern antibiotics, the way in which it works is so different that it can kill strains of bacteria that have become antibiotic-resistant. Garlic and onions generally have great antifungal and antiviral properties, and they play their part in maintaining a healthy intestinal flora and fauna.

Research is also progressing to examine the link between garlic and cancer. Garlic certainly has antioxidant properties and contains selenium, which is known to strengthen the body's ability to resist cancer. Clinical tests have also shown that garlic reduces the size of certain tumours in animals or prevents them from growing. Most experts agree that even a small amount of garlic every day – say one clove – will help maintain good health and strengthen the immune system. Garlic can also help thin the blood and prevent blood clotting.

Lore, remedies and old wives' tales
• As a remedy for corns, bandage a cut slice of garlic over the corn and replace it every day until the corn drops off.
• A syrup made from garlic steeped in vinegar and honey is good for asthma, coughs and general bronchial problems.
• To soothe a dry and painful cough, take a spoonful of honey mixed with a little crushed raw onion or garlic.
• It was once recommended that a roasted onion be applied to the affected ear as a cure for earache; it was also said to be good for boils.
• All onions are good for getting rid of moles in the garden. Drop peeled garlic or cut onions into their holes.
• Chopped garlic, bandaged to the soles of the feet and renewed daily, was thought a remedy for smallpox and even leprosy.
• Cut garlic rubbed over the lips will prevent them being burned by the sun.
• Mixed with lard or white cooking fat and applied to the chest or back as a poultice, garlic is thought good for chest conditions.
• A cut onion will rid a room of other strong smells, such as paint.
• An Irish folk-belief is that garlic planted on a Good Friday will protect people from fever during the whole year.
• A cut onion is said to attract all infection from the air into it and will kill air-borne infection.
• To cure baldness, rub the sap of a cut onion mixed with honey on the bald patch until the skin reddens – then wait.
• According to Brewer's *Dictionary of Phrase & Fable*, the phrase "to know your onions" is probably derived from Cockney rhyming slang, as in "onion rings" – "things". However, some have suggested that it refers to the man who edited the *Oxford English Dictionary* – C. T. Onions.

THE WORLD OF ONIONS

While we tend to think of onions as being more or less the same, there are many different varieties, colours and sizes. Some are better suited to roasting, others to frying; some are delicious cooked whole, others are better for chopping, slicing and eating raw. The same is true of the other members of the onion family — especially shallots, garlic and leeks. This fully illustrated reference section will help you to identify all the main varieties of edible alliums and give guidance on how best to use them in the kitchen.

THE ALLIUM FAMILY

There are more than 300 distinct species in the allium family, many of which have been used as food plants. For culinary purposes the best-known species are the onion (*Allium cepa*), the shallot (*Allium cepa*, Aggregatum Group), the leek (*Allium ampeloprasum* var. *porrum*), bunching onions (*Allium fistulosum* and *Allium cepa*, Proliferum Group), garlic (*Allium sativum*) and, finally, the various chives (*Allium schoenoprasum* and *Allium tuberosum*).

Onions, shallots, leeks and garlic are commonly known only in their cultivated forms. Although we do not know the wild forms of many of these plants, we can make informed guesses as to their origins. Many wild forms of edible alliums still exist around the world, as well as many varieties of allium that are purely ornamental.

The one thing that connects all the members of the allium family is their characteristic smell. Alliums contain chemical compounds known as alliins. When a plant is bruised or damaged, the alliins immediately begin to break down into the sulphur compounds known as allicins, which produce the instantly recognizable smell and flavour. The release of these volatile compounds can make us cry when we chop onions. If you wander through a woodland carpeted with wild garlic (*Allium ursinum*) in the late spring, the acrid, pungent smell is almost overpowering. Place a bunch of unwrapped garlic chives in the refrigerator, and you will find that within a few hours the eggs, milk and butter will be tainted with their strong smell. Onions are some of the most potent flavouring ingredients available for use in the kitchen, so it is no wonder they have been used by cooks for countless generations.

WILD ALLIUMS

Ramsons (*Allium ursinum*) are one of the commonest wild alliums in Britain and they grow in damp, shady areas throughout Europe. They form broad, fresh green leaves and have lacy heads of white flowers in late spring. The whole plant is very odorous and will affect the milk of any goats or cattle that graze on it. Ramsons used to be fed to chickens before they started laying, as a spring tonic and to "kick-start" them into productivity. The leaves are good wrapped around fish before cooking over charcoal. The flowers may be added to salads, and young leaves may be shredded into omelettes or rice dishes; they were commonly used in place of scarce onions during World War II. Ramsons have left their mark in a number of English place names, such as Ramsbottom in Lancashire and Ramsey on the Isle of Man.

Rocambole *Allium scorodoprasum* and *Allium sativum* var. *ophioscorodon* have both been called rocambole. The first is commonly called the sand leek, for it likes to grow in sandy soils; the second is a form of garlic. Both have coiled or twisted stems and grow widely across Europe. They have a good, mild flavour and were once exceedingly popular in salads and for flavouring cheese. John Evelyn, the 17th-century diarist and gardener who was quite against garlic, thought rocambole far more socially acceptable: "a clove or two of roccombo, of a yet milder and delicate nature, which by rubbing the [salad] dish only, imparts its vertue agreeably enough" (*Acetaria*, 1699).

Above: The pink-flowered wild sand leek has a mild, garlic flavour, which has been popular with cooks for centuries.

Babbington leek or kurrat (*Allium ampeloprasum* var. *babbingtonii* or *Allium ampeloprasum* var. *kurrat*) is probably related to the elephant garlic (*Allium ampeloprasum*). It is grown in the Near East for its narrow leaves. The sectioned bulb may be used as a mild version of garlic.
Other wild onions that have been used in the kitchen are crow garlic (*Allium vineale*) in Europe; *A. canadense*, *A. tricconum* and *A. cernum* in America.

Left: The flowers of ramsons can be found in European woodlands in spring.

Left: Spanish (Bermuda) onions are usually large and have a mild flavour.

Above: French onions tend to have a stronger, more pungent flavour than Spanish (Bermuda) onions.

ONIONS

These are all varieties of *Allium cepa*. Onions are grown for the bulb, formed by layers of fleshy, swollen leaf bases; the actual stem of an onion is the small layer of hard tissue at the top of the roots. The onion probably originated in western and central Asia, in an area stretching from modern-day Israel to India, and has been cultivated since the earliest times. It is likely that various kinds of onion were first cultivated around the Middle and Near East.

The uses of onions in the kitchen are myriad. They are used in the savoury cooking of almost every country and culture. They are fried, boiled, roasted, baked, stuffed and grilled (broiled).

There are many different kinds of onion and they are classified for kitchen use according to size, shape and colour.

Yellow onions

These are the most usual type of onion and are characterized by a light brown skin and a greenish white to pale yellow flesh. There are different varieties within this basic type, but they are commonly known as Spanish onions, regardless of their place of origin; Bermuda is the similar generic title for this kind of large, mild onion in the United States. For culinary purposes, Spanish onions are usually large, round and mild. Other types of yellow onions include brown onions, which have thick brown skins, and French onions, which have a stronger flavour.

Generally, the younger and greener the onion, the more pungent the flesh. Several varieties of yellow onion have been favoured for the mild sweetness of their flesh, such as the Vidalia from the north-western states of America and the Maui from Hawaii. The Walla Walla, named after the town in Washington State where it was first grown, was brought to the United States by Corsican immigrants in the early 20th century. Most onions in the northern hemisphere are autumn-cropping from a spring sowing, but some varieties have been bred to overwinter from an autumn sowing and crop in summer. Of these, the Japanese varieties are best known in Europe. The Vidalia is a summer-cropping onion in America.

Below: Brown onions have a thick, brown skin.

Uses in the kitchen Yellow onions are suitable for most kitchen purposes. Choose large round onions for baking, stuffing or cutting into rings. Longer or squatter onions are better for slicing or roasting whole. Some people consider them too strong to eat raw, although a mild yellow onion is good in potato salad or in marinated fish dishes, such as ceviche and soused herrings.

Uses in the kitchen

Red onions usually have a much milder, sweeter flavour than yellow onions and they are popular in salads; this is, no doubt, also because of their attractive pink-tinged flesh. They are frequently used raw in salsas, relishes, antipasti and marinated dishes. Red onions are also good roasted, either whole or cut into wedges, which concentrates the sweetness of their flesh. They are less useful for basic frying, when they have less flavour than other varieties and their lovely pink colour tends to turn to a murky mauve or dull brown.

Above: Red onions have beautiful purple-red skins and pink-tinged, mild flavoured flesh that is excellent in salads and salsas.

Red onions

As with yellow onions, there is a great variety of size and shape among red onions, but all are characterized by shiny, papery skins of a glorious purple-red. The flesh is basically white, stained red at the edges of each layer. The colour is released by contact with acids, such as vinegar or citrus juice, and red onion slices tossed in vinegar will soon turn a beautiful, uniform deep pink.

White onions

These are usually medium to large onions with a papery, white outer skin and white flesh. They tend not to vary so much in size, shape and flavour as yellow and red onions. They are usually fairly strong in taste.

Uses in the kitchen White onions may be used for all general cooking purposes, although many people consider them too strong for eating raw. Their even size and shape make them good for baking whole or stuffing.

Cipolla or borettane onions

These are quite small, flattish or squat onions with a pale golden skin and pale yellow flesh, while some varieties are tinged with pink. Cipolla or borettane onions are popular in Italy and some varieties are grown in France, too. They have an excellent, sweet flavour combined with an agreeable strength of taste.

Left: Evenly shaped white onions have a stronger flavour than red onions and are good for stuffing.

Right: A string of mixed onions makes an attractive sight hanging in a cool spot, and will cover all your onion needs in the kitchen.

Left: Cipolla onions are common in Italian markets and are excellent for braising, pickling and in salads.

Above: Small yellow pickling onions are good for adding whole to stews and casseroles.

Uses in the kitchen

Because they are generally small and have such a characteristic shape it would be a shame to use these onions for slicing or chopping so, generally, they are peeled and cooked whole. They are excellent caramelized or cooked *à la grecque* in a mixture of olive oil, wine and spices. They are also excellent for roasting whole, bottling and pickling.

Below: Tiny silverskin onions have a strong flavour and crisp texture.

Pickling onions

This is a general term for many different varieties of small onion. Some varieties may simply be immature yellow or red onions; others have been specially bred to produce small onions.

White silverskin pickling onions These strong-flavoured tiny "pearl" onions are nearly always used for pickling. When a small, pickled silverskin onion is added to a Martini, the drink is called a Gibson.

Yellow and red pickling onions These are usually larger and milder than the silverskin varieties. They also keep much better than silverskins. Store them as you would normal onions.

Uses in the kitchen These onions are excellent for pickling whole in spiced vinegar and for roasting whole, or for caramelizing. Small onions are good added whole to casseroles and stews. Typically, the bourguignonne garnish, characteristic of the cooking of Burgundy in France, uses fried onions and small mushrooms to finish stews.

Grelots

This is the French term for small, flattish onions with a green skin and very white flesh. They are very like a bulbous spring onion (scallion). Various types of this kind of fresh onion (they must be eaten fresh as they will not store well) are often labelled salad onions in supermarkets and food stores. They have a generally mild-flavoured flesh with a crisp bite.

Uses in the kitchen Grelots are used extensively sliced raw in salads, but are good in many quick-cooked dishes, such as omelettes and frittatas, or sliced into stir-fries. They are less useful for general frying or long-cooked recipes, when they tend to disintegrate.

Below: Pickling onions are favourites for traditional English pickled onions.

SHALLOTS

These are a distinct sub-species of *Allium cepa*, and are grouped botanically under the umbrella term Aggregatum Group, from the Latin meaning "a whole formed from several units". This is what distinguishes shallots from onions: they form clusters of several bulbs at the leaf bases. Their name comes from the ancient Palestinian port of Ascalon (now the port of Ashkelon in southern Israel), where it is thought they were first grown, but it is more likely to have been the port from where they were first exported to Rome. There is quite a variety of different shallots, but most are smaller than onions, composed of finer layers and they contain less water. As a result, they have a more concentrated flavour than onions, which makes them useful in the kitchen.

Banana shallots are the largest variety and get their name from their elongated shape. They have a smooth tan skin and a slightly milder flavour than other shallots.

Pink shallots and *échalote grise* are perhaps the most strongly flavoured shallots and are the most popular varieties in France. Pink shallots have a reddish

Left: Banana shallots (or frog's leg shallots) are large and mild, and may be used in the same way as small onions in most recipes.

skin and pink-tinged flesh; *échalote grise* are paler, but still have a pinkish cast to the flesh. They have a crisp texture and pungent, but not harsh, flavour, which is good raw and cooked.

Brown, English or Dutch shallots are probably the most common shallots found in food stores. These small, tan-skinned shallots often separate into subsidiary bulbs when they are peeled. They are good general-purpose shallots with well-flavoured but reasonably mild flesh.

Asian or Thai red shallots are small, round red bulbs, which are used extensively in the cooking of many South-east Asian countries. They vary from the strong to exceptionally strong in taste and are used most commonly in spice pastes, when they are pounded with other ingredients. Because of their low water content they are also excellent for slicing and frying to make crisp-fried shallots, which are common as a garnish on Thai salads and curries.

Chinese "shallots" are actually a different species (*Allium chinense*) and not a shallot at all. It is a wild species that is cultivated in China (*jiao tou* in Cantonese or *rakkyo* in Japanese).

Below: French shallots generally have a good, strong flavour and separate into several small sections when peeled. They are excellent in raw and cooked sauces and in salad dressings.

Left: Pink Thai shallots are used extensively in Thai curry pastes and are also used as salad garnishes. They are exceptionally pretty pickled in rice vinegar with herbs and spices.

Uses in the kitchen Shallots are excellent roasted whole, caramelized or pickled. Raw, they are essential in salad dressings and a wide range of French dishes. Chopped raw shallot is often sprinkled over a seared, rare steak *à la bordelaise*. Cooked, shallots are an essential ingredient in many sauces that need the flavour of onion but not its bulk. Shallots have a low water content, which means that they can burn and toughen easily, so care should be taken when frying. Potato onions may be used like ordinary onions.

They are grown mainly for pickling, and that is the form in which they are usually seen in the West.

Potato onions are related to shallots and belong to the Aggregatum Group of *Allium cepa*. The species is peculiar among the onions in that it develops entirely underground, in the same way as garlic. Because of this, it is a little hardier than other onions and shallots and, in the past, it was often planted in autumn. It forms clumps of small, yellow-skinned onions that store well. As many as eight small onions may form per clump.

Potato onions were once far more popular than they are now, especially in the mild west of England and Ireland, from where they were taken to the United States. They filled a gap between the end of the stored autumn-cropping onions and the new crop of shallots in late summer. Today, the potato onion is regarded as a bit of an oddity, mainly restricted to the herb patch, but the bulbs are of good flavour and are just as useful as ordinary onions in the kitchen. It is an interesting rarity that keen gardener-cooks might like to consider growing.

Right: English or Dutch shallots are generally brown skinned and have a mild flavour.

LEEKS

As a cultivated vegetable, the leek has even more ancient origins than the onion. It is probably derived from the wild *Allium ampeloprasum*, although some botanists call it a species in its own right (*Allium porrum*). The wild leek is a native of the Mediterranean and islands such as the Azores, Madeira and the Canaries. This wild leek has been traced back as far as Jericho 7,000 years ago. "Leeks" of a different species – *Allium ramosum* – have also been cultivated in China for thousands of years. Although there are many hundreds of varieties of cultivated leek, in fact, they vary only in size and winter hardiness. Some leeks have been bred to grow to vast dimensions and others to withstand quite severe winter frosts.

In the kitchen, the cook is mainly concerned with size. Traditionally in the northern hemisphere, leeks have been seen as a winter vegetable. These large leeks are one of the few vegetables to survive outdoors without protection. In recent years, baby leeks have increased in popularity, and while these may simply be immature, miniature versions of ordinary leeks, there are now special

Below: Baby leeks are good for serving whole. Steam, then brown in a hot griddle pan to bring out their flavour.

varieties that are grown to mature quickly and provide slender, tender leeks throughout the summer.

In leeks, the "bulb" or layers of leaf base are elongated to form what is commonly regarded as a stem, although botanically the stem is strictly the sometimes slightly bulbous base of the leek just above the roots. The leek divides into the white, fleshy basal portion and the green leaves or "flags". All the fleshy part of the leek may be used, but the green part is tougher and requires more cooking. Leeks have an almost universally popular flavour that is both milder and more rounded than that of onions. It lacks the pungency of onions, but makes up for it in the gentle depth of its flavour.

Uses in the kitchen Young, fresh leeks may be used raw, shredded in salads (a favourite with the Romans), but their chief use in the kitchen is when they are cooked. They are superlative in soups. Leeks cook more quickly than onions, so they should be added to stews towards the end of cooking. Whole, they are good braised or blanched then grilled (broiled). Baby leeks are usually cooked whole. They are excellent briefly boiled or steamed, then dressed in oil and vinegar.

Below: Large leeks, with their sweet, mild flavour, are among the most popular of alliums in the modern kitchen. They are excellent in soups and cooked salads.

Left: Bulb spring onions (scallions) are the best ones to use for grilling (broiling) whole or for cooking in stir-fries, or deep-frying whole in batter.

Uses in the kitchen In Britain, spring onions have traditionally been served whole (trimmed) in salads. They are good as crudités with a black olive tapenade and are excellent chopped or sliced into mixed or composite salads; they are widely used like this in the Middle East. They are a good addition to Mexican salsas. Spring onions are also excellent cooked, and are an essential ingredient in Asian stir-fries because they cook quickly. They grill (broil) well, taking only a few minutes to cook. In Cataluña, in north-east Spain, they are widely used in this way: known as *calçots*, they are grilled over hot coals and served with all sorts of grilled meats and a nut/chilli sauce called *salsa romesco*. The tops of young spring onions may be used as a garnish in the same way as chives, and spring onions curls and brushes are popular garnishes in Chinese food.

Below: Thin spring onions (scallions) are excellent in salads, whether left whole or chopped small.

SPRING ONIONS

Most of what are sold as spring or salad onions (scallions in the United States) are simply early-maturing varieties of onion (*Allium cepa*). However, the need for a year-round supply and recent breeding, especially by the Japanese, means that some spring onion varieties now have genes from Welsh onions (*Allium fistulosum*) in their makeup. If the cross-section of the leaf is circular, then the onion is a variety based on *Allium fistulosum*; if the cross-section of the leaf is crescent-shaped, then it is derived from *Allium cepa*.

As the English name suggests, these onions probably started out as the spring thinnings from ordinary onions. In culinary terms, the distinction between the different types of spring onion is purely one of size – they vary from the really tiny (thinner than a pencil) to those that are as large as, if not larger than, a baby leek. Some varieties of spring onion have a markedly bulbous base, and show a relation to the type of salad onions the French call *grelotes*; others are more leek-like, with no particular basal swelling.

Spring onions have a mild, sweet flavour with a fresh green snap, which makes them good in salads. Use thinner spring onions for salads and thicker ones for cooking. Red spring onions have been developed: these look pretty in salads, but do not differ significantly in flavour from white spring onions.

BUNCHING, WELSH AND TREE ONIONS

Bunching or Welsh onions (*Allium fistulosum*) are very popular in China and Japan. They are called Welsh as a corruption of the Germanic *welsche*, meaning foreign. This label was probably given when they were first introduced into Europe from Asia. In Wales itself they used to be known as "holtzers" and they were once a popular flavouring because they grew in early spring when few other vegetables were available. They are also known as *chiboules* or *cibols*. In Chinese cooking, they are used in stir-fries in place of spring onions (scallions). The onion grows in clusters of bulbs, so individual onions may be removed, leaving the plant growing. The flavour is mild.

Right: Tree onions, or Egyptian onions, are vigorous, clumping onions that grow well in the herb patch.

Below: Bunching or Welsh onions are the most popular type of onion in China and Japan.

Tree onions (*Allium cepa*, Proliferum Group) are true perennials for the herb patch. As with bunching onions, individual onions may be removed from the plant for use in the kitchen. Tree onions also form little bulblets at the tips of the stem, which may also be used in the kitchen or may be planted to form new plants. A particularly vigorous and tall form of the tree onion, known as the Catawissa onion, was a popular pot herb in America during the 19th and early 20th centuries.

Uses in the kitchen Both the basal stem and the green flags may be used in sauces, stir-fries and salads, but because tree onions are slightly tougher than spring onions, they do not grill (broil) well. The bulblets are good chopped in sauces and salad dressings.

Above: Chive flowers have a surprisingly oniony flavour and make a pretty addition to salads in early summer.

CHIVES

European chive (*Allium schoenoprasum*) is a common wild plant, occurring from northern Russia to the Mediterranean and as far east as the Himalayas. Various larger-growing varieties have been selected for domestication. Chives are one of the first herbs to start into growth in the early spring, and the first shoots are remarkably strong and pungent; later on, as the plants develop, they become milder. The flowers also have a mild oniony taste and are good in salads and as a garnish. Chives are usually eaten raw or very lightly cooked.

Chinese chives (*Allium tuberosum*) are also known as *kuchai* (*gow choy* in Cantonese) or garlic chives. They have a much more pungent smell and taste than European chives and because of their strong flavour are usually cooked. They come in two forms: the leaf form has flat, slightly twisted leaves with a pronounced garlic smell; the flowering stalk with a round, hollow stem is normally sold with flower buds intact. A third kind, Chinese yellow chives (*gow wong*), are simply a version of Chinese chives that have been blanched by excluding all natural light. They are highly regarded by the Chinese as a vegetable in their own right for stir-

frying. Garlic shoots are also used in Chinese cookery and are sometimes known as garlic chives.

Uses in the kitchen European chives are widely used as a garnish, but they have a surprising amount of flavour, especially when picked young from the garden. They are excellent in egg and cheese dishes, but care should be taken that they are not left in contact with eggs or dairy products as they will taint them. Chives are useful for adding a mild oniony taste to salad dressings, soups and sauces, and are particularly good in potato dishes. Chinese chives are more robust and need brief cooking. They are excellent in stir-fries, in rice dishes and stirred into soups and stews.

Right: Chinese chives are often sold in tight bud and may be chopped and used in stir-fries.

*Below: Chives (*Allium schoenoprasum*) are popular throughout Europe and North America, and give a mild, oniony flavour that is particularly good in cheese and egg dishes.*

Left: Young, new-season or wet garlic that has not been dried has a particularly sweet and mild flavour.

There are many different varieties of garlic, most of them geographically specific and therefore adapted to local climate and conditions. Garlic stores well when it is dried, but has a different taste from when it is used green and freshly pulled. There are some garlics with very white skin, while others are stained or mottled deep pink. Some garlic varieties separate naturally into tiny cloves, while others are characterized by large, fat cloves. Generally, the larger and less dried the clove, the milder and less pungent it is, but this is not an unbroken rule.

Above: Solo garlic is a mild form of garlic in which each small bulb comprises a single clove.

Below: Garlic is often sold in strings and will keep for several months if hung in a cool, dry place.

GARLIC

At various times, garlic (*Allium sativum*) has been the most lauded and the most despised of all the onion tribe because it is the fieriest and most pungent. It is one of the few culinary alliums that forms its bulb underground rather than on the surface of the soil.

Typically, a garlic bulb, or head, is formed of several separate cloves, each wrapped in its own papery skin, and the whole head is enclosed in a further papery skin. Garlic is widely cultivated, but needs a long growing season and a period of cold weather to initiate proper bulb development.

Most cultures consider it a herb or flavouring rather than a vegetable in its own right, but many dishes exist that include several whole heads of garlic rather than the odd clove that more timid cooks employ. A whole head of garlic, gently roasted until it becomes sweet, mellow and purée-soft, may easily be consumed by one person at a sitting. There are French recipes for chicken or lamb with forty cloves of garlic, which achieved an almost mythical status in garlic-phobic Britain of the 1950s. Some Asian dishes contain huge quantities of garlic by Western standards, such as southern Indian dishes of whole garlic cloves cooked with spices and coconut milk.

Middle East and in all Mediterranean countries. Crisp, fried garlic is a popular garnish to Burmese food, and in both Thailand and Korea pickled garlic is an accompaniment to many meals.

Garlic alters in flavour according to how it is prepared and for how long it is cooked. Crushed garlic, either raw or briefly cooked, is the most pungent and strongly flavoured; a whole head of garlic, slowly roasted, will have a mellow, nutty, toasty flavour. Garlic may be fried, baked, roasted or braised. It is a ubiquitous ingredient in most spice pastes, Spanish salsas, Italian pestos and Mexican moles. It is also widely used in all types of cuisine in dressings, marinades, soups and stews.

Left: Smoked garlic is infused (steeped) over wood smoke. It is good in garlic mayonnaise, marinades and dressings.

Below: There are many different kinds of garlic, which are often geographically specific: white garlic is popular in California. California Late and Silverskin are well-known varieties.

Elephant garlic (*Allium ampeloprasm*) There is some confusion in food stores between this variety and large-growing varieties of true garlic. Elephant garlic is actually more closely related to the leek than to garlic proper. It has a mild, creamy, garlic flavour and the cloves are very large in comparison with ordinary garlic. Another variety of allium (*Allium gigantum*) has also been known as elephant garlic, but most gardeners grow this as an ornamental, for its very large, purple drumstick flowers, rather than as a food plant.

Solo is a variety of garlic that has been specially bred to develop just one, large clove, making it easy to peel and prepare. It is useful for dishes using a lot of garlic, but expensive to use in any quantity. The flavour is fairly mild.

Wet or new season garlic may simply be labelled "fresh" or "green" garlic. Typically, in the northern hemisphere, this is ready in late spring to early summer, when the papery skin has not fully developed and dried out. Usually the head is used whole: it is creamy white, streaked and flushed with green and pink, and has a delicious mild flavour that is ideal for European garlic soups and to roast whole.

Smoked garlic usually consists of large, whole heads of garlic that have been hot-smoked so that they are partly cooked and infused (steeped) with wood smoke. They have a light, tan-brown exterior skin that should be peeled before the cloves are used for crushing into mayonnaise, for making garlic butter, or for tossing with pasta.

Garlic shoots – the first shoots of early spring – are considered a great delicacy in many areas of southern Europe (Italy, France and Spain) and are used in much the same way as chives or spring onions (scallions). They are also much used in Chinese stir-fries. Soup made from garlic shoots is a great favourite and is considered a splendid health tonic – a sort of "spring clean" for the blood and circulation. The shoots are also pickled for use later in the season in relishes, salads and sauces.

Uses in the kitchen Garlic is an almost universal favourite for flavouring in cuisines all around the world. It is widely used, both raw and cooked, to flavour all kinds of dishes. It is used raw in dressings, salsas, butters and salads. Cooked, it is used in huge quantities in most Asian countries (apart from Japan), Mexico and South America, the

ALLIUM FLAVOURINGS AND INGREDIENTS

There are a large number of allium flavourings and ingredients available. Some are made from onions, while others are not even related to the alliums but impart an oniony flavour.

Asafoetida

This is a pungent spice obtained from a resin from the root of a giant fennel (*Ferula asafoetida*). It is not related to the alliums, but does give a distinct garlicky taste to the dishes in which it is used. It was favoured in Roman cooking and was used by the Roman epicurean Apicius in the 1st century AD. Today, asafoetida is used in Afghanistan, India and Pakistan. It is usually bought ground and should be kept well sealed, because the smell of the uncooked spice is disagreeable. It is used in Indian Brahman cooking in place of the forbidden onions and garlic.

Onion seed or kalonji

The name onion seed is a complete misnomer, because the Indian spice kalonji is not a relation of the alliums, but is related to the familiar, blue-flowered annual "love-in-the-mist" (*Nigella sativa*) of our flower borders. It is much used in India, especially in Bengali cooking. It is good stir-fried with green vegetables, and sprinkled on the top of Indian breads and pancakes.

Dried onion flakes

These are simply dehydrated thin slices of onion, but as onions are available all year round, they are rarely used today. They should be rehydrated in warm water for 15–20 minutes before using, or they may be gently fried, to form crisp fried onions, which are much used as a garnish for Thai salads and curries. Dried shallot flakes are also available.

Crisp fried onion flakes

These are ready-fried crisp scraps of onion, which are useful as a garnish in salads, soups and rice dishes, or may be added to egg dishes. Once the pack is opened, the flakes should be used quickly or they will go rancid.

Left: Pungent asafoetida is much used in Indian vegetarian cooking.

Above right: Dry-roasting kalonji seeds will bring out their nutty flavour.

Right: Fried onion flakes are good sprinkled over salads and rice dishes.

Below: Dried shallot flakes may be added directly to slow-cooked stews.

Garlic salt

This is a mix of dried garlic and salt. It can be used to add instant garlic flavour to dishes such as garlic bread, but the drying process alters garlic's flavour, and many cooks prefer to use fresh garlic.

Garlic pastes

Ready-prepared garlic pastes are widely available. However, as with dried garlic, some of the preservatives used in the preparation of commercial garlic pastes alter the flavour and can give a slightly metallic tang to the finished dish. It is better to make your own roasted garlic paste, which will keep for 1–2 weeks covered with olive oil in a screw-top jar in the refrigerator.

Above left: Garlic salt is used in Cajun cooking for their blackened dishes.

Above: Fried garlic and garlic granules

Below: Small onions, garlic and shallots are popular in pickles.

Right: Minced (ground) garlic

Bottled or pickled alliums

In many countries, onions, garlic and shallots are pickled or bottled in vinegar or oil. These preserved alliums make a delicious addition to mixed salads, egg and rice dishes. Bottled green shoots of sprouting garlic are a popular spring flavouring in Spain, Italy and China. They are occasionally available fresh from Asian food stores.

CULTIVATION

The fact that the onion family has been cultivated since the earliest times and that it has spread far and wide across the globe suggests that onions are easy to grow. This is largely true: for the most part, onions are easily grown, hardy plants that are adaptable to a wide range of climates and soils. Certain varieties have been bred that are more suited to specific climatic conditions, and these different types vary in flavour and strength. Generally, the quicker an onion grows, the milder its flavour will be. Ideal quick-growing conditions, such as those found in large parts of Spain, the west-coast of the United States and Hawaii, foster sweet, mild onions, such as the Vidalia from Washington State and the Maui from the Hawaiian island of the same name. Onions that grow more slowly, say in northern Europe, tend to be stronger and more pungent. Home-grown onions, which have had to survive the

Below: Seedlings of the onion Vera Prima, ready for planting out.

vicissitudes of the garden, possibly with periods of drought and neglect, tend to be stronger in flavour and odour than commercially grown onions, which have led a pampered and well-watered life.

Onions can be grown in almost any type of soil, but most members of the onion family like a friable, open, slightly sandy soil. The best way is to plant in ground that has been manured in the autumn before planting. All members of the onion family prefer an open, sunny position: they do not grow well under the shade of trees or buildings, nor do they like the competition of roots from trees or large shrubs. Onions like to be well fed, but not with a fertilizer with a high nitrogen content, as this will make them grow large leaves rather than foster the formation of the bulb or stem. They also need to be well watered, as this helps the bulb to swell, but they can stand short periods of drought.

Onions (*Allium cepa* vars.) are biennial plants, which means that they form a bulb or storage organ one year, in order to flower and set seed the next. If the climate is mild enough, onions left in the ground over winter will shoot, flower and set seed in late spring.

The gardener grows the onion for the bulb it produces in its first year of growth. If it is properly dried off and stored, this bulb will survive throughout the winter dormant period and will not attempt to grow again until the following spring. Onions that are kept in a place that is too warm or damp may well shoot while they are in storage. An onion that does this is still edible, but the winter dormancy has been broken and it will not keep.

Onions are grown by two methods: either from seed, or from small, infant onions called sets. Shallots and garlic are, effectively, grown only from sets, while leeks and spring onions (scallions) are grown from seed. Bunching onions and chives are perennial plants (they live for several years and do not die upon flowering) and may be grown either from seed, division (when the plants are separated to make new plants) or from little bulblets.

GROWING ONIONS FROM SEED

Onions are fairly hardy plants, and small seedlings, growing outdoors, will survive a mild frost. Therefore, seed may be sown outdoors in mid- to late spring, or, with some varieties in mild climates (zones 7–8), in the early autumn.

Sowing onions outside

1 Prepare the ground by removing all weeds, then fork it over and rake it to form a fine tilth and a level surface.

2 Make a drill about 5mm/¼in deep with a thin stick or the corner of the rake head.

3 If the soil is dry, water the bottom of the drill before sowing.

4 Sow the seeds thinly along the bottom. Cover with the soil and firm it lightly with a rake. If sowing on a heavy, clay soil, a thin layer of sharp sand trickled along the bottom of the seed drill will prevent the seed from rotting before it starts to shoot.

5 The seedlings should germinate within 10–15 days. When they are 5–7.5cm/2–3in high, thin them to 7.5–10cm/3–4in apart. Water if conditions are very dry and keep free from weeds.

6 When the seedlings are growing strongly and the leaves are beginning to meet, thin them again to 13–15cm/5–6in apart. The thinnings at this stage of growth may be used as salad or spring onions (scallions). Unless you are intending to grow very large onions, you will not need to thin them again.

7 If you prefer small onions, space them closer together or let them grow as clumps of seedlings – you will then get clumps of small bulbs. Autumn-sown onions are often left to grow as clumps, as they overwinter better than the single seedlings.

Sowing onions indoors

In colder climates or on cold, heavy soils, sow onion seeds indoors under glass and then plant them outside in the garden in late spring. The seeds may be sown in early to mid-spring.

1 Fill a seed tray with sterilized seed compost (growing medium), level the surface and firm it slightly by pressing down gently with your finger.

2 Sprinkle the seed thinly over the surface of the compost.

3 Cover with either a thin layer of sifted seed compost or sprinkle with a thin layer of fine vermiculite to a depth of about 5mm/¼in.

Above: North Holland Blood and Red Mate are both good growing varieties of onions.

4 Using a watering can with a fine rose on the spout, lightly water the seeds, label and cover with a propagator lid or a plastic bag. Gentle heat under the tray will aid germination, but is not essential. As soon as the seedlings begin to emerge, move the tray into full light, but protect the delicate leaves from scorching in strong sunlight.

5 When the seedlings are 5–6cm/2–2½in high, prick them out into trays of compost, spacing them 5–6cm/2–2½in apart.

6 Alternatively, sow the seeds in divided trays or seed modules, 3–4 seeds per module. When the seedlings are growing strongly, thin to one seedling.

Planting onion seedlings outside

Seedlings grown inside will need to be planted outside in late spring. Harden off the seedlings before planting out by standing the trays outside for about 12 days. Cover and protect from heavy rain or frosty weather in a cold frame or greenhouse. When the seedlings have been hardened off, plant out 15–18cm/6–7in apart, in rows 25cm/10in apart. The tiny bulb should be no deeper than it was in the seed tray. Water well and protect from birds.

Some varieties of onion have been specially bred (mainly in Japan) to overwinter in a mild, temperate climate. These should be sown in late summer/early autumn. The seedlings or young plants overwinter, then grow in the spring. These onions are ready for harvesting in the early summer of the year following sowing, and usefully fill the gap between the end of the stored onions and the new season's crop of spring-sown onions. The most famous of these onions are the Vidalia onions, which are grown in the town of the same name in Washington State. The Vidalia onion is famous for being particularly sweet and mild.

GROWING ONIONS FROM SETS

Onions can also be grown from sets, which are small, immature bulbs. Sets have been grown and treated so that, once planted, they will continue to grow to form a full-size onion. Because onions are biennial there is a danger that the set will bolt, that is run to flower, rather than grow to make a fair-size bulb. However, some sets have been heat-treated to kill the flower and prevent bolting. Onion sets are planted in early to mid-spring and will stand a little light frost. They are best planted in open, well-dug soil which has been manured the autumn before planting.

If the soil is heavy, put a little sharp sand beneath each set. Push into the soil in rows, allowing 10cm/4in between sets and 25cm/10in between rows. The top of the set should be just visible. Apart from watering in extremely dry weather and weeding, they should need no more care.

Sometimes birds will work their way down a row pulling out the sets before they have time to root. If this happens, simply push them back into the soil, making sure that they are firm. If birds are proving to be a particular problem, try laying twigs over the soil, or covering the sets with netting. This may well be the best solution to the problem.

Good varieties of onion

Spring sowing: Buffalo, Giant Fen Globe, Ailsa Craig, Sturon, North Holland Blood, Long Red Florence, Red Baron, Southport Red Globe, Red Mate. Autumn sowing: Express Yellow, Imai Early Yellow, Vidalia, Senshyu Yellow. Pickling onions: Paris Silver Skin, Shakespeare.

Championship onions and leeks

Around the world, specialist and competitive growers prepare deep beds of special soil in which to grow mammoth onions and leeks. There is great competition between growers. Show leeks are blanched by growing them through drainpipes or wrapping them in thick, corrugated cardboard, and they are fed with "secret" compounds of liquid fertilizer to encourage growth. Some onions can grow to over 2.75kg/6lb, while leeks can grow up to 1m/1yd long, with a stem as thick as a person's arm. Good varieties for championship onions are Mammoth and Beacon.

GROWING LEEKS

Leeks are grown from seed in exactly the same way as onions. Sow outside in mid- to late spring or inside under glass in early spring. Sowing seeds indoors provides a longer growing season and produces bigger leeks. Leeks sown outside should be thinned to about 2.5cm/1in apart. Inside, prick out the seedlings into trays or modules about 2.5cm/1in apart. In early summer, plant the leeks outside. Indoor-sown leeks should be hardened off first.

1 If you want long, blanched leeks, dig a trench of prepared soil. The trench should be about 30cm/12in across and about 25cm/10in deep. Fork over the bottom of the trench thoroughly and dig in some well-rotted manure or fertilizer. Heap the removed soil alongside the trench for infilling later.

2 Half-fill the trench with removed soil, then make holes with a stick or dibber 20–25cm/8–10in apart. They should be about 2.5–4cm/1–1½in across and 13–15cm/5–6in deep.

3 Drop the seedlings into the holes so that the leaves poke out of the top.

4 Water the leeks well, by pouring water into the hole to wash soil over the roots.

5 As the leeks grow, gradually return the remaining soil to the trench. This blanches the stem, and forces the leeks to grow a longer, white stem.

6 For leeks for general cooking, holes may be made in well-prepared soil, rather than a trench. Drop in the leek seedlings and water in as above. Some gardeners on heavy clay soil find they get better results if they grow leeks in raised beds of deeply prepared soil.

Below: De Saint Victor leeks have distinctive blue-purple leaves; they are winter-hardy and have excellent flavour.

This aids drainage, whereas a trench may fill with water on badly draining land. Support the sides with planks of wood, bricks or old railway sleepers (railroad ties). The beds should be about 1.2m/4ft wide so that they can be cultivated without stepping on the soil.

Good varieties of leek

Bleu de Solaise: a handsome leek with blue-purple foliage; Autumn Giant: an early maturing leek that will last to late winter in the ground; Musselborough Improved: a good winter-hardy variety; King Richard: a quick-growing variety, good for harvesting as baby leeks; Jolant; De Saint Victor: winter-hardy.

Fertilizing onions and leeks

In ordinary conditions, onions need little or no feeding during the growing period, although they may be fed with a potash fertilizer when the bulb is well formed. This helps the bulb ripen and prevents it developing "thick neck". Leeks need no extra feeding during the growing season as long as the ground was manured to start with.

GROWING SHALLOTS

Shallots are generally grown from sets rather than from seed. They grow as clumps of bulbs, each one of which may be grown on as a set. They are grown in exactly the same way as onion sets but they grow much more quickly.

1 In late winter to early spring, plant shallot sets in open, well-dug soil that has been well manured the autumn before planting.

2 If the soil is very heavy, place a little sharp sand under every shallot to aid drainage and prevent the bulb from rotting in the wet earth.

3 If any of the sets are pulled up by birds, press them back into the soil. Alternatively, protect the sets with a layer of netting or by laying a few twigs over the soil.

4 The shallots will be ready to harvest by midsummer.

Good varieties of shallot

Atlantic: golden-skinned shallots with a high yield; Pikant: a pink-fleshed shallot of fine flavour; Giant Iona; Topper.

Pests and diseases

The potent chemicals that alliums produce generally give them an in-built defence against pests and diseases. Garlic, in particular, seems resistant to most garden pests.

Rabbits, rodents and deer give all alliums a wide berth because they find the smell and taste offensive. Moles, too, avoid making their runs near an onion or garlic bed. Despite this, mice or rats are known to eat onions in store, so, when alliums are stored, they should be protected against these vermin.

In very wet summers, and on heavy, poorly drained land, onions can be susceptible to downy mildew, which can cause rotting. Affected onions should be pulled up and discarded, but not on the compost heap. Onions should not be grown on the same patch of ground for about three years.

The major pest of onions is onion fly. They lay their eggs in the bulb, which is then eaten by the maggots that hatch from the eggs. There are no chemical treatments that protect onions against this harmful pest, but companion planting is said to be effective in deterring them. Plant tagetes (French marigolds) and parsley in rows among the onions if the pest is known to be prevalent.

Leeks sometimes get a rust disease, which causes rust-coloured spots on the foliage. However, it does not affect the leek stem so there is no need to spray or discard the leek plants, but do not put affected leaves on the compost heap.

Above: Once harvested, shallots are best strung for storage and kept in a dry, frost-free place. They should keep throughout the winter if stored in this way.

GROWING GARLIC

Garlic is grown from individual cloves in a similar way to onion and shallot sets. There are many different varieties of garlic that have been specially bred to suit specific climates. It is better to order an appropriate variety from a seed firm, rather than using a head of garlic from the supermarket as it may have been imported. These will, however, often grow. Garlic needs a long growing season and also a period of 1–2 months of cold weather (0–10°C/32–50°F) to make a good-size head.

Garlic is different from other alliums (apart from the seldom-grown potato onion) in that the head, or bulb, grows underground rather than on the surface of the soil. Because of this, garlic is best planted in the autumn, to be harvested in mid- to late summer the following year. It will tolerate some frost. Little or no growth will be visible above ground until the following spring.

1 Plant individual cloves 10–15cm/ 4–6in apart in rows 25cm/10in apart just below the surface in well-dug soil. Place a little sand beneath each clove if gardening on heavy, clay soil to help drainage and prevent rotting.

Growing garlic shoots

Garlic shoots can easily be grown by planting cloves of garlic in pots of good, free-draining compost (soil mix) from early spring onwards. Keep well watered in a sunny, open position. Harvest the young shoots when they are about 15–20cm/6–8in high. More shoots will soon grow to replace them.

Good varieties of garlic

Moraluz: large white heads; Cristo; Mediterranean.

GROWING SPRING ONIONS

Spring onions (scallions) are grown from seed. Sow as for bulb onions in rows about 20cm/8in apart. Spring onions mature quickly, so sow short rows in succession every 3–4 weeks during spring and early summer. If you sow the seed thinly, there is no need to thin out spring onions, simply pull the onions as you need them.

Good varieties of spring onion

Santa Claus: a Japanese variety with deep-red stems; White Lisbon: a traditional, white, quick-growing spring onion.

GROWING BUNCHING ONIONS

Asian varieties of bunching onions are grown in a similar way to spring onions, but you can keep on harvesting them over a longer period, so thin the plants to about 10cm/4in apart.

Good varieties of bunching onion

Summer Isle; White Evergreen; Ishikura, Kujo Green.

GROWING WELSH ONIONS AND TREE ONIONS

These perennial onions are best bought as small plants from a herb nursery, although it is possible to grow them from seed sown indoors in early spring. If growing from seed, prick out clumps of little seedlings in 7.5-cm/3-in pots. Harden off the seedlings and plant them out in early summer. If you have a mature plant, you can create more by simply digging the plant up and dividing it into smaller plants. Replant small

Above: Freshly harvested garlic ready for cleaning and stringing for storage.

sections from the healthy, outer edge of the clumps, rather than from the congested centre. Bulblets from the top of the stem of tree onions will also grow into new plants if pushed into a pot of good compost.

GROWING CHIVES

Chives are propagated by division. They prefer a good, moist soil, but will grow more or less anywhere. Divide the plant when it is actively growing in early or mid-spring and set the divisions about 25cm/10in apart. Chives should be harvested as you need them. During the growing season, they can be cut down to ground level two or three times and they will sprout again, with fresh, full-flavoured leaves. Water well after cutting back. In the autumn, pot up chive plants, cut them back and keep them in a cool, frost-free place indoors where there is plenty of good light. This is a good way to have fresh chives available for use throughout the winter.

HARVESTING AND STORAGE

The harvesting of alliums depends on the length of time that they can be stored. Onions, shallots and garlic, which, if stored correctly, can keep throughout the winter, should be harvested when they are fully grown. Leeks, spring onions (scallions) and chives, which have a shorter shelf life, are better left in the ground until they are needed.

ONIONS, SHALLOTS AND GARLIC

It is obvious when onions, shallots and garlic are ready to be harvested. With onions and shallots, the leaf stem keels over at the top (neck) of the bulb. With garlic, the leaves start to die back, wither and keel over. When this happens, it is fairly certain that the bulb has finished its growth for the season.

Sometimes onions develop a "fat" or "thick" neck. This is not a disease, but a physiological condition. Some varieties are more susceptible than others; wet weather is an additional factor. The neck of the onion becomes thick and remains green, and the leaves do not keel over but stay upright and healthy. The onion still continues to grow, rather than to ripen and dry off. If left in the soil, the onion would eventually bolt, or run to flower. Such onions are perfectly good to eat, but they will not keep for a great length of time, so use them as quickly as possible.

When the onion leaves keel over, it is best to leave them in the soil for a week or so, especially if the weather is dry and sunny. After that, gently pull the onions up to expose the roots to the air and leave them on the ground to finish drying and for the root to wither. If the weather is cold and wet, remove the bulbs to a dry but well-ventilated place: lying on the greenhouse staging is ideal, or on a frame made of netting. Do not remove stems at this time. When the onions have thoroughly dried, the stems may be twisted off and the onions placed in trays with ventilation holes.

Above: Stringing garlic is an excellent way of making sure that it stays dry and well ventilated.

Left: Lift onions with a fork, then let the bulbs dry off either on the ground, if dry, or on a rack under cover.

Stringing onions, shallots and garlic

If the stems are left intact, the onions may be strung together to form ropes or skeins, either by plaiting (braiding) the stalks or tying them together with string or raffia. Shallots and garlic should be treated in the same way. An alternative method of "stringing" garlic is simply to thread a stiff wire through the dry necks of the bulbs.

Strung onions, shallots and garlic may then be hung up for storage, which is an excellent way of keeping them well aired. All three should keep through to the following spring if stored in a dry, well-ventilated room or shed that is cool and just frost-free. Check your store of onions throughout winter and discard any that feel soft. Towards the end of winter, some onions may begin to sprout. Use these immediately. Do not try to store garlic ropes in the kitchen, however decorative, or they will sprout.

How to string onions, shallots and garlic

Onions, shallots and garlic can all be strung together in the same way. Either tie them into a skein with string or raffia, or plait (braid) the dried stems.

1 Take the first bulb and tie a loop of string around the neck. Pull the string tight to allow for shrinkage later.

2 Add more bulbs, each one just above the last, forming a loop of string around the neck of each. Bind any surplus stem into the skein.

3 When you have reached the end of the skein – usually about 12–15 onions – tie all the stalks together firmly, folding over any surplus.

Above: Young leeks, like these 4-month-old De Saint Victors, may be harvested as soon as they begin to thicken.

LEEKS

These are best left in the ground rather than lifting them as they mature. Simply harvest as and when you need them in the kitchen. They will withstand quite hard frosts and can be left in the ground throughout the autumn. When dug, the leeks will keep for about a week in a dry, well-ventilated room. Washed and prepared, leeks should be stored in a plastic bag in the vegetable drawer of the refrigerator.

SPRING ONIONS AND CHIVES

If the spring onions (scallions) have been sown thinly enough then, as they mature, you can simply pull them from the ground when you need them. Once pulled, they should be stored in the refrigerator, wrapped in a plastic bag.

CHIVES

These should not be pulled, but can be snipped near to the soil with a pair of kitchen scissors. Harvest chives as they are required in the kitchen. They will keep for a few days, well-wrapped in a plastic bag or in a plastic tub in the refrigerator.

PREPARING ONIONS AND OTHER ALLIUMS

This section looks at most of the basic techniques for preparing and cooking onions, leeks and other alliums. It is worthwhile spending a little of your time studying and mastering these techniques, since they ultimately help to save time and tears.

CHOOSING ONIONS AND OTHER ALLIUMS

When buying onions, choose firm, undamaged specimens with light skins. Reject any that feel soft when gently squeezed, show signs of dampness or with green shoots at the top. These rules apply to shallots and garlic too, except new season's garlic which should have moist, fresh skins.

Examine the leaves of spring onions (scallions) and leeks – they should be fresh and not brown or slimy. Be careful when buying leeks in late spring and early summer, since they may well have a hard, central core. This core is the developing flower stalk and it will not soften on cooking.

When preparing onions, discard any that have brown patches or are brown or slimy at the centre. The onion will be tainted, and even if the bad portion is cut away and discarded, the onion will still taste nasty.

Green shoots at the centre of a garlic clove, and dried-out, old or withered garlic cloves should be discarded – they will give a bitter or musty taste to the finished dish.

PEELING ONIONS

1 The easiest way to peel an onion is first to cut off the top and bottom.

2 Slit the skin with a sharp knife and peel it off.

Peeling whole onions

Onions or shallots used for braising or for adding to a *boeuf bourguignonne*, for example, must be left whole. Some cooks even find it easier to slice onions, which can be quite slippery and tough, if the root end is temporarily left intact.

1 To peel an onion or shallot, when it is important that the onion stays whole, trim any root from the base, making sure you leave the base intact.

2 Then, working from the neck down, make a shallow slit in the skin from top to bottom with a small, sharp knife.

3 Pull the skin off the onion, working from the neck down.

Peeling small onions and shallots

If you are peeling a lot of small onions or shallots, it is easier if you first blanch them in boiling water. This is particularly helpful when peeling varieties that have tenaciously clinging, tight skins. This also works with garlic cloves.

1 Cut off the neck of the onions or shallots and cut a thin slice off the bottom, but leave the root base intact or the onions may fall apart in cooking.

2 Place in a bowl and add enough boiling water to cover.

3 Leave for about 3 minutes, drain, then slip the onions or shallots out of their skins.

TRIMMING AND CLEANING LEEKS

Particles of soil can easily become trapped in between the leaf layers of a leek. The tighter the layers, the less likelihood there is that soil will have managed to penetrate.

Baby leeks and tight, ready-trimmed leeks from the supermarket are unlikely to be very gritty, but it is still worth checking before cooking, since nothing ruins a leek dish more than the mere trace of grittiness from hidden soil. Leeks fresh from the garden are always the worst culprits and therefore need to be washed thoroughly.

Trimming and cleaning large leeks

1 When preparing large leeks, trim off most of the loose green leaves, or flags, cutting at the point where the layers begin to get tighter.

2 Discard any loose green leaves but, unless the recipe specifies the white part of the leek only, do not discard the green part of the bulb.

3 Trim off excess root. Discard one or two outer layers of the leek, which are tough, fibrous and quite likely to have been damaged.

4 Make a slit starting about 2.5cm/1in from the base of the leek to the top, cutting through to the centre.

5 Carefully wash the leek under cold running water, fanning out the layers with your fingers to make sure you wash away all the dirt. Hold the leek so that the water runs from the base to the top, so dirt will not be washed back into the layers of leaves.

Trimming and cleaning baby leeks

1 Cut off as little of the green leaf as possible, as it is tender enough to eat.

2 Baby leeks are usually clean enough to cook whole, but check one by cutting a slit through to the centre.

3 Peel off the outer layer of the leek if it looks tough or damaged.

4 Wash the leeks by shaking them well in a bowl of cold water.

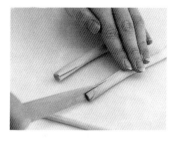

5 If leeks appear dirty only at the top end and you want to cook the leek whole, cut a short slit in the leek. Either wash the leeks under cold running water or soak them in a bowl of cold, well-salted water for 30 minutes to draw out the dirt. Soaking also leaches out vitamins, so this should be a last resort.

> **Preparing in advance**
> It is unwise to prepare any of the onion family too far in advance. Raw alliums can develop "off-flavours" as a result of the sulphur compounds that are released when their cell walls are broken. Although safe to eat, they can taint delicate dishes of eggs, cream and butter. If you want to prepare alliums ahead of time, cook them briefly in a little fat from the recipe (or blanch them in boiling water for a few minutes).

SLICING AND CHOPPING ONIONS, SHALLOTS AND LEEKS

1 The easiest way to slice an onion is to cut it in half with a sharp knife, from neck to root.

2 Place the halves, cut sides down, on the chopping board.

3 Hold down one half firmly, but tuck your fingertips in, away from the blade of the knife, then, using the knuckles to guide the knife blade, cut down to make slices. Repeat with the other half.

Cutting crescent-shaped slices

Crescent-shaped slices of onion are good in salads and stir-fries. Thicker wedges are excellent for roasting.

1 Leave the root end of the onion intact and cut the bulb in half vertically, from neck to root.

2 Lay the onion, cut side down, on a board and, using a sharp knife, cut thin slices following the curve of the onion.

3 Leave these thin slices attached at the base for frying or separate them into layers for salad garnishes.

Cutting onion rings

1 Choose evenly shaped round onions. Look at the neck of the bulb and check that there is only one shoot, or neck – this means that there is more chance of getting perfectly round onion rings.

2 Cut a thin slice from one side so that it will not slip on the chopping board.

3 Cut down to form thin or thick slices. Push out to separate into rings.

Chopping onions

1 Slice the onion in half from top to bottom and lay it cut side down.

2 Slice across the onion, leaving a small section uncut at the root end.

3 Slice down through the onion at right angles to these cuts from neck to root. Leave the root end uncut to prevent the onion falling apart.

4 Finally, slice across the onion at right angles to the second set of cuts and the onion will fall into dice on the chopping board as you cut.

Slicing leeks

1 Cut across the width of the leek in the thickness you require.

COOK'S TIP

The green part of the leek often takes a little longer to cook than the tender white part, so put it into the pan a few minutes earlier.

2 When stir-frying, cut across the leek obliquely in a series of diagonal cuts. This exposes a larger surface area of the central portion of the leek to the heat, so that it cooks quickly.

Chopping leeks

1 Using a sharp knife, carefully cut the leek in half vertically, from top to root. Lay the leek, cut side down, on the chopping board.

2 Make a series of cuts along the length of the leek from bottom to top, leaving the root end intact to prevent the leek from falling apart.

3 Cut across the leek and it will fall into dice on the chopping board.

PREPARING SPRING ONIONS AND BUNCHING ONIONS

Spring onions (scallions) and bunching onions are easily prepared. Cut off only tough or damaged green leaves. Peel the thin, outer layer from the onion and trim the root end. Wash in a bowl of cold water or under running water. For stir-frying, simply slice at an oblique angle, holding the knife blade at about 40 degrees to the length of the onion.

Spring onion brushes

These are traditionally served with Peking duck. The fringed end of the onion may be used to dip into the plum sauce for brushing it on to the pancakes.

1 Cut the spring onion into 6–7.5cm/ 2½–3in lengths.

2 Make a series of lengthways cuts at one end of the spring onion, using a sharp knife or kitchen scissors to produce a tassel effect. Leave at least half the onion uncut to form a handle.

3 Place the spring onions in a bowl of iced water and chill in the refrigerator for 30–45 minutes to allow them to curl.

Making spring onion curls

1 Cut the spring onion into 6–7.5cm/ 2½–3in lengths.

2 Cut each piece in half lengthways, then cut these pieces lengthways into long, thin shreds.

3 Place in a bowl of iced water and chill in the refrigerator for 30 minutes to allow the shreds to curl.

Making spring onion tassels

1 Make a series of short, lengthways cuts at each end of the onions using a sharp knife or kitchen scissors to produce a tassel effect. Make sure you leave at least 2.5cm/1in of onion uncut at the centre.

2 Chill the spring onions in iced water for 30–45 minutes until the ends curl.

CUTTING CHIVES

1 Hold a bunch of chives in your hand, snip the bunch level at one end with kitchen scissors, then snip off the amount you require.

2 Cut straight across to form little rings, or obliquely to form slanting chives.

PREPARING GARLIC

The taste of garlic differs depending on how it is prepared. This is because varying amounts of the natural sulphur compounds, which are contained in garlic, are released depending on how you cut it. The finer you chop or crush garlic, the stronger the flavour will be.

Peeling garlic

The easiest way to peel garlic is to place it on a chopping board and use the blade of a wide-bladed knife flat to crush the clove.

1 Lay the blade of a knife flat on the clove and press down firmly on the blade with your fist or the heel of your hand, breaking the skin of the garlic.

2 The skin will then peel off easily. This also bruises the garlic, which allows the flavour to come out.

COOK'S TIP

To remove the smell of garlic from your hands, sprinkle them with salt, then rinse in cold water before washing them with hot water and soap. Alternatively, rub them all over with the cut side of a lemon before washing in hot water.

Blanching garlic

If peeling a lot of garlic, you can blanch the cloves to make them easier to peel.

1 Cut off the top and bottom of each garlic clove and place in a bowl of boiling water for 2–3 minutes. Drain, then slip the cloves out of their skins.

Chopping garlic

1 When chopping or crushing garlic, first remove any green shoot at the centre of the cloves. The shoot is most apparent in late winter/spring and can taste bitter. Cut out the shoot with the tip of a knife or pinch it out.

2 For a mild flavour, slice garlic thinly, across the clove, or chop coarsely.

3 For a stronger flavour, finely chop the garlic by first cutting the clove in half from top to bottom, then cutting along and then across the clove.

Crushing garlic

To attain a much stronger flavour, crush the garlic rather than chopping it.

1 Crush the garlic in a mortar with a pestle or, alternatively, crush it on a chopping board with the flat blade of a knife to make a paste. Adding a few flakes of sea salt to the garlic will make crushing much easier.

2 Easier still, press the peeled clove through a specially designed garlic press or crusher.

GARLIC GADGETS

The only tools you really need to prepare garlic are a good, small, sharp knife, a chopping board and, of course, your hands. However, there are plenty of pieces of equipment on the market that are designed to help with the preparation of garlic. Most of this equipment has just one aim in mind – to minimize handling the garlic and therefore preventing the hands from smelling of it.

Garlic peeler

Garlic peelers are made of a simple rubber tube with a textured inside surface. The garlic clove is placed inside the tube, which is then pressed down on and rolled back and forth on the work surface to loosen the skin for easier peeling.

Garlic press (pump action)

A pump action garlic press is the most familiar type of garlic crusher. Some presses have a very useful reverse action that helps to extract the garlic that can become trapped in the holes. Garlic presses can also be used for preparing onion and ginger juice.

Garlic press (screw action)

A different type of press from the pump action, but the result is basically the same. As you screw down the handle, the garlic is pressed out of the head. It is easy to use, but not so easy to clean.

Mortar and pestle

These are very useful pieces of general kitchen equipment and are excellent for crushing large quantities of garlic or making garlicky pastes, such as aioli.

Below: A mortar and pestle are the traditional devices for crushing garlic.

Garlic crush

A garlic crush is similar to a pestle but has a larger domed base. It is most effective when used with a bowl-shaped board. It produces a similar result to garlic crushed with the flat blade of a large knife.

Garlic slicer

A garlic slicer acts like a miniature mandolin. The garlic clove is placed in the holder, then slid back and forth over the sharp blade. This gadget is particularly useful if you are slicing large quantities of garlic or ginger.

COOKING ONIONS AND OTHER ALLIUMS

There are many ways of cooking onions, all of which will produce very different results both in the flavour of the onion and in the dish in which it is used.

FRYING ONIONS

Onions can be fried in a number of different ways and each gives its own unique result. Onions that are quickly fried until they are brown will retain all the pungency of the raw onion and may taste quite bitter if allowed to get too brown. Quick-fried onions are generally used in dishes where they will receive further cooking, such as stews and casseroles – dishes that also benefit from the dark colour the browned onions impart to the sauce.

Slow-cooked onions, cooked over a low heat in a covered pan and not allowed to brown at all, will develop a wonderful, mellow, sweet taste that can add a great depth of flavour to the finished dish. This process is called sweating, and is an essential first step in preparing many soups and sauces. It works well with leeks, too.

Caramelizing onions is a combination of these two methods. First the onions are cooked slowly until soft but not browned, then the heat is turned up and the onions are cooked uncovered until they brown. In some recipes, a little sugar is added to speed up the caramelizing process. When the onions are cooked slowly to a mahogany brown, they are used as the base of many rich, brown soups and many classic sauces. They are also good to eat just as they are as an accompaniment to meat, poultry or cheese.

Different kinds of onion, or onions at different stages of growth, react in different ways to these basic cooking techniques. Green, unripened onions will not fry to a dry crispness. Red onions tend to be "wetter" than yellow Spanish (Bermuda) onions and so they tend not to brown and caramelize so easily. Shallots are quite dry-fleshed and will soon dry out and turn bitter and hard if they are fried and browned too quickly. To keep onions soft and prevent them from browning when frying, add a pinch of salt to draw out their moisture.

Quick frying

1 Heat whatever fat the recipe calls for in a large, heavy frying pan over a medium heat until hot. Add the thinly sliced or chopped onions and cook for about 5 minutes, stirring frequently to prevent them from sticking to the pan, until the onions begin to turn brown at the edges. Do not allow to burn as this will spoil the flavour.

Slow frying

1 Cook the onions over a very low heat for 10–15 minutes, until they collapse and turn a deep golden yellow colour. Stir the onions occasionally while they cook to prevent them from sticking to the pan and browning, as this will spoil their mellow flavour.

Sweating

This cooking process can be used for onions or leeks and is often the first step in soup making, as it concentrates and mellows the flavour, producing a rounder taste. Sweating or slow-frying requires a very low heat that cooks, but does not brown the onions or leeks, as this destroys the mellow, sweet flavour.

1 Cook the onions as for shallow frying, but cover the pan with a lid to produce a much softer, sweeter result.

2 Some cooks like to press a piece of greaseproof (waxed) paper or baking parchment on top of the onions before covering them with the lid. This sweats the onions even more intensely.

Remedies for onion odours
• Try rubbing the soles of your feet with pure peppermint oil. Within 30 minutes the smell on your breath should be of mint.
• Chewing fresh parsley is the best-known antidote to onions and garlic on the breath. The chlorophyll in the parsley neutralizes the sulphur chemicals released by the alliums, which cause odours.
• Cover over the onion smells by chewing cardamom or fennel seeds – these seeds are traditionally offered after Indian meals as breath fresheners and an aid to digestion.
• Drink a herbal infusion or tea of mint, fennel and/or sage.

Thai crisp-fried shallots

These are excellent for garnishing salads, rice and soups.

1 Peel the shallots and slice to a medium thickness.

2 Cook the shallots gently in oil for about 8 minutes, until they soften.

3 Raise the heat and fry the shallots briskly until they brown and crisp. Remove with a slotted spoon and drain well on kitchen paper.

COOK'S TIP
Dried shallot or onion slices can be fried from dry to form a crisp-fried garnish. Take care not to burn them.

CARAMELIZING

To caramelize onions or shallots, they need to be cooked slowly until their natural sugars turn an appetizing brown colour. Caramelized onions or shallots add a depth of flavour to soups, sauces and stews. They are also good served with liver, steak or sausages.

The speed with which onions will caramelize depends on the heat of the pan. Onions or shallots caramelized over a very low heat for 45 minutes will slowly turn a deep mahogany brown. The cooking time will depend on the onions' sugar content. Caramelized onions are used most famously in *soupe à l'oignon*. For a quicker result, raise the heat and add just a little sugar to aid caramelization, but stir frequently to prevent the onions from sticking.

Caramelizing onions in a pan

1 Cook onions slowly, covered, in butter or oil until they soften and turn golden.

2 Continue cooking, uncovered, until they begin to brown at the edges, stirring them frequently.

3 Add 2.5–5ml/½–1 tsp sugar to help the onions to caramelize more quickly.

Caramelizing onions in the oven

This technique can be quite useful if you are busy, because the onions do not need to be stirred quite so often as onions caramelized in a pan.

1 Place thickly sliced onions in a roasting pan or on a baking tray, season with salt and pepper to taste, add herbs, such as thyme or rosemary, and sprinkle with a little olive oil.

2 Cover the onions with foil and cook at 190°C/375°F/Gas 5 for 30 minutes.

3 Uncover the pan or tray, stir in 5ml/ 1 tsp sugar and sprinkle a little wine or balsamic vinegar over the onions.

4 Return the pan or tray to the oven, uncovered this time, and cook for another 25–35 minutes, stirring once or twice, by which time the onions should be very soft and browned.

COOK'S TIP
A thick layer of onions will caramelize better than a thin layer, which will brown too quickly. Keep an eye on them in the oven. If they brown too quickly, lower the heat and be sure to stir once or twice.

Caramelizing shallots or baby onions

Shallots and baby (pearl) onions are usually caramelized whole, but they can also be cooked in thick slices.

1 Brown the shallots or baby onions lightly on all sides in a little butter or oil. Raise the heat slightly, sprinkle in a little sugar, then cook the shallots until the sugar begins to caramelize.

2 Add seasoning, herbs, if using, and a fairly shallow layer of a liquid to suit the recipe, such as wine, stock or vinegar. Cook gently, covered, until the shallots or onions are tender but still whole.

3 Then cook, uncovered, at a higher heat, until all the liquid has evaporated.

FRYING GARLIC

Because of garlic's relatively low moisture content, it fries and browns more quickly than onions. It will burn easily and develops a bitter, acrid taste. Therefore, when a recipe calls for onions and garlic to be fried together, add the garlic to the pan when the onions are almost cooked.

In Chinese and Asian cooking, garlic is often fried in oil at the beginning of cooking. Sometimes it is removed and discarded afterwards because only the flavoured oil is wanted in the dish; at other times, the garlic is an integral part of the dish. Again, care needs to be taken that the garlic cooks to an even, light brown, when it has a delicious toasty flavour.

Frying garlic slices

1 Heat a wok or deep frying pan until hot, add some cooking oil and allow it to become hot.

2 Add finely sliced garlic to the wok or pan and immediately stir it through the oil. It will begin to colour at once.

3 Remove the garlic with a slotted spoon as soon as it is a light brown.

Frying whole garlic cloves

Fried cloves of garlic make a delicious addition to green salads, especially those with goat's cheese.

1 Choose large, plump garlic cloves and peel them. Bring a large pan of water to the boil and throw in the garlic, cook for 3–4 minutes, then drain.

2 Repeat the blanching process, then drain and dry thoroughly.

3 Heat a shallow layer of oil in a wok or frying pan, then fry the garlic gently until it turns an even, medium brown.

4 Remove with a slotted spoon and drain well on kitchen paper.

GRILLING

Cooking onions, leeks and spring onions (scallions) in this way gives a delicious result. They are perfect for serving as an accompaniment. Grilling (broiling) – either under a grill (broiler), over hot coals or using a griddle pan – gives onions, leeks and spring onions a sweet, mellow flavour.

Grilling onions

Onions, particularly mild, sweet onions, grill very successfully and are especially good when cooked over hot coals.

1 Peel the onions and slice them horizontally into thick slices, discarding the thin slices from the top and bottom of the onion. Carefully spear the slices on an oiled metal skewer, passing the skewer through the slices so that all the layers are kept flat.

2 Brush the skewered onion slices with oil, season, then grill for 5–6 minutes on each side or until the onions are soft and slightly charred.

3 Alternatively, place the onion slices in a grill cage, brush with oil and season, then grill each side for 5–6 minutes.

Grilling spring onions

Spring onions are delicious grilled and are very good as an accompaniment to grilled fish, poultry and meat dishes or served with cheese. They are very popular in Mexico and Cataluña where they are known as *calçots* and eaten with a spicy chilli sauce.

1 Choose big, fat spring onions with large bulbs for grilling.

2 Trim off any damaged leaves and the outer skin; trim off the root, too, but leave the end intact.

3 Brush with a little oil and grill, either over charcoal on a barbecue or on a cast-iron, ridged grill pan, for about 2 minutes each side, or until softened and browned but not too charred. In Cataluña the outer skin is often peeled off before eating.

COOK'S TIP
Whole grilled cipolla onions make unusual and delicious canapés. After cooking, marinate the grilled cipolla onions in French dressing and serve on rounds of toasted bread or simply with thick slices of fresh crusty bread.

Grilling leeks

Baby leeks, when very small, may be grilled in a similar way to spring onions. However, leeks are usually blanched for a few minutes in boiling water before grilling, since they have tougher skins than spring onions.

1 Bring a large pan of lightly salted water to the boil and throw in the trimmed leeks. Cook baby leeks for 2–3 minutes and cook larger leeks for 4–5 minutes, then drain.

2 Cool a little, then gently squeeze the excess water out of the leeks. Leave baby leeks whole. Cut large leeks in half lengthways or into short logs. Dry on a clean dishtowel or kitchen paper.

3 Brush the leeks with oil, season with salt and pepper to taste, then grill baby leeks as for spring onions, allowing 3–4 minutes each side. Grill large leeks for about 4–5 minutes each side.

COOK'S TIP
Grilled leeks may be served hot, warm or cold. They are particularly delicious with a simple dressing of oil, tarragon vinegar and a little mustard.

ROASTING ONIONS

Onions are delicious roasted. They can be roasted in their skins, which will produce a soft, juicy, sweet centre, or they can be peeled, which produces a more caramelized taste and a much crisper texture.

Roasting onions in their skins

1 Remove any damaged skin and cut off excess root, leaving the base intact.

2 Brush with oil if you like, then roast at 190°C/375°F/Gas 5 until they feel soft when gently squeezed (1–1½ hours).

3 To serve, cut a cross in the top and add butter or cheese. A flavoured butter with herbs or chilli is especially good.

Roasting peeled onions

1 Small, peeled onions may be roasted whole. Larger onions may be cut into wedges (leaving them attached at the root base, so they don't fall apart on cooking) or, alternatively, they can be cut into halves or quarters.

2 Alternatively, make 2–3 cross-cuts from the top down to 1cm/½in from the root base. As they roast, the layers of the onion will open out.

3 Whole onions will roast more quickly if first blanched in boiling water for 3–4 minutes. Toss in oil, season, and cook, uncovered at 190–200°C/375–400°F/Gas 5–6. Whole onions take 40 minutes; wedges about 30 minutes.

STUFFING ONIONS

Onions make natural containers for stuffings, and these may be prepared in two ways.

Preparing raw onion cups for stuffing

1 Choose round, even-shaped onions, not flat or pointed onions. Large Spanish (Bermuda) onions are best.

2 Peel and cut a thin slice off each end so that the cups will stay upright.

3 Using a sharp knife, cut the onion in half horizontally.

4 Using a sharp, pointed knife, cut round the second or third layer of onion, counting in from the outer layer.

5 Gradually loosen the centre of the onion from the outer layers, leaving a cup of two or three layers.

6 If any of the cups has a hole in the base, cover it with a small piece of the removed onion. Fill with stuffing and cook according to the recipe.

To prepare whole onions for stuffing

Whole onions need to be blanched first so that they will cook evenly. The flesh can then be scooped out and mixed with the stuffing. Allow one large onion per person.

1 Choose round, even-shaped onions, peel, but leave the top and especially the root base intact.

2 Cover in lightly salted, boiling water and cook for 15 minutes, then drain thoroughly and set aside until cool enough to handle.

3 Cut off and remove a cap from the top of the onion.

4 Using a small, sharp knife and a pointed or serrated teaspoon, remove the centre of the onion to leave a shell two or three layers thick.

Making stuffing

The most popular stuffings for onions are either meat, or breadcrumbs with herbs, spices and cheese. The stuffing usually incorporates the chopped onion that has been removed.

Raw onion cups are best suited to meaty fillings as they need cooking for 1–1½ hours at 180–190°C/350–375°F/Gas 4–5. They cook best if sat on a bed of sauce or a mixture of olive oil and lemon juice, so that the onions may be basted while they cook. This helps to stop them drying out and keeps them moist. Blanched, partially cooked whole onions should be brushed with a little oil or melted butter and baked for 45–60 minutes.

Watering eyes

Peeling and chopping onions makes you cry because these actions release the volatile chemicals that give onions their strength and bite. They travel to the eyes and nasal cavities through the water vapour in juicy onions. The stronger and juicier the onion, the more it will make you cry. Shallots and garlic, although often containing more of the offending allicins, contain less water, so produce less vapour and hence fewer tears. Leeks are very mild and hardly ever cause tears during preparation.

Most cures for onion tears have to be taken with a pinch of salt, but here are a few that people claim help.
- Chilling an onion for several hours in the refrigerator (or the freezer for a few minutes) is said to "lock-in" the water vapour and prevent it from reaching your eyes.
- Peeling onions under water will prevent the water vapour reaching your nose and eyes, but no one's suggesting you try chopping onions underwater!
- The chemicals mostly reach your tear ducts through your nose, so try breathing through your mouth rather than your nose.
- If you are preparing a lot of small onions, try peeling them by the blanching method – this reduces the chemical spray that's released when onions are peeled.
- When preparing onions, try leaving the base (root) end intact, or cut it last of all. This basal portion of the onion contains the highest concentration of tear-causing allicins.
- An old wives' tale suggests that if you bite on a crust of bread while preparing onions, then you won't cry. Maybe the crust forms a barrier to prevent the onion's water vapour from reaching your nose and eyes.

PICKLING AND PRESERVING

Once, pickling was an important way of storing vegetables through the lean winter months, but nowadays onions are pickled because people like the taste. Although onions, shallots and garlic keep well in their natural state, pickling has always been a popular way of keeping them because their naturally strong flavour survives the pickling process so well and stands up to the strong tastes of vinegar and spices.

Pickling onions

Choose small, firm even-shaped onions for pickling and peel them by the blanching method. Onions to be pickled are usually salted to remove water and to make sure they keep well.

For crisp pickled onions, cover with cold vinegar. For a softer pickle, the onions may be cooked in the hot vinegar for up to 10 minutes.

1 The onions can be layered with sea salt in a non-reactive (i.e. non-metallic) bowl.

2 Alternatively, put the onions in a bowl and cover with a strong brine solution. Set aside to soak.

3 Weight the onions to make sure that they are covered by the brine.

4 After 1–2 days in the brine (this depends on the size of the onions), the onions should be rinsed and patted dry, then packed into clean, sterilized jars.

5 Pour spiced vinegar over the onions.

6 Extra spices can be added to the jar if you like, then tightly seal the jars for storage.

COOK'S TIP

Spices, which can be added for extra flavouring, may include mustard seeds, peppercorns, coriander seeds, allspice, chillies and cloves.

Simple spiced vinegar

Heat together 1.2 litres/2 pints/5 cups vinegar (light or dark malt has the best keeping qualities) with 2 pieces of dried ginger root, 2 blades of mace, 2–3 dried red chillies and 15ml/1 tbsp each mustard seeds, coriander seeds and black peppercorns. Add a few bay leaves, a piece of cinnamon stick or 2–3 star anise to taste. The longer you heat the flavourings with the vinegar, the stronger the taste will become. For a sweeter vinegar, dissolve 45ml/3 tbsp of muscovado (molasses) sugar in the vinegar.

To sterilize jars

Wash, rinse and dry thoroughly. Heat the oven to 180°C/350°F/Gas 4. Making sure you remove any rubber seals first, place the jars on a tray, then heat the jars for about 20 minutes. Cool a little before handling them – the jars will be very hot.

Jars can also be sterilized by putting them in a pan of boiling water for 10 minutes. Stand them on a trivet so that they are not directly over the heat.

OTHER WAYS OF PRESERVING ALLIUMS

Drying onions

In the past, drying was a popular way of preserving onions, but it is less so now, since onions are available fresh all year round. However, dried onions can make a useful store-cupboard (pantry) ingredient for emergencies. To use dried onions, add them directly to stews or casseroles, or reconstitute them in a little warm water for 10–15 minutes first. Dried shallots may be fried in a little oil over a medium heat to produce excellent crisp-fried shallots, which are useful as a garnish for many Thai and South-east Asian dishes.

1 Peel and thinly slice the onions, then lay them on racks.

2 Leave them in a very low oven (110°C/225°F/Gas ¼) until very dry. This will take anything up to 12 hours. Turn the slices once as they dry.

3 Store the onions in a cloth or paper bag in a dry place or in a jar with a cloth or paper lid to absorb any residual moisture. Shallots may be dried in the same way.

Making roasted garlic purée

This makes a very useful flavouring to have in the refrigerator. It will store for several weeks as long as you keep the purée covered with at least 1cm/½in of oil. Top up the oil when you remove some purée. As a guide, one head of garlic will yield about 15–30ml/1–2 tbsp of purée.

The purée is useful in many dishes. To make a simple sauce for pasta, stir 2–3 tbsp of the purée into 150ml/¼ pint/⅔ cup of heated, bubbling double (heavy) cream, season with salt and pepper to taste and add a little lemon juice and some chopped thyme or basil. This is good with many vegetarian dishes too. The purée is also good in soufflés, omelettes and tarts, or simply spread on good bread and eaten with some grilled (broiled) or baked goat's cheese.

Roasted garlic purée

The following quantities make 120ml/4fl oz/½ cup purée.

5 large heads garlic
2–3 sprigs thyme or rosemary
  or both
extra virgin olive oil
salt and ground black pepper

COOK'S TIP
When puréeing this amount of garlic, it is easier to purée the garlic, skins and all, in a food mill or mouli legumes. The mill will force through the soft garlic, leaving all the papery skins and debris behind.

Using a dehydrator

If you are planning on drying a lot of onions, it may be worthwhile for you to invest in a domestic dehydrator. They are easy to use and will enable you to dry large quantities of onions quickly and efficiently. They are also useful for drying other vegetables and fruit, as well as being handy for quick-drying fresh herbs. Follow the manufacturer's instructions for timing.

1 Cut a thin slice off the top of each head of garlic.

2 Wrap the garlic heads in foil with the herbs and drizzle over 45ml/3 tbsp oil. Bake at 190°C/3/5°F/Gas 5 for 50–60 minutes, or until the garlic is soft, then cool.

3 Squeeze the garlic out of its skin into a bowl, then mash, beat in the oil and season.

4 Spoon into a sterilized jar. Pour over oil to cover by about 1cm/½in. Cover and store in the refrigerator for up to 3 weeks.

Freezing

It is not recommended to freeze raw alliums, since they can develop "off-flavours" because of the sulphur compounds that are released when they are cut. Sauces that contain raw garlic or onion should also be frozen with caution. With pesto, for instance, prepare and freeze the basil, pine nut and oil paste and add the garlic and grated cheeses only on thawing.

We add onions to marinades, to stews and casseroles, to roasts and braises, and we give them a starring role in soups, flans and baked dishes. Certain classics stand out: French Onion Soup with Gruyère Croûtes, Onion Tart, Jansson's Temptation and Lamb Smothered in Onions and North African Spices. Try to imagine a Spanish tortilla or a dish of Italian pasta without onions — it doesn't bear thinking about. In fact, it is hard to think of many savoury recipes in which onions aren't an essential ingredient.

Onion Dishes

FRENCH ONION SOUP
WITH GRUYÈRE CROÛTES

*THIS IS PERHAPS THE MOST FAMOUS OF ALL ONION SOUPS. TRADITIONALLY, IT WAS SERVED AS A
SUSTAINING EARLY MORNING MEAL TO THE PORTERS AND WORKERS OF LES HALLES MARKET IN PARIS.*

SERVES SIX

INGREDIENTS
  50g/2oz/¼ cup butter
  15ml/1 tbsp olive oil
  2kg/4½lb yellow onions, peeled
    and sliced
  5ml/1 tsp chopped fresh thyme
  5ml/1 tsp caster (superfine) sugar
  15ml/1 tbsp sherry vinegar
  1.5 litres/2½ pints/6¼ cups good
    beef, chicken or duck stock
  25ml/1½ tbsp plain (all-
    purpose) flour
  150ml/¼ pint/⅔ cup dry white wine
  45ml/3 tbsp brandy
  salt and ground black pepper
For the croûtes
  6–12 thick slices day-old French
    stick, about 2.5cm/1in thick
  1 garlic clove, halved
  15ml/1 tbsp French mustard
  115g/4oz/1 cup coarsely grated
    Gruyère cheese

1 Melt the butter with the oil in a large pan. Add the onions and stir to coat them in the fat. Cook over a medium heat for 5–8 minutes, stirring once or twice, until the onions begin to soften. Stir in the thyme.

2 Reduce the heat to very low, cover the pan and cook the onions for 20–30 minutes, stirring frequently, until they are very soft and golden yellow.

4 Meanwhile, bring the stock to the boil in another pan. Stir the flour into the onions and cook for about 2 minutes, then gradually pour in the hot stock. Add the wine and brandy and season the soup to taste with salt and pepper. Simmer for 10–15 minutes.

3 Uncover the pan and increase the heat slightly. Stir in the sugar and cook for 5–10 minutes, until the onions start to brown. Add the sherry vinegar and increase the heat again, then continue cooking, stirring frequently, until the onions turn a deep, golden brown – this could take up to 20 minutes.

COOK'S TIP
The long slow cooking of the onions is the key to success with this soup. If the onions brown too quickly, the soup will be bitter.

5 For the croûtes, preheat the oven to 150°C/300°F/Gas 2. Place the slices of bread on a greased baking tray and bake for 15–20 minutes, until dry and lightly browned. Rub the bread with the cut surface of the garlic and spread with the mustard, then sprinkle the grated Gruyère cheese over the slices.

6 Preheat the grill (broiler) on the hottest setting. Ladle the soup into a large flameproof pan or six flameproof bowls. Float the croûtes on the soup, then grill (broil) until the cheese melts, bubbles and browns. Serve immediately.

CEVICHE WITH RED ONION, AVOCADO AND SWEET POTATO

CEVICHE IS A SOUTH AMERICAN DISH OF FISH MARINATED IN CITRUS JUICE AND ONION, WHICH HAS A SIMILAR EFFECT TO COOKING, MAKING THE FISH OPAQUE AND FIRM IN TEXTURE.

SERVES SIX AS AN APPETIZER

INGREDIENTS

675g/1½lb white fish fillets, skinned
1 red onion, thinly sliced
pinch of dried red chilli flakes
grated rind of 1 small lime and
  juice of 5 limes
450–500g/1–1¼lb sweet potatoes
75ml/5 tbsp mild olive oil
15–25ml/3–5 tsp rice vinegar
2.5–5ml/½–1 tsp caster
  (superfine) sugar
2.5 ml/½ tsp ground toasted
  cumin seeds
½–1 fresh red or green chilli, seeded
  and finely chopped
1 large or 2 small avocados, peeled,
  stoned (pitted) and sliced
225g/8oz peeled cooked prawns
  (shrimp)
45ml/3 tbsp chopped fresh
  coriander (cilantro)
30ml/2 tbsp roasted peanuts, chopped
salt and ground black pepper

1 Cut the fish into strips or chunks. Sprinkle half the onion over the base of a glass dish and lay the fish on top. Sprinkle on the dried red chilli flakes and pour in the lime juice. Cover and chill for 2–3 hours, spooning the lime juice over the fish once or twice. Drain, and discard the onion.

2 Steam or boil the sweet potatoes for 20–25 minutes, or until just tender. Peel and slice, or cut into wedges.

3 Place the oil in a bowl and whisk in the rice vinegar and sugar to taste, then add the cumin, season and whisk in the fresh chilli and grated lime rind.

4 In a glass bowl, toss together the fish, sweet potatoes, avocado slices, prawns and most of the coriander, and the dressing.

5 Toss in the remaining half of the sliced red onion. Sprinkle with the remaining coriander and the peanuts and serve immediately.

COOK'S TIP
Choose orange-fleshed sweet potatoes if you can for this dish.

POTATO AND ONION TORTILLA WITH BROAD BEANS

THE CLASSIC TORTILLA OR SPANISH OMELETTE INCLUDES NOTHING MORE THAN ONIONS, POTATO, EGGS AND OLIVE OIL. ADDING CHOPPED HERBS AND A FEW SKINNED BROAD BEANS MAKES THIS A VERY SUMMERY DISH TO ENJOY AT LUNCH, OR CUT IT INTO SMALL PIECES AND SERVE AS A SPANISH TAPAS.

SERVES TWO

INGREDIENTS
  45ml/3 tbsp olive oil
  2 Spanish (Bermuda) onions,
    thinly sliced
  300g/11oz waxy potatoes, cut into
    1cm/½in dice
  250g/9oz/1¾ cups shelled broad
    (fava) beans
  5ml/1 tsp chopped fresh thyme
  6 large (US extra large) eggs
  45ml/3 tbsp mixed chopped chives
    and chopped flat leaf parsley
  salt and ground black pepper

1 Heat 30ml/2 tbsp of the oil in a 23cm/9in deep non-stick frying pan. Add the onions and potatoes and stir to coat. Cover and cook gently, stirring frequently, for 20–25 minutes, until the potatoes are cooked and the onions collapsed. Do not let the mixture brown.

2 Meanwhile, cook the beans in boiling salted water for 5 minutes. Drain well and set aside to cool.

3 When the beans are cool enough to handle, peel off the grey outer skins. Add the beans to the frying pan, together with the chopped thyme and season with salt and pepper to taste. Stir well to mix and cook for a further 2–3 minutes.

4 Beat the eggs with salt and pepper to taste and the mixed herbs, then pour the mixture over the potatoes and onions and increase the heat slightly. Cook gently until the egg on the bottom sets and browns, gently pulling the omelette away from the sides of the pan and tilting it to allow the uncooked egg to run underneath.

5 Invert the tortilla on to a plate. Add the remaining oil to the pan and heat until hot. Slip the tortilla back into the pan, uncooked side down, and cook for another 3–5 minutes to allow the underneath to brown. Slide the tortilla out on to a plate. Divide as you like, and serve warm rather than piping hot.

SPICED ONION KOFTAS

THESE DELICIOUS INDIAN ONION FRITTERS ARE MADE WITH CHICKPEA FLOUR, OTHERWISE KNOWN AS GRAM FLOUR OR BESAN. SERVE WITH CHUTNEY OR YOGURT DIP.

SERVES FOUR TO FIVE

INGREDIENTS
  675g/1½lb onions, halved and
    thinly sliced
  5ml/1 tsp salt
  5ml/1 tsp ground coriander
  5ml/1 tsp ground cumin
  2.5ml/½ tsp ground turmeric
  1–2 green chillies, seeded and
    finely chopped
  45ml/3 tbsp chopped fresh
    coriander (cilantro)
  90g/3½oz/¾ cup chickpea flour
  2.5ml/½ tsp baking powder
  vegetable oil, for deep-frying
To serve
  lemon wedges (optional)
  fresh coriander (cilantro) sprigs
  yogurt and herb dip or yogurt and
    cucumber dip

1 Place the onions in a colander, add the salt and toss. Place on a plate and leave to stand for 45 minutes, tossing once or twice. Rinse the onions, then squeeze out any excess moisture.

2 Place the onions in a bowl. Add the ground coriander, cumin, turmeric, chillies and fresh coriander. Mix well.

COOK'S TIPS
• To make a yogurt and herb dip, stir 30ml/2 tbsp each of chopped fresh coriander (cilantro) and mint into about 250ml/8fl oz/1 cup set yogurt. Season with salt, ground toasted cumin seeds and a pinch of sugar.
• For a cucumber dip, stir half a diced cucumber and 1 seeded and chopped fresh green chilli into 250ml/8fl oz/1 cup set yogurt. Season with salt and cumin.

3 Add the chickpea flour and baking powder, then use your hand to mix all the ingredients thoroughly.

4 Shape the mixture by hand into 12–15 koftas about the size of golf balls.

5 Heat the oil for deep-frying to 180–190°C/350–375°F or until a cube of day-old bread browns in about 30–45 seconds. Fry the koftas, four or five at a time, until deep golden brown all over. Drain on kitchen paper and keep warm until all the koftas are cooked. Serve with lemon wedges, coriander sprigs and a yogurt dip.

GRILLED POLENTA <u>WITH</u> CARAMELIZED ONIONS, RADICCHIO <u>AND</u> TALEGGIO CHEESE

SLICES OF GRILLED POLENTA, ONE OF THE STAPLES OF NORTH ITALIAN COOKING, ARE TASTY TOPPED WITH SLOWLY CARAMELIZED ONIONS AND BUBBLING TALEGGIO CHEESE, ALSO FROM NORTH ITALY.

SERVES FOUR

INGREDIENTS
900ml/1½ pints/3¾ cups water
5ml/1 tsp salt
150g/5oz/generous 1 cup polenta
  or corn meal
50g/2oz/⅔ cup freshly grated
  Parmesan cheese
5ml/1 tsp chopped fresh thyme
90ml/6 tbsp olive oil
675g/1½lb onions, halved and sliced
2 garlic cloves, chopped
a few fresh thyme sprigs
5ml/1 tsp brown sugar
15–30ml/1–2 tbsp balsamic vinegar
2 heads radicchio, cut into thick
  slices or wedges
225g/8oz Taleggio cheese, sliced
salt and ground black pepper

1 In a large pan, bring the water to the boil and add the salt. Adjust the heat so that it simmers. Stirring constantly, add the polenta in a steady stream, then bring to the boil. Cook over a very low heat, stirring frequently, for 30–40 minutes, until thick and smooth.

2 Beat in the Parmesan and chopped thyme, then turn on to a work surface or tray. Spread evenly, then leave to cool.

3 Heat 30ml/2 tbsp of the oil in a frying pan over a moderate heat. Add the onions and stir to coat in the oil, then cover and cook over a very low heat for 15 minutes, stirring occasionally.

4 Add the garlic and most of the thyme sprigs and cook, uncovered, for another 10 minutes, or until light brown.

5 Add the sugar, 15ml/1 tbsp of the vinegar and salt and pepper. Cook for another 5–10 minutes, until soft and well-browned. Taste and add more vinegar and seasoning as necessary.

6 Preheat the grill (broiler). Cut the polenta into thick slices and brush with a little of the remaining oil, then grill (broil) until crusty and lightly browned.

7 Turn over the polenta and add the radicchio to the grill rack or pan. Season the radicchio and brush with a little oil. Grill for about 5 minutes, until the polenta and radicchio are browned. Drizzle a little vinegar over the radicchio.

8 Heap the onions on to the polenta. Sprinkle the cheese and a few sprigs of thyme over both polenta and radicchio. Grill until the cheese is bubbling. Season with pepper and serve immediately.

ONION TART

NO BOOK ON ONION COOKING WOULD BE COMPLETE WITHOUT A RECIPE FOR THIS CLASSIC TART FROM ALSACE IN EASTERN FRANCE. TRADITIONALLY SERVED IN SMALL SLICES AS A FIRST COURSE, IT ALSO MAKES A DELICIOUS MAIN COURSE WHEN SERVED WARM AND ACCOMPANIED BY A GREEN SALAD.

SERVES FOUR TO SIX

INGREDIENTS
  175g/6oz/1½ cups plain (all-
    purpose) flour
  75g/3oz/6 tbsp butter, chilled
  30–45ml/2–3 tbsp iced water
For the filling
  50g/2oz/¼ cup butter
  900g/2lb Spanish (Bermuda) onions,
    thinly sliced
  1 egg plus 2 egg yolks
  250ml/8fl oz/1 cup double
    (heavy) cream
  1.5ml/¼ tsp freshly grated nutmeg
  salt and ground black pepper

VARIATIONS
There are endless variations on this tart: try adding chopped fresh herbs such as thyme. The tart is also delicious made with cheese pastry; add 50g/2oz/⅔ cup grated Parmesan to the flour.

1 Process the flour, a pinch of salt and the chilled butter in a food processor until reduced to fine crumbs. Add the iced water and process briefly to form a dough. Wrap in clear film (plastic wrap) and chill for 40 minutes.

2 Melt the butter in a large pan and add the onions and a pinch of salt. Turn them in the butter. Cover and cook very gently, stirring frequently, for 30–40 minutes. Cool slightly.

3 Preheat the oven to 190°C/375°F/ Gas 5. Roll out the dough thinly and use to line a 23–25cm/9–10in loose-based flan tin (tart pan). Line with foil or baking parchment and baking beans, then bake blind for 10 minutes.

4 Remove the foil or parchment and baking beans, and bake for another 4–5 minutes, until the pastry is lightly cooked to a pale brown colour (blonde is a good description). Reduce the oven temperature to 180°C/350°F/Gas 4.

5 Beat the egg, egg yolks and cream together. Season with salt, pepper and the grated nutmeg. Place half the onions in the pastry case (pie shell) and add half the egg mixture. Add the remaining onions, then pour in as much of the remaining custard as you can.

6 Place on a baking sheet and bake on the middle shelf for 40–50 minutes, or until the custard is risen, browned and set in the centre. Serve warm rather than piping hot.

BEAN SALAD WITH TUNA AND RED ONION

THIS MAKES A GREAT FIRST COURSE OR EVEN A LIGHT MAIN MEAL IF SERVED WITH A GREEN SALAD, SOME GARLIC MAYONNAISE AND PLENTY OF WARM, CRUSTY BREAD.

SERVES FOUR

INGREDIENTS

250g/9oz/1⅓ cups dried haricot
  (navy) or cannellini beans, soaked
  overnight in cold water
1 bay leaf
200–250g/7–9oz fine green
  beans, trimmed
1 large red onion, very thinly sliced
45ml/3 tbsp chopped fresh flat
  leaf parsley
200–250g/7–9oz good-quality
  canned tuna in olive oil, drained
200g/7oz cherry tomatoes, halved
salt and ground black pepper
a few onion rings, to garnish
For the dressing
90ml/6 tbsp extra virgin olive oil
15ml/1 tbsp tarragon vinegar
5ml/1 tsp tarragon mustard
1 garlic clove, finely chopped
5ml/1 tsp grated lemon rind
a little lemon juice
pinch of caster (superfine) sugar

1 Drain the beans and bring them to the boil in fresh water with the bay leaf added. Boil rapidly for 10 minutes, then reduce the heat and boil steadily for 1–1½ hours, until tender. The cooking time depends on the age of the beans. Drain well. Discard the bay leaf.

3 Blanch the green beans in plenty of boiling water for 3–4 minutes. Drain, refresh under cold water and drain thoroughly again.

2 Meanwhile, place all the dressing ingredients apart from the lemon juice and sugar in a jug (pitcher) or bowl and whisk until mixed. Season to taste with salt, pepper, lemon juice and a pinch of sugar. Leave to stand.

4 Place both types of beans in a bowl. Add half the dressing and toss to mix. Stir in the onion and half the chopped parsley, then season to taste with salt and pepper.

5 Flake the tuna into large chunks with a knife and toss it into the beans with the tomato halves.

6 Arrange the salad on four individual plates. Drizzle the remaining dressing over the salad and sprinkle the remaining chopped parsley on top. Garnish with a few onion rings and serve immediately, at room temperature.

BAKED STUFFED ONIONS
WITH TOMATO SAUCE

THESE ARE IDEAL COMFORT FOOD FOR SUPPER ON COLD WINTER EVENINGS. SERVE WITH BUTTERED CABBAGE AND RICE OR THICK SLICES OF BREAD TO MOP UP THE SAUCE.

SERVES EIGHT

INGREDIENTS
8 onions, each about 8.5cm/3½in
in diameter, peeled but left whole
60ml/4 tbsp olive oil
2.5ml/½ tsp ground allspice
50g/2oz pancetta or bacon, chopped
250g/9oz minced (ground) pork
115g/4oz/2 cups fresh breadcrumbs
45ml/3 tbsp chopped fresh parsley
15ml/1 tbsp chopped fresh oregano
1.5ml/½ tsp ground cinnamon
75ml/5 tbsp water
25g/1oz/2 tbsp butter
For the tomato sauce
30ml/2 tbsp olive oil
1 garlic clove, finely chopped
2.5ml/½ tsp ground allspice
400g/14oz can chopped tomatoes
small piece of cinnamon stick
1 fresh bay leaf
30ml/2 tbsp chopped fresh oregano
30ml/2 tbsp double (heavy) cream
1.5–2.5ml/¼–½ tsp harissa or other
chilli paste
pinch of brown sugar (optional)
salt and ground black pepper

1 Place the onions in a large pan, pour in water to cover and bring to the boil. Reduce the heat and simmer gently for 10–15 minutes. Drain and cool.

2 Cut a small cap off the top of each onion. Use a small, sharp knife and a teaspoon to hollow out the centres, leaving a shell of two or three layers.

3 Stand the onion shells in a large ovenproof dish and patch any holes in their bases with pieces of onion. Chop the flesh removed from the centres and set aside 45ml/3 tbsp for the sauce. Heat 30ml/2 tbsp of the oil in a frying pan and cook the chopped onion over a low heat until just beginning to brown. Add the allspice and cook for a little longer. Remove and set aside.

4 Cook the pancetta or bacon in the pan until the fat melts. Add the pork and cook until it is beginning to brown. Preheat the oven to 190°C/375°F/Gas 5.

5 Place 75g/3oz/1½ cups of the breadcrumbs in a bowl and add the cooked onions, pork, half the parsley, the oregano and the ground cinnamon. Season well and mix to form a stuffing.

6 Fill the onions with the stuffing. Spoon the water around the onions and dot the butter on top of them. Cover with foil and bake for 30 minutes.

7 To make the sauce, heat the oil and cook the reserved onion and the garlic until soft and just beginning to brown. Add the allspice and cook for about 2 minutes, then add the tomatoes, cinnamon stick, bay leaf and oregano. Cook, uncovered, for 15–20 minutes.

8 Remove the cinnamon and bay leaf. Process the sauce in a blender or food processor until smooth. Add 45–60ml/ 3–4 tbsp water to thin to a pouring consistency. Add the cream with seasoning, harissa and sugar to taste.

9 Pour the sauce around the onions and use it to baste them. Cover the dish and bake for 20–25 minutes, then uncover and baste again. Mix together the remaining breadcrumbs and parsley. Sprinkle the crumbs over the onions, then drizzle with the remaining 30ml/2 tbsp of oil. Return the dish to the oven and bake for 15–20 minutes, until the topping is browned and crisp. Serve immediately.

JANSSON'S TEMPTATION

*A TRADITIONAL SWEDISH FAVOURITE, THIS RICH GRATIN IS THOUGHT TO BE NAMED AFTER ADOLF
JANZON, A STAR OF THE ROYAL OPERA HOUSE, STOCKHOLM. JANZON WOULD INVITE HIS FRIENDS TO
DINNER AFTER A PERFORMANCE, SERVING THEM THIS DELICIOUS POTATO DISH.*

SERVES FOUR TO SIX

INGREDIENTS
   50g/2oz/¼ cup butter
   900g/2lb waxy potatoes
   2 large sweet Spanish (Bermuda)
   onions, sliced
   2 × 50g/2oz cans anchovies in olive
   oil, drained
   450ml/¾ pint/scant 2 cups whipping
   cream or half and half double
   (heavy) and single (light) cream
   a little milk (optional)
   salt and ground black pepper

1 Preheat the oven to 200°C/400°F/
Gas 6. Use 15g/½oz/1 tbsp of the butter
to grease a 1.5 litre/2½ pint/6¼ cup
ovenproof dish.

2 Using a sharp knife, carefully cut the
potatoes into fine batons.

3 Toss the potato batons with salt
and freshly ground black pepper and
sprinkle half of them in the base of the
prepared ovenproof dish.

4 Lay half of the onions on top of the
potatoes, season with black pepper and
dot with butter. Lay the anchovies on
top of the onions, then add the rest of
the sliced onions and top with the
remaining potatoes.

5 Mix the cream with 30ml/2 tbsp cold
water and pour this over the potatoes.
Add a little milk, if necessary, to bring
the liquid to just below the top of the
final layer of potatoes.

6 Dot the potatoes with the remaining
butter then cover with foil and bake for
1 hour.

7 Reduce the heat to 180°C/350°F/
Gas 4 and uncover the dish. Bake for
a further 40–50 minutes or until the
potatoes are tender and brown.

COOK'S TIPS
• Cover the gratin with foil for the first
half of cooking so that the potatoes don't
brown or dry out too much. If using
whole, salted anchovies or Swedish
salted sprats they will need to be boned.
If they are very salty, soak in a little milk
for 30 minutes before using.
• Serve with small glasses of chilled
schnapps and cold beer for an authentic
Swedish flavour.

PASTA <u>WITH</u> SLOWLY COOKED ONIONS, CABBAGE, PARMESAN <u>AND</u> PINE NUTS

THIS IS AN UNUSUAL, BUT QUITE DELICIOUS, WAY OF SERVING PASTA. CAVOLO NERO, TUSCAN BLACK CABBAGE, IS A CLOSE RELATIVE OF CURLY KALE, WITH LONG LEAVES AND A SPICY FLAVOUR.

SERVES FOUR

INGREDIENTS

25g/1oz/2 tbsp butter
15ml/1 tbsp extra virgin olive oil,
  plus extra for drizzling (optional)
500g/1¼lb Spanish (Bermuda)
  onions, halved and thinly sliced
5–10ml/1–2 tsp balsamic vinegar
400–500g/14oz–20oz cavolo nero,
  spring greens (collards), kale or
  Brussels sprout tops, shredded
400–500g/14–20oz dried pasta (such
  as penne or fusilli)
75g/3oz/1 cup freshly grated
  Parmesan cheese
50g/2oz/½ cup pine nuts, toasted
salt and ground black pepper

VARIATION
To make a delicious pilaff, cook 250g/
9oz/1¼ cups brown basmati rice and use
in place of the pasta.

1 Heat the butter and olive oil together in a large, heavy pan. Stir in the onions, cover and cook very gently, stirring occasionally, for about 20 minutes, until very soft.

2 Uncover, and continue to cook gently, until the onions have turned golden yellow. Add the balsamic vinegar and season well, then cook for a further 1–2 minutes. Set aside.

3 Blanch the cavolo nero, spring greens, kale or Brussels sprout tops in lightly salted, boiling water for about 3 minutes. Drain well and add to the onions, then cook over a low heat for 3–4 minutes.

4 Cook the pasta in lightly salted, boiling water for 8–12 minutes, or according to the packet instructions, until just tender. Drain, then add to the pan of onions and greens and toss thoroughly to mix.

5 Season well with salt and pepper and stir in half the Parmesan. Transfer the pasta to warmed plates. Sprinkle the pine nuts and more Parmesan on top and serve immediately, offering extra olive oil for drizzling over to taste.

LAMB SMOTHERED IN ONIONS AND NORTH AFRICAN SPICES

THIS IS A WONDERFUL WAY OF COOKING A LEG OR SHOULDER OF LAMB, BY FIRST MARINATING IT IN YOGURT WITH NORTH AFRICAN SPICES, THEN COVERING WITH SLICED ONIONS AND POT-ROASTING. SERVE A COUSCOUS PILAFF AND YOGURT FLAVOURED WITH GARLIC AS ACCOMPANIMENTS.

SERVES SIX

INGREDIENTS
  2kg/4½lb leg or shoulder of lamb
  30ml/2 tbsp olive oil
  2 large onions, halved and sliced
  3 fresh bay leaves
  300ml/½ pint/1¼ cups water
  500g/1¼lb butternut squash, peeled,
    seeded and cut into thick chunks
  2–3 green or red (bell) peppers,
    seeded and cut into thick slices
  chopped fresh coriander (cilantro)
For the spice paste
  15ml/1 tbsp cumin seeds
  15ml/1 tbsp coriander seeds
  2.5cm/1in piece cinnamon stick
  7.5ml/1½ tsp paprika
  good pinch of saffron threads
  1 green chilli, seeded and chopped
  2 garlic cloves, chopped
  15g/½oz fresh coriander
    (cilantro), chopped
  30ml/2 tbsp fresh mint, chopped
  45ml/3 tbsp extra virgin olive oil
  grated rind and juice of 1 lemon
  250ml/8fl oz/1 cup plain
    (natural) yogurt
  salt and ground black pepper

1 First prepare the spice paste. Set 5ml/1 tsp each of the cumin and coriander seeds aside and toast the remainder separately in a small dry pan until they are aromatic. Take care not to overcook the spices or cook them too quickly or they will taste bitter.

2 Grind the toasted spices with the cinnamon in a spice or coffee grinder. Then process them with all the paste ingredients, apart from the yogurt, in a food processor or blender to make a paste. Season with salt and pepper.

3 Use a sharp knife to make deep slits all over the lamb, then rub the spice paste all over, forcing it into the slits. Place the lamb in a roasting pan and rub the yogurt all over. Cover and marinate for several hours, preferably overnight, turning once or twice.

4 Preheat the oven to 180°C/350°F/ Gas 4. Scrape the marinade off the meat and reserve. Heat a large roasting pan in the oven and brown the lamb all over. Remove it and set aside. Add the oil and cook the onions for 6–8 minutes, until softened. Coarsely grind the reserved coriander and cumin seeds, add to the onions and cook for 2–3 minutes. Transfer the onions to a plate.

5 Add the marinade to the pan with the bay leaves and water. Bring to the boil. Return the lamb to the pan and turn it in the liquid. Cover with the onions, then cover the pan tightly with foil and cook in the oven for 1¾–2 hours, until tender. Baste the lamb occasionally and add a little more water if the dish seems dry. Remove the lamb and onions, cover and keep warm. Increase the oven temperature to 200°C/400°F/Gas 6.

6 Add the squash and peppers to the pan and toss in the lamb juices. Roast, uncovered, for 30–35 minutes, stirring once or twice, until the squash is tender. Return the lamb for the last 15 minutes.

7 Transfer the lamb and vegetables to a warmed serving dish and sprinkle with the fresh coriander. Serve immediately, cut into thick slices.

The delicate flavour of leeks adds subtle undertones and the gentlest hint of that special allium quality to dishes as diverse as soups, salads, gratins and pies. One of the most versatile members of the onion family, the unassuming leek complements and enhances a wide range of other ingredients, from chicken to fish and from mushrooms to cheese — characteristics superbly demonstrated in this delicious collection of international recipes.

Cooking with Leeks

CHICKEN <u>AND</u> LEEK SOUP
<u>WITH</u> PRUNES <u>AND</u> BARLEY

THIS RECIPE IS BASED ON THE TRADITIONAL SCOTTISH SOUP, COCK-A-LEEKIE. THE UNUSUAL COMBINATION OF LEEKS AND PRUNES IS SURPRISINGLY DELICIOUS.

SERVES SIX

INGREDIENTS

1 chicken, weighing about 2kg/4¼lb
900g/2lb leeks
1 fresh bay leaf
a few each fresh parsley stalks and
    thyme sprigs
1 large carrot, thickly sliced
2.4 litres/4 pints/10 cups chicken or
    beef stock
115g/4oz/generous ½ cup
    pearl barley
400g/14oz ready-to-eat prunes
salt and ground black pepper
chopped fresh parsley, to garnish

1 Cut off the chicken breast portions and set aside. Place the remaining chicken carcass in a large pan. Cut half the leeks into 5cm/2in lengths and add them to the pan. Tie the bay leaf, parsley and thyme into a bouquet garni and add to the pan with the carrot and the stock. Bring to the boil, then reduce the heat and cover. Simmer gently for 1 hour. Skim off any scum when the water first boils and occasionally during simmering.

2 Add the breast portions and cook for another 30 minutes, until they are just cooked. Leave until cool enough to handle, then strain the stock. Reserve the breast portions and meat from the chicken carcass. Discard all the skin, bones, cooked vegetables and herbs. Skim as much fat as you can from the stock, then return it to the pan.

3 Meanwhile, rinse the pearl barley thoroughly in a sieve under cold running water, then cook it in a large pan of boiling water for about 10 minutes. Drain, rinse well again and drain thoroughly.

4 Add the pearl barley to the stock. Bring to the boil over a medium heat, then lower the heat and cook very gently for 15–20 minutes, until the barley is just cooked and tender. Season the soup with 5ml/1 tsp salt and black pepper.

5 Add the prunes. Slice the remaining leeks and add them to the pan. Bring to the boil, then simmer for 10 minutes or until the leeks are just cooked.

6 Slice the chicken breast portions and add them to the soup with the remaining chicken meat, sliced or cut into neat pieces. Reheat if necessary, then ladle the soup into deep plates and sprinkle with chopped parsley.

MEDITERRANEAN LEEK AND FISH SOUP WITH TOMATOES

THIS CHUNKY SOUP, WHICH IS ALMOST A STEW, MAKES A ROBUST AND WONDERFULLY AROMATIC MEAL IN A BOWL. SERVE IT WITH CRISP-BAKED CROÛTES SPREAD WITH A SPICY GARLIC MAYONNAISE.

SERVES FOUR

INGREDIENTS
  30ml/2 tbsp olive oil
  2 large thick leeks, white and green
    parts separated, both thinly sliced
  5ml/1 tsp crushed coriander seeds
  good pinch of dried red chilli flakes
  300g/11oz small salad potatoes,
    thickly sliced
  200g/7oz can chopped tomatoes
  600ml/1 pint/2½ cups fish stock
  150ml/¼ pint/⅔ cup fruity white wine
  1 fresh bay leaf
  1 star anise
  strip of pared orange rind
  good pinch of saffron threads
  450g/1lb white fish fillets, such as
    monkfish, sea bass, cod or haddock
  450g/1lb small squid, cleaned
  250g/9oz uncooked peeled
    prawns (shrimp)
  30–45ml/2–3 tbsp chopped parsley
  salt and ground black pepper
To serve
  1 short French loaf, sliced and toasted
  spicy garlic mayonnaise

1 Gently heat the oil in a pan, then add the green part of the leeks, the coriander and the chilli, and cook for 5 minutes.

2 Add the potatoes and tomatoes and pour in the stock and wine. Add the bay leaf, star anise, orange rind and saffron.

3 Bring to the boil, reduce the heat and part-cover the pan. Simmer for 20 minutes or until the potatoes are tender. Taste and adjust the seasoning.

4 Cut the fish into chunks. Cut the squid sacs into rectangles and score a criss-cross pattern into them without cutting right through.

5 Add the fish to the stew and cook gently for 4 minutes. Add the prawns and cook for 1 minute. Add the squid and the shredded white part of the leek and cook, stirring occasionally, for 2 minutes.

6 Stir in the chopped parsley and serve with toasted French bread and spicy garlic mayonnaise.

GRILLED LEEK AND FENNEL SALAD WITH SPICY TOMATO DRESSING

THIS IS AN EXCELLENT SALAD TO MAKE IN THE EARLY AUTUMN WHEN YOUNG LEEKS ARE AT THEIR BEST AND RIPE TOMATOES ARE FULL OF FLAVOUR. SERVE WITH GOOD BREAD AS AN APPETIZER OR SERVE TO ACCOMPANY SIMPLY GRILLED WHITE FISH FOR A MAIN COURSE.

SERVES SIX AS AN APPETIZER

INGREDIENTS
675g/1½lb leeks
2 large fennel bulbs
120ml/4fl oz/½ cup extra virgin
    olive oil
2 shallots, chopped
150ml/¼ pint/⅔ cup dry white wine or
    white vermouth
5ml/1 tsp fennel seeds, crushed
6 fresh thyme sprigs
2–3 bay leaves
good pinch of dried red chilli flakes
350g/12oz tomatoes, peeled, seeded
    and diced
5ml/1 tsp sun-dried tomato paste
good pinch of caster (superfine)
    sugar (optional)
75g/3oz/¾ cup small black olives
salt and ground black pepper

2 Trim the fennel bulbs, reserving any feathery tops for the garnish and cut the bulbs either into thin slices or into thicker wedges, according to taste.

3 Cook the fennel in the reserved cooking water for about 5 minutes, then drain thoroughly and toss with 30ml/2 tbsp of the olive oil. Season to taste with black pepper.

6 Add the diced tomatoes and cook briskly for 5–8 minutes, or until reduced and thickened.

7 Add the tomato paste and adjust the seasoning to taste, adding a good pinch of caster sugar if you think the dressing needs it.

1 Cook the leeks in salted, boiling water for 4–5 minutes. Use a slotted spoon to remove the leeks and place them in a colander to drain thoroughly and cool. Reserve the cooking water in the pan. Squeeze out excess water and cut the leeks into 7.5cm/3in lengths.

COOK'S TIP
When buying fennel, look for rounded bulbs; they have a better shape for this dish. The flesh should be crisp and white, with no signs of bruising. Avoid specimens with broken leaves or with brown or dried out patches.

4 Heat a ridged cast-iron griddle. Arrange the leeks and fennel on the griddle and cook until tinged deep brown, turning once. Remove the vegetables from the griddle, place in a large shallow dish and set aside.

5 Place the remaining olive oil, the shallots, white wine or vermouth, crushed fennel seeds, thyme, bay leaves and chilli flakes in a large pan and bring to the boil over a medium heat. Lower the heat and simmer for 10 minutes.

8 Pour the dressing over the leeks and fennel, toss to mix and leave to cool. The salad may be made several hours in advance and kept in the refrigerator, but bring it back to room temperature before serving.

9 When ready to serve, stir the salad then sprinkle the chopped fennel tops and black olives over the top.

LEEK, SQUASH AND TOMATO GRATIN

THIS AUTUMNAL GRATIN COMPLEMENTS ROAST OR GRILLED LAMB OR CHICKEN. OR SERVE IT AS A SIMPLE SUPPER DISH ACCOMPANIED BY A GREEN SALAD AND GOOD BREAD.

4 Heat the cream in a small pan with the chilli and garlic. Bring to the boil, then stir in the mint and pour over the gratin, thoroughly scraping the contents out of the pan.

SERVES FOUR TO SIX

INGREDIENTS
    450g/1lb peeled and seeded squash,
      cut into 1cm/½in slices
    60ml/4 tbsp olive oil
    450g/1lb leeks, cut into thick,
      diagonal slices
    675g/1½lb tomatoes, peeled and
      thickly sliced
    2.5ml/½ tsp ground toasted cumin seeds
    450ml/¾ pint/scant 2 cups single
      (light) cream
    1 fresh red chilli, seeded and sliced
    1 garlic clove, finely chopped
    15ml/1 tbsp chopped fresh mint
    30ml/2 tbsp chopped fresh parsley
    60ml/4 tbsp fine white breadcrumbs
    salt and ground black pepper

1 Steam the squash over boiling salted water for 10 minutes.

2 Heat half the oil in a frying pan and cook the leeks gently for 5–6 minutes, until lightly coloured. Try to keep the slices intact. Preheat the oven to 190°C/375°F/Gas 5.

3 Layer the squash, leeks and tomatoes in a 2 litre/3½ pint/8¾ cup gratin dish, arranging them in rows. Season with salt, pepper and cumin.

5 Bake for 50–55 minutes, or until the gratin is bubbling and the vegetables are tender. Sprinkle the parsley and breadcrumbs on top and drizzle over the remaining oil. Then bake for another 15–20 minutes until the breadcrumbs are browned and crisp. Serve immediately.

BRAISED LEEKS WITH CARROTS

SWEET CARROTS AND LEEKS GO WELL TOGETHER AND ARE GOOD FINISHED WITH A LITTLE CHOPPED MINT, CHERVIL OR PARSLEY. THIS IS A GOOD ACCOMPANIMENT TO ROAST BEEF, LAMB OR CHICKEN.

SERVES SIX

INGREDIENTS
65g/2½oz/5 tbsp butter
675g/1½lb carrots, thickly sliced
2 fresh bay leaves
pinch of caster (superfine) sugar
75ml/5 tbsp water
675g/1½lb leeks, cut into 5cm/
   2in lengths
120ml/4fl oz/½ cup white wine
30ml/2 tbsp chopped fresh mint,
   chervil or parsley
salt and ground black pepper

1 Melt 25g/1oz/2 tbsp of the butter in a pan and cook the carrots gently, without allowing them to brown, for 4–5 minutes.

2 Add the bay leaves, seasoning, the sugar and water. Bring to the boil, cover and cook for 10–15 minutes, until the carrots are tender. Uncover, then boil until the juices have evaporated, leaving the carrots moist and glazed.

3 Meanwhile, melt another 25g/1oz/ 2 tbsp of the remaining butter in a wide pan or deep frying pan that will take the leeks in a single layer. Add the leeks and cook them in the butter over a low heat for 4–5 minutes, without allowing them to brown.

4 Add seasoning, a good pinch of sugar, the wine and half the chopped herb. Heat until simmering, then cover and cook gently for 5–8 minutes, until the leeks are tender, but not collapsed.

5 Uncover the leeks and turn them in the buttery juices. Increase the heat, then boil the liquid rapidly until reduced to a few tablespoons.

VARIATION
Braised leeks in tarragon cream
Cook 900g/2lb leeks in 40g/1½oz/3 tbsp butter as above. Season, add a pinch of sugar, 45ml/3 tbsp tarragon vinegar, 6 fresh tarragon sprigs or 5ml/1 tsp dried tarragon and 60ml/4 tbsp white wine. Cover and cook as above. Add 150ml/ ¼ pint/⅔ cup double (heavy) cream and allow to bubble. Adjust the seasoning and serve sprinkled with chopped fresh tarragon. A spoonful of tarragon-flavoured mustard is good stirred into these leeks.

6 Add the carrots to the leeks and reheat them gently, then swirl in the remaining butter. Adjust the seasoning, if necessary. Transfer to a warmed serving dish and serve sprinkled with the remaining chopped herb.

LEEKS BAKED WITH HAM, CREAM AND MINT

CHOOSE LEEKS THAT ARE NOT TOO THICK FOR THIS VERY EASY BUT DELICIOUS SUPPER DISH.
SERVE GOOD BREAD TO MOP UP THE SAUCE AND A GREEN SALAD TO REFRESH THE PALATE.

SERVES FOUR

INGREDIENTS
  8–12 slender leeks
  8–12 large, medium-thick slices
    prosciutto or Serrano ham
  15g/½oz/1 tbsp butter
  75g/3oz/1 cup freshly grated
    Parmesan cheese
  250ml/8fl oz/1 cup double
    (heavy) cream
  15ml/1 tbsp chopped fresh mint
  pinch of cayenne pepper
  45ml/3 tbsp fine white breadcrumbs
  salt and ground black pepper

1 Trim the leeks so that they are all the same size. Bring a large pan of lightly salted water to the boil, add the leeks and cook for 5–8 minutes. Test the leeks with the tip of a sharp knife to check if they are cooked. Drain, reserving 60ml/4 tbsp of the cooking water. Squeeze the excess water out of the leeks. Preheat the oven to 190°C/375°F/Gas 5.

2 Wrap each leek in a slice of ham. Butter an ovenproof gratin dish just large enough to take the leeks in one layer and arrange the leeks in it. Season to taste with salt and pepper and sprinkle half the grated Parmesan cheese over the leeks.

3 Mix the cream, cooking water and mint. Season with salt, pepper and cayenne and pour over the leeks. Sprinkle the breadcrumbs and the remaining Parmesan on top. Bake for 30–35 minutes, until bubbling and browned. Serve immediately.

VARIATIONS
• Arrange the leeks on a bed of 350g/12oz ripe tomatoes, peeled, seeded and finely chopped.
• Wrap the cooked leeks in fried, but not crisp, bacon. Then pour over a cheese sauce made with equal quantities of the reserved cooking water and milk. Season the sauce to taste with Dijon mustard, grated Cheddar cheese and nutmeg. Sprinkle with grated Parmesan and fine white breadcrumbs and bake as above.
• Wrap 8 raw, slender leeks in slices of pancetta or prosciutto, then fry gently in 25g/1oz/2 tbsp butter for 5 minutes. Add 90ml/6 tbsp white wine and some sprigs of thyme and season to taste with salt and pepper. Cover and cook very gently for 15–20 minutes, until the leeks are cooked. Remove the leeks from the pan, increase the heat and add 60ml/4 tbsp double (heavy) cream, then bubble to make a sauce. Adjust the seasoning and pour over the leeks. Sprinkle with a little chopped parsley before serving.

SALMON EN PAPILLOTE WITH LEEKS AND YELLOW PEPPERS

COOKING FISH "EN PAPILLOTE" MAKES A LOT OF SENSE, MAKING SURE THAT THE FISH RETAINS ITS FLAVOUR WHILE IT COOKS IN ITS PARCEL WITH AROMATIC INGREDIENTS SUCH AS LEEKS AND HERBS. IT IS ALSO EXCELLENT WHEN ENTERTAINING, AS THE PARCELS MAY BE PREPARED AHEAD OF COOKING.

SERVES SIX

INGREDIENTS

25ml/1½ tbsp groundnut (peanut) oil
2 yellow (bell) peppers, seeded and
   thinly sliced
4cm/1½in fresh root ginger, peeled
   and finely shredded
1 large fennel bulb, thinly sliced,
   feathery tops chopped and reserved
1 green chilli, seeded and
   finely shredded
2 large leeks, cut into 10cm/4in
   lengths and shredded lengthways
30ml/2 tbsp chopped chives
10ml/2 tsp light soy sauce
6 portions salmon fillet, each
   weighing 150–175g/5–6oz, skinned
10ml/2 tsp toasted sesame oil
salt and ground black pepper

1 Heat the oil in a large non-stick frying pan and cook the peppers, ginger and fennel for 5–6 minutes, until they are softened but not browned. Add the chilli and leeks and cook for a further 2–3 minutes. Stir in half the chives and the soy sauce with seasoning to taste. Set aside to cool.

2 Preheat the oven to 190°C/375°F/ Gas 5. Cut 6 x 35cm/14in rounds of baking parchment or foil. Divide the vegetable mixture between the 6 rounds and place a portion of salmon on each pile of vegetables. Drizzle with sesame oil and sprinkle with the remaining chives and the chopped fennel tops. Season with salt and pepper.

3 Fold the paper or foil over to enclose the fish, rolling and twisting the edges together to seal the parcels. Place the parcels on a baking sheet and bake for 15–20 minutes, until the parcels are puffed up and, if made with paper, lightly browned. Transfer the parcels to warmed individual plates and serve immediately.

POTATO AND LEEK FILO PIE

THIS FILO PASTRY PIE MAKES AN ATTRACTIVE AND UNUSUAL CENTREPIECE FOR A VEGETARIAN BUFFET.
SERVE IT COOL, WITH A CHOICE OF SALADS.

SERVES EIGHT

INGREDIENTS
  800g/1¾lb new potatoes, sliced
  400g/14oz leeks (trimmed weight)
  75g/3oz/6 tbsp butter
  15g/½oz parsley, finely chopped
  60ml/4 tbsp chopped mixed fresh
    herbs (such as chervil, chives, a
    little tarragon and basil)
  12 sheets filo pastry
  150g/5oz white Cheshire,
    Lancashire or Cantal
    cheese, sliced
  2 garlic cloves, finely chopped
  250ml/8fl oz/1 cup double
    (heavy) cream
  2 large (US extra large) egg yolks
  salt and ground black pepper

1 Preheat the oven to 190°C/375°F/
Gas 5. Cook the potatoes in lightly
salted, boiling water for 3–4 minutes,
then drain and set aside.

2 Slice the leeks. Melt 25g/1oz/2 tbsp
of the butter in a frying pan and cook
the leeks gently, stirring occasionally,
until softened. Remove from the heat,
season with pepper and stir in half the
parsley and half the mixed herbs.

3 Melt the remaining butter. Line a
23cm/9in loose-based metal cake tin
(pan) with six or seven sheets of filo
pastry, brushing each layer with butter.
Let the edges overhang the rim.

4 Layer the potatoes, leeks and cheese
in the tin, sprinkling a few herbs and
the garlic between the layers. Season.

5 Flip the overhanging pastry over the
filling and cover with two sheets of filo,
tucking in the sides to fit and brushing
with melted butter as before. Cover
the pie loosely with foil and bake for
35 minutes. (Keep the remaining pastry
covered with a plastic bag and a clean,
damp cloth.)

6 Meanwhile beat the cream, egg yolks
and remaining herbs together. Make a
hole in the centre of the pie and
gradually pour in the eggs and cream.

7 Arrange the remaining pastry on top,
teasing it into swirls and folds, then
brush with melted butter. Reduce the
oven temperature to 180°C/350°F/
Gas 4 and bake the pie for another
25–30 minutes, until the top is golden
and crisp. Allow to cool before serving.

LEEK AND ROQUEFORT TART WITH WALNUT PASTRY

MILD LEEKS GO EXCEPTIONALLY WELL WITH THE SALTY FLAVOUR OF THE ROQUEFORT CHEESE, AND THE NUTTINESS OF THE PASTRY MARRIES THE INGREDIENTS PERFECTLY IN THIS TART. SERVE THE TART WARM WITH A PEPPERY GREEN SALAD OF ROCKET, MIZUNA OR WATERCRESS.

SERVES FOUR TO SIX

INGREDIENTS
25g/1oz/2 tbsp butter
450g/1lb leeks, sliced
175g/6oz Roquefort cheese, sliced
2 large (US extra large) eggs
250ml/8fl oz/1 cup double
  (heavy) cream
10ml/2 tsp chopped fresh tarragon
salt and ground black pepper
For the pastry
175g/6oz/1½ cups plain (all-
  purpose) flour
50g/2oz/¼ cup butter
75g/3oz/¾ cup walnuts, ground
15ml/1 tbsp lemon juice
30ml/2 tbsp iced water

1 First make the pastry. Sift the flour, 2.5ml/½ tsp salt and some black pepper into a bowl. Rub in the butter until the mixture looks like breadcrumbs, then stir in the ground walnuts. Bind with the lemon juice and iced water. Gather into a ball, wrap and chill for 30–40 minutes.

2 Preheat the oven to 190°C/375°F/ Gas 5. Roll out the pastry and use to line a 21–23cm/8½–9in loose-based metal flan tin (tart pan).

COOK'S TIP
Grind walnuts in a small food processor or clean coffee mill with a little of the pastry flour.

3 Protect the sides of the pastry with foil, prick the base with a fork and bake for 15 minutes. Remove the foil and bake for a further 5–10 minutes, until just firm to the touch. Reduce the oven temperature to 180°C/350°F/Gas 4.

4 Meanwhile, to make the filling, melt the butter in a pan, add the leeks, cover and cook for 10 minutes. Season and cook for a further 10 minutes. Cool.

5 Spoon the leeks into the pastry case and arrange the slices of Roquefort on top. Beat the eggs with the cream and season with pepper (the cheese will probably be sufficiently salty). Beat in the tarragon and carefully pour the mixture into the tart.

6 Bake the tart on the centre shelf of the oven for 30–40 minutes, until the filling has risen and browned and become firm to a gentle touch. Leave to cool for 10 minutes before serving.

BARLEY RISOTTO <u>WITH</u> ROASTED SQUASH <u>AND</u> LEEKS

THIS IS MORE LIKE A PILAFF, MADE WITH SLIGHTLY CHEWY, NUTTY-FLAVOURED PEARL BARLEY, THAN A CLASSIC RISOTTO. SWEET LEEKS AND ROASTED SQUASH ARE SUPERB WITH THIS EARTHY GRAIN.

3 Heat half the butter with the remaining oil in a large frying pan. Cook the leeks and garlic gently for 5 minutes. Add the mushrooms and remaining thyme, then cook until the liquid from the mushrooms evaporates and they begin to colour.

4 Stir in the carrots and cook for 2 minutes, then add the barley and most of the stock. Season well and part-cover the pan. Cook for a further 5 minutes. Pour in the remaining stock if the mixture seems dry.

5 Stir in the parsley, the remaining butter and half the Pecorino. Then stir in the squash. Add seasoning to taste and serve immediately, sprinkled with the toasted pumpkin seeds or walnuts and the remaining Pecorino.

SERVES FOUR TO FIVE

INGREDIENTS
200g/7oz/1 cup pearl barley
1 butternut squash, peeled, seeded
 and cut into chunks
10ml/2 tsp chopped fresh thyme
60ml/4 tbsp olive oil
25g/1oz/2 tbsp butter
4 leeks, cut into fairly thick
 diagonal slices
2 garlic cloves, finely chopped
175g/6oz chestnut mushrooms, sliced
2 carrots, coarsely grated
about 120ml/4fl oz/½ cup
 vegetable stock
30ml/2 tbsp chopped fresh flat
 leaf parsley
50g/2oz Pecorino cheese, grated
 or shaved
45ml/3 tbsp pumpkin seeds, toasted,
 or chopped walnuts
salt and ground black pepper

1 Rinse the barley, then cook it in simmering water, keeping the pan part-covered, for 35–45 minutes, or until tender. Drain. Preheat the oven to 200°C/400°F/Gas 6.

2 Place the squash in a roasting pan with half the thyme. Season with pepper and toss with half the oil. Roast, stirring once, for 30–35 minutes, until tender and beginning to brown.

Here is conclusive proof that garlic can be so much more

than a mere accent, as it takes a starring role in soups,

sauces, main course dishes and accompaniments. It

complements fish and shellfish superbly, gives a much-

needed lift to chicken, adds character to beef and turns

routine vegetables into a taste sensation. And don't

overlook tried and tested favourites, such as Garlic and

Herb Bread, Aioli and Salsa Verde.

Dishes with Garlic

GARLIC AND CORIANDER SOUP

THIS RECIPE IS BASED ON THE WONDERFUL BREAD SOUPS OR AÇORDAS OF PORTUGAL. BEING A SIMPLE SOUP, IT SHOULD BE MADE WITH THE BEST INGREDIENTS — PLUMP GARLIC, FRESH CORIANDER, HIGH-QUALITY CRUSTY COUNTRY BREAD AND EXTRA VIRGIN OLIVE OIL.

SERVES SIX

INGREDIENTS

25g/1oz/1 cup fresh coriander
(cilantro), leaves and stalks
chopped separately
1.5 litres/2½ pints/6¼ cups vegetable
or chicken stock
5–6 plump garlic cloves, peeled
6 eggs
275g/10oz day-old bread, most of
the crust removed and torn into
bitesize pieces
salt and ground black pepper
90ml/6 tbsp extra virgin olive oil,
plus extra to serve

1 Place the coriander stalks in a pan. Add the stock and bring to the boil, then simmer for 10 minutes. Process in a blender or food processor and sieve back into the pan.

2 Crush the garlic with 5ml/1 tsp salt, then stir in 120ml/4fl oz/½ cup hot soup. Return the mixture to the pan.

3 Meanwhile, poach the eggs in a frying pan of simmering water for about 3–4 minutes, until just set. Use a slotted spoon to remove them from the pan and transfer to a warmed plate. Trim off any untidy pieces of white.

4 Bring the soup back to the boil and add seasoning. Stir in the chopped coriander leaves and remove from the heat.

5 Place the bread in six soup plates or bowls and drizzle the oil over it. Ladle in the soup and stir. Add a poached egg to each bowl and serve immediately, offering olive oil at the table so that it can be drizzled over the soup to taste.

ROASTED GARLIC AND BUTTERNUT SQUASH SOUP WITH TOMATO SALSA

THIS IS A WONDERFUL, RICHLY FLAVOURED DISH. A SPOONFUL OF THE HOT AND SPICY TOMATO SALSA GIVES BITE TO THE SWEET-TASTING SQUASH AND GARLIC SOUP.

SERVES FOUR TO FIVE

INGREDIENTS
2 garlic bulbs, outer papery
    skin removed
75ml/5 tbsp olive oil
a few fresh thyme sprigs
1 large butternut squash, halved
    and seeded
2 onions, chopped
5ml/1 tsp ground coriander
1.2 litres/2 pints/5 cups vegetable or
    chicken stock
30–45ml/2–3 tbsp chopped fresh
    oregano or marjoram
salt and ground black pepper
For the salsa
4 large ripe tomatoes, halved
    and seeded
1 red (bell) pepper, halved
    and seeded
1 large fresh red chilli, halved
    and seeded
30–45ml/2–3 tbsp olive oil
15ml/1 tbsp balsamic vinegar
pinch of caster (superfine) sugar

1 Preheat the oven to 220°C/425°F/Gas 7. Place the garlic bulbs on a piece of foil and pour over half the olive oil. Add the thyme sprigs, then fold the foil around the garlic bulbs to enclose them completely. Place the foil parcel on a baking sheet with the butternut squash and brush the squash with 15ml/1 tbsp of the remaining olive oil. Add the tomatoes, red pepper and fresh chilli for the salsa.

2 Roast the vegetables for 25 minutes, then remove the tomatoes, pepper and chilli. Reduce the temperature to 190°C/375°F/Gas 5 and cook the squash and garlic for 20–25 minutes more, or until the squash is tender.

3 Heat the remaining oil in a large, heavy pan and cook the onions and ground coriander gently for about 10 minutes, or until softened.

4 Peel the pepper and chilli and process in a food processor or blender with the tomatoes and 30ml/2 tbsp olive oil. Stir in the vinegar and seasoning to taste, adding a pinch of caster sugar. Add the remaining oil if you think the salsa needs it.

5 Squeeze the roasted garlic out of its papery skin into the onions and scoop the squash out of its skin, adding it to the pan. Add the stock, 5ml/1 tsp salt and plenty of black pepper. Bring to the boil and simmer for 10 minutes.

6 Stir in half the oregano or marjoram and cool the soup slightly, then process it in a blender or food processor. Alternatively, press the soup through a fine sieve.

7 Reheat the soup without allowing it to boil, then taste for seasoning before ladling it into warmed bowls. Top each with a spoonful of salsa and sprinkle over the remaining chopped oregano or marjoram. Serve immediately.

MUSSELS IN GARLIC BUTTER

GARLIC AND HERB BUTTER IS A CLASSIC TREATMENT FOR SNAILS IN BURGUNDY, BUT BECAME VERY POPULAR IN THE 1960S WITH MUSSELS, AND MAKES A DELICIOUS FIRST COURSE.

SERVES FOUR

INGREDIENTS
2kg/4½lb mussels, scrubbed
2 large shallots, finely chopped
200ml/7fl oz/scant 1 cup dry
  white wine
115g/4oz/½ cup unsalted (sweet)
  butter, softened
2–3 garlic cloves, finely chopped
grated rind of 1 lemon
60ml/4 tbsp finely chopped mixed
  herbs, such as parsley, chervil,
  tarragon and chives
115g/4oz/1 cup fresh
  white breadcrumbs
salt and ground black pepper
lemon wedges, to serve

1 Check that all the mussels are closed after cleaning and discard any that remain open when sharply tapped.

2 Place the shallots and wine in a large pan and bring to the boil. Throw in the mussels and cover tightly. Cook over a high heat for 4–5 minutes, shaking the pan vigorously 2–3 times.

3 The mussels should be cooked and gaping open. Discard any that do not open after 5 minutes' cooking. Drain, reserving the cooking liquid.

4 Discard the top (empty) half of each shell. Place the mussels in a large roasting pan or heatproof dish.

5 Pour the cooking liquid into a clean pan and boil it vigorously until reduced to about 45ml/3 tbsp. Remove from the heat and leave to cool.

6 Cream the butter with the shallots from the reduced liquid, the garlic, lemon rind and herbs. Season well and chill until firm.

7 Distribute the flavoured butter among the mussels. Sprinkle with the cooking liquid, then sprinkle the breadcrumbs over the top.

8 Preheat the grill (broiler) and position the shelf about 10cm/4in below the heat. Grill (broil) the mussels until the butter is bubbling and the breadcrumbs are golden and crisp. Serve immediately, with wedges of lemon.

FLASH-FRIED SQUID <u>WITH</u> PAPRIKA <u>AND</u> GARLIC

THESE QUICK-FRIED SQUID ARE GOOD SERVED WITH A DRY SHERRY OR MANZANILLA AS AN APPETIZER OR AS PART OF MIXED TAPAS. ALTERNATIVELY, SERVE THEM ON A BED OF SALAD LEAVES AND OFFER WARM BREAD AS AN ACCOMPANIMENT FOR A MORE SUBSTANTIAL FIRST COURSE.

SERVES SIX TO EIGHT AS AN APPETIZER,
FOUR AS A FIRST COURSE

INGREDIENTS

500g/1¼lb very small squid, cleaned
90ml/6 tbsp olive oil, plus extra
1 red chilli, seeded and
  finely chopped
10ml/2 tsp Spanish mild smoked
  paprika (*pimentón*)
30ml/2 tbsp plain (all-purpose) flour
2 garlic cloves, finely chopped
15ml/1 tbsp sherry vinegar
5ml/1 tsp grated lemon rind
30–45ml/2–3 tbsp fincly chopped
  fresh parsley
salt and ground black pepper

1 Choose small squid that are no longer than 10cm/4in. Cut the body sacs into rings and cut the tentacles into bitesize pieces.

2 Place the squid in a bowl and add 30ml/2 tbsp of the oil, half the chilli and the paprika. Season with a little salt and some pepper, cover and marinate for 2–4 hours in the refrigerator.

COOK'S TIPS
• Make sure the wok or pan is very hot as the squid should cook for only 1–2 minutes: any longer and it will begin to toughen.
• Smoked paprika, known as *pimentón* in Spain, has a wonderful smoky flavour. If you cannot find it, use mild paprika.

3 Toss the squid in the flour and divide it into two batches. Heat the remaining oil in a preheated wok or deep frying pan over a high heat until very hot. Add the first batch of squid and stir-fry for 1–2 minutes, or until it becomes opaque and the tentacles have curled.

4 Sprinkle in half the garlic. Stir, then turn out on to a plate. Repeat with the second batch, adding more oil if needed.

5 Sprinkle over the sherry vinegar, lemon rind, remaining chilli and parsley. Season and serve hot or cool.

Salt Cod Fritters with Aioli

Aioli is a fiercely garlicky, olive oil mayonnaise from Provence in the south of France and is a traditional accompaniment to salt cod.

SERVES SIX

INGREDIENTS
450g/1lb salt cod
500g/1¼lb floury potatoes
300ml/½ pint/1¼ cups milk
6 spring onions (scallions),
    finely chopped
30ml/2 tbsp extra virgin olive oil
30ml/2 tbsp chopped fresh parsley
juice of ½ lemon, to taste
2 eggs, beaten
60ml/4 tbsp plain (all-purpose) flour
90g/3½oz/1½ cups dry
    white breadcrumbs
vegetable oil, for shallow frying
salt and ground black pepper
lemon wedges and salad, to serve
For the aioli
2 large garlic cloves
2 egg yolks
300ml/½ pint/1¼ cups olive oil
lemon juice, to taste

1 Soak the salt cod in cold water for 24–36 hours, changing the water five or six times. The cod should swell as it rehydrates and should not taste unpleasantly salty when tried. Drain.

2 Cook the potatoes, unpeeled, in a pan of boiling salted water for about 20 minutes, until tender. Drain, then peel and mash the potatoes.

3 Poach the cod very gently in the milk with half the spring onions for 10–15 minutes, or until it flakes easily. Remove the cod and flake it with a fork into a bowl, discarding bones and skin.

4 Add 60ml/4 tbsp mashed potato to the flaked cod and beat with a wooden spoon. Work in the olive oil, then gradually add the remaining potato. Beat in the remaining spring onions and the parsley. Season with lemon juice and pepper to taste – the mixture may need a little salt. Beat in one egg, then chill the mixture until firm.

5 Shape the mixture into 12–18 small round cakes. Coat them in flour, then dip them in the remaining egg and coat with the breadcrumbs. Chill until ready to fry.

COOK'S TIPS
• Try to find a thick, creamy white piece of salt cod, preferably cut from the middle of the fish rather than the tail and fin ends. Avoid thin, yellowish salt cod, as it will be too dry and salty.
• Mash potatoes by hand, never in a food processor, as it makes them gluey.
• Aioli traditionally has a sharp bite from the raw garlic. However, if you prefer a milder flavour, blanch the garlic once or twice in boiling water for about 3 minutes each time before using it.

6 Meanwhile, make the aioli. Place the garlic and a good pinch of salt in a mortar and pound to a paste with a pestle. Using a small whisk or a wooden spoon, gradually work in the egg yolks.

7 Add the olive oil, a drop at a time, until about half is incorporated. When the sauce is as thick as soft butter, beat in 5–10ml/1–2 tsp lemon juice, then continue adding oil until the aioli is very thick. Adjust the seasoning, adding lemon juice to taste.

8 Heat about 2cm/¾in depth of oil in a large, heavy frying pan. Add the fritters and cook over a medium-high heat for about 4 minutes. Turn them over and cook for a further 4 minutes on the other side, until crisp and golden. Drain thoroughly on crumpled kitchen paper, then serve with the aioli, lemon wedges and salad leaves.

ROASTED GARLIC AND GOAT'S CHEESE SOUFFLÉ

THE MELLOW FLAVOUR OF ROASTED GARLIC PERVADES THIS SIMPLE SOUFFLÉ. BALANCE THE RICH SOUFFLÉ WITH A CRISP GREEN SALAD, INCLUDING PEPPERY LEAVES, SUCH AS MIZUNA AND WATERCRESS.

5 Cook the sauce very gently for 10 minutes, stirring frequently. Season with salt, pepper and a pinch of cayenne. Cool slightly. Preheat the oven to 200°C/400°F/Gas 6.

6 Beat in the egg yolks one at a time. Then beat in the goat's cheese, all but 15ml/1 tbsp of the Parmesan and the chopped thyme. Use the remaining butter to grease one large soufflé dish (1 litre/1¾ pints/4 cups) or four large ramekins (about 250ml/8fl oz/1 cup).

7 Whisk the egg whites and cream of tartar in a scrupulously clean bowl until firm, but not dry. Stir 45ml/3 tbsp of the whites into the sauce, then gently, but thoroughly, fold in the remainder.

8 Pour the mixture into the prepared dish or dishes. Run a knife around the edge of each dish, pushing the mixture away from the rim. Sprinkle with the reserved Parmesan.

9 Place the dish or dishes on a baking sheet and cook for 25–30 minutes for a large soufflé or 20 minutes for small soufflés. The mixture should be risen and firm to a light touch in the centre; it should not wobble excessively when given a light push. Serve immediately.

SERVES THREE TO FOUR

INGREDIENTS
2 large heads of garlic (choose heads with plump cloves)
3 fresh thyme sprigs
15ml/1 tbsp olive oil
250ml/8fl oz/1 cup milk
1 fresh bay leaf
2 × 1cm/½in thick onion slices
2 cloves
50g/2oz/¼ cup butter
40g/1½oz/⅓ cup plain (all-purpose) flour, sifted
cayenne pepper
3 eggs, separated, plus 1 egg white
150g/5oz goat's cheese, crumbled
50g/2oz/⅔ cup freshly grated Parmesan cheese
5ml/1 tsp chopped fresh thyme
2.5ml/½ tsp cream of tartar
salt and ground black pepper

1 Preheat the oven to 180°C/350°F/ Gas 4. Place the garlic and thyme sprigs on a piece of foil. Sprinkle with the oil and close the foil around the garlic, then bake for about 1 hour, until the garlic is soft. Leave to cool.

2 Squeeze the garlic out of its skin. Discard the thyme and garlic skins, then purée the garlic flesh with the oil.

3 Meanwhile, place the milk, bay leaf, onion slices and cloves in a small pan. Bring to the boil, then remove from the heat. Cover and leave to stand for 30 minutes.

4 Melt 40g/1½oz/3 tbsp of the butter in another pan. Stir in the flour and cook gently for 2 minutes, stirring. Reheat and strain the milk, then gradually stir it into the flour and butter.

PASTA WITH GARLIC AND CHILLI

THIS IS THE SIMPLEST OF PASTA DISHES AND ONE OF THE BEST. MINT AND OREGANO GIVE VERY DIFFERENT RESULTS, BOTH GOOD. THERE IS NO NEED TO SERVE GRATED PARMESAN WITH THIS DISH — INSTEAD, LET THE CLEAR FLAVOUR OF THE GARLIC AND OLIVE OIL SING OUT.

SERVES THREE TO FOUR

INGREDIENTS
  400g/14oz dried spaghetti
  105ml/7 tbsp extra virgin olive oil,
    plus extra to taste
  1.5ml/¼ tsp dried red chilli flakes or
    2 small whole dried red chillies
  6 large garlic cloves, finely chopped
  15ml/1 tbsp chopped fresh mint
    or oregano
  15g/½ oz chopped fresh flat
    leaf parsley
  salt and ground black pepper

1 Cook the spaghetti in lightly salted, boiling water for 9–11 minutes, or according to the packet instructions, until just tender.

2 Meanwhile, warm the oil in a large frying pan or other suitable pan over a very gentle heat. Add the chilli flakes or whole chillies and cook very gently for 2–3 minutes.

COOK'S TIP
If you use fresh spaghetti, cook for only 2–3 minutes in salted, boiling water.

3 Add the garlic to the pan. Keep the heat very low, so that the garlic barely bubbles and does not brown, then cook, shaking the pan occasionally, for about 2 minutes. Remove the pan from the heat and cool a little, then add the fresh mint or oregano.

4 Drain the pasta, then immediately add it to the oil and garlic mixture, with the parsley. Toss thoroughly. Season with freshly ground black pepper and transfer to warmed serving bowls. Serve immediately, offering more olive oil at the table.

VARIATION
Cook 250g/9oz broccoli florets in boiling salted water for 4 minutes. Add to the chilli oil and gently fry for 5–8 minutes.

CHICKEN WITH FORTY CLOVES OF GARLIC

THIS DISH DOES NOT HAVE TO BE MATHEMATICALLY EXACT, SO DO NOT WORRY IF YOU HAVE 35 OR EVEN 50 CLOVES OF GARLIC – THE IMPORTANT THING IS THAT THERE SHOULD BE LOTS. THE SMELL THAT EMANATES FROM THE OVEN AS THE CHICKEN AND GARLIC COOK IS INDESCRIBABLY DELICIOUS.

3 Sprinkle in 5ml/1 tsp flour and cook for 1 minute. Add the port or wine. Tuck in the whole heads of garlic and the peeled cloves with the herb sprigs. Pour over the remaining oil and season to taste with salt and pepper.

4 Mix the main batch of flour with sufficient water to make a firm dough. Roll it out into a long sausage and press it around the rim of the casserole, then press on the lid, folding the dough up and over it to create a tight seal. Cook in the oven for 1½ hours.

5 To serve, lift off the lid to break the seal and remove the chicken and whole garlic to a serving platter and keep warm. Remove and discard the herb sprigs, then place the casserole on the hob (stovetop) and whisk to combine the garlic cloves with the cooking juices. Add the crème fraîche, if using, and lemon juice to taste. Process the sauce in a food processor or blender or press through a sieve. Serve the garlic purée with the chicken.

SERVES FOUR TO FIVE

INGREDIENTS
  5–6 whole heads of garlic
  15g/½oz/1 tbsp butter
  45ml/3 tbsp olive oil
  1.8–2kg/4–4½lb chicken
  150g/5oz/1¼ cups plain (all-purpose)
    flour, plus 5ml/1 tsp
  75ml/5 tbsp white port, Pineau
    de Charentes or other white,
    fortified wine
  2–3 fresh tarragon or rosemary sprigs
  30ml/2 tbsp crème fraîche (optional)
  few drops of lemon juice (optional)
  salt and ground black pepper

1 Separate three of the heads of garlic into cloves and peel them. Remove the first layer of papery skin from the remaining heads of garlic and cut off the tops to expose the cloves, if you like, or leave them whole. Preheat the oven to 180°C/350°F/Gas 4.

2 Heat the butter and 15ml/1 tbsp of the olive oil in a flameproof casserole that is just large enough to take the chicken and garlic. Add the chicken and cook over a medium heat, turning frequently using two large forks, for 10–15 minutes, until it is golden brown all over.

GARLIC AND CHILLI MARINATED BEEF WITH CORN-CRUSTED ONION RINGS

FRUITY, SMOKY AND MILD MEXICAN CHILLIES COMBINE WELL WITH GARLIC IN THIS MARINADE FOR GRILLED STEAK. POLENTA MAKES A CRISP COATING FOR THE ACCOMPANYING FRIED ONION RINGS.

SERVES FOUR

INGREDIENTS
    20g/¾oz large mild dried red chillies
        (such as *mulato* or *pasilla*)
    2 garlic cloves, plain or smoked,
        finely chopped
    5ml/1 tsp ground toasted
        cumin seeds
    5ml/1 tsp dried oregano
    60ml/4 tbsp olive oil
    4 × 175–225g/6–8oz beef steaks:
        rump (round) or rib-eye
    salt and ground black pepper
For the onion rings
    2 onions, sliced into rings
    250ml/8fl oz/1 cup milk
    75g/3oz/¾ cup polenta or
        coarse corn meal
    2.5ml/½ tsp dried red
        chilli flakes
    5ml/1 tsp ground toasted
        cumin seeds
    5ml/1 tsp dried oregano
    vegetable oil, for deep-frying

3 Wash and dry the steaks, rub the chilli paste all over them and leave to marinate for up to 12 hours.

4 For the onion rings, soak the onions in the milk for 30 minutes. Mix the corn meal, chilli, cumin and oregano and season with salt and pepper.

5 Heat the oil for deep-frying to 160–180°C/325–350°F, or until a cube of day-old bread turns brown in about a minute.

6 Drain the onion rings and dip each one into the corn meal mixture, coating it thoroughly. Fry for 2–4 minutes, until browned and crisp. Do not overcrowd the pan, but cook in batches. Lift the onion rings out of the pan with a slotted spoon and drain on kitchen paper.

7 Heat a barbecue or cast-iron griddle pan. Season the steaks with salt and cook for about 4 minutes on each side for a medium result; reduce or increase this time according to how rare or well done you like steak. Serve the steaks with the onion rings.

1 Cut the stalks from the chillies and discard the seeds. Toast the chillies in a dry frying pan for 2–4 minutes, until they give off their aroma. Place the chillies in a bowl, cover with warm water and leave to soak for 20–30 minutes. Drain and reserve the water.

2 Process the chillies to a paste with the garlic, cumin, oregano and oil in a food processor. Add a little soaking water, if needed. Season with pepper.

FENNEL, POTATO AND GARLIC MASH

THIS FLAVOURSOME MASH OF POTATO, FENNEL AND GARLIC GOES PARTICULARLY WELL WITH FISH OR CHICKEN. IT IS ALSO EXTREMELY DELICIOUS WITH ROAST PORK.

SERVES FOUR

INGREDIENTS

   1 head of garlic, separated
     into cloves
   800g/1¾lb boiling potatoes, cut
     into chunks
   2 large fennel bulbs
   65g/2½oz/5 tbsp butter or 90ml/
     6 tbsp extra virgin olive oil
   120–150ml/4–5fl oz/½–⅔ cup milk
     or single (light) cream
   freshly grated nutmeg
   salt and ground black pepper

1 If using a food mill to mash the potato, leave the garlic unpeeled, otherwise peel it. Boil the garlic with the potatoes in salted water for 20 minutes.

2 Meanwhile, trim and coarsely chop the fennel, reserving any feathery tops. Chop the tops and set them aside. Heat 25g/1oz/2 tbsp of the butter or 30ml/ 2 tbsp of the oil in a heavy pan. Add the fennel, cover and cook over a low heat for 20–30 minutes, until soft but not browned.

3 Drain and mash the potatoes and garlic. Purée the fennel in a food mill or blender and beat it into the potato with the remaining butter or olive oil.

COOK'S TIP

A food mill is good for mashing potatoes as it guarantees a smooth texture. Never mash potatoes in a food processor or blender as this releases the starch, giving a result that resembles wallpaper paste.

4 Warm the milk or cream and beat sufficient into the potato and fennel to make a creamy, light mixture. Season to taste and add a little grated nutmeg.

5 Reheat gently, then beat in any chopped fennel tops. Transfer to a warmed dish and serve immediately.

VARIATIONS

• For a stronger garlic flavour, use 30–45ml/2–3 tbsp roasted garlic purée.
• To give a stronger fennel flavour, cook 2.5–5ml/½–1 tsp ground fennel seeds with the fennel.
• For a slightly less rich mash, substitute hot stock for some or all of the milk or cream. Mash made with fish stock is particularly good with grilled (broiled) fish or as a topping for fish pie.

GARLIC AND HERB BREAD

EXCELLENT WITH SOUPS OR VEGETABLE FIRST COURSES, GARLIC BREAD IS ALSO IRRESISTIBLE JUST ON ITS OWN. THE BETTER THE BREAD, THE BETTER THE FINAL, BAKED VERSION WILL BE.

SERVES THREE TO FOUR

INGREDIENTS
1 baguette or bloomer loaf
For the garlic and herb butter
115g/4oz/½ cup unsalted (sweet)
butter, softened
5–6 large garlic cloves, finely
chopped or crushed
30–45ml/2–3 tbsp chopped fresh
herbs (such as parsley, chervil and
a little tarragon)
15ml/1 tbsp chopped fresh chives
sea salt and ground black pepper

1 Preheat the oven to 200°C/400°F/
Gas 6. Make the garlic and herb butter
by beating the butter with the garlic,
herbs, chives and seasoning.

2 Cut the bread into 1cm/½in thick
diagonal slices, but leave them attached
at the base so that the loaf stays intact.

3 Spread the butter between the slices,
being careful not to detach them, and
spread any remaining butter over the
top of the loaf.

4 Wrap the loaf in foil and bake for
20–25 minutes, until the garlic and
herb butter is melted and the crust is
crisp. Cut into slices to serve.

VARIATIONS
• Use 105ml/7 tbsp extra virgin olive oil
instead of butter.
• Flavour the butter with garlic, chopped
fresh chilli, grated lime rind and
chopped fresh coriander (cilantro).

• Add chopped, pitted black olives or
sun-dried tomatoes to the butter with a
little grated lemon rind.
• To make bruschetta, take thick slices
of good country bread. Toast on a ridged
cast-iron griddle pan, then rub with
garlic and drizzle with extra virgin olive
oil. For a stronger garlic taste, toast one
side of the bread, spread some finely
chopped garlic on the untoasted side,
drizzle oil over, then toast until golden.

WALNUT AND GARLIC SAUCE

THIS SAUCE, SEVERAL VERSIONS OF WHICH CAN BE FOUND AROUND THE MEDITERRANEAN, IS EXCELLENT WITH ROAST OR POACHED CHICKEN OR STEAMED CAULIFLOWER OR POTATOES.

SERVES FOUR

INGREDIENTS
2 × 1cm/½in slices good white bread, crusts removed
60ml/4 tbsp milk
150g/5oz/1¼ cups shelled walnuts
4 garlic cloves, chopped
120ml/4fl oz/½ cup mild olive oil
15–30ml/1–2 tbsp walnut oil (optional)
juice of 1 lemon
salt and ground black pepper
walnut or olive oil, for drizzling
paprika, for dusting (optional)

VARIATION
For an Italian *salsa di noci* for pasta, process 90g/3½oz/scant 1 cup walnuts with 2 garlic cloves and 15g/½oz/½ cup flat leaf parsley. Blend in 1 slice white bread (crusts removed), soaked in milk, and 120ml/4fl oz/½ cup fruity olive oil as above. Season with salt, pepper and lemon juice. Thin with more milk or single (light) cream if very thick.

1 Soak the slices of white bread in the milk for about 5 minutes, then process with the walnuts and chopped garlic in a food processor or blender, to make a coarse paste.

2 Gradually add the olive oil to the paste with the motor still running, until the mixture forms a smooth thick sauce. Blend in the walnut oil, if using.

3 Scoop the sauce into a bowl and squeeze in lemon juice to taste, season with salt and pepper and beat well.

4 Transfer to a serving bowl, drizzle over a little more walnut or olive oil, then dust lightly with paprika, if using.

COOK'S TIP
Once opened, walnut oil has a fairly short shelf life. Buy it in small bottles and keep it in a cool, dark place. It is delicious in many salad dressings.

SALSA VERDE

THIS SIMPLE ITALIAN SAUCE IS A PURÉE OF FRESH HERBS WITH OLIVE OIL AND FLAVOURINGS. IT IS GOOD WITH POACHED OR ROAST BEEF AND CHICKEN, GRILLED STEAK OR GRILLED POLENTA.

SERVES FOUR

INGREDIENTS
1–2 garlic cloves, finely chopped
25g/1oz/1 cup flat leaf parsley leaves
15g/½oz fresh coriander (cilantro), basil or mint or a mixture of herbs
15ml/1 tbsp chopped chives
15ml/1 tbsp salted capers, rinsed
5 anchovy fillets in olive oil, drained and rinsed
10ml/2 tsp French mustard (tarragon or *fines herbes* mustard are both good)
120ml/4fl oz/½ cup extra virgin olive oil
a little grated lemon rind and juice (optional)
ground black pepper

1 Process the garlic, parsley, coriander, basil or mint, chives, capers, anchovies, mustard and 15ml/1 tbsp of the oil in a blender or food processor.

2 Gradually add the remaining oil in a thin stream with the motor running.

3 Transfer to a bowl and adjust the seasoning to taste – there should be enough salt from the capers and anchovies. Add a little lemon juice and rind if you like (especially if serving with fish). Serve immediately.

VARIATIONS
• Whisk in 30–45ml/2–3 tbsp crème fraîche to make a mild sauce that goes well with grilled (broiled) polenta, cauliflower and potatoes.
• Substitute fresh chervil, tarragon, dill or fennel – or a mixture of aniseed-flavoured herbs – for the coriander (cilantro), basil or mint to make a sauce that goes particularly well with poached or baked fish. It is also good with prawns (shrimp) and langoustines.

YOGURT WITH GARLIC, CUCUMBER AND MINT

VERSIONS OF THIS COOL, MINTY RELISH ARE FOUND IN GREECE (TZATZIKI), TURKEY (CACIK) AND THROUGHOUT THE MIDDLE EAST. IN INDIA, THE EQUIVALENT IS CALLED RAITA.

SERVES FOUR

INGREDIENTS
  15cm/6in piece cucumber
  5ml/1 tsp sea salt
  300ml/½ pint/1¼ cups Greek
  (US strained plain) yogurt
  3–4 garlic cloves, crushed
  45ml/3 tbsp chopped fresh mint
  ground black pepper
  chopped fresh mint and/or ground
  toasted cumin seeds, to garnish

1 Slice, chop or grate the cucumber, then place it in a sieve and sprinkle with half the salt. Place the sieve on a deep plate and set aside for 30 minutes to drip.

2 Rinse the cucumber in cold water, pat dry and mix with the yogurt, garlic and mint. Season with salt and pepper. Leave for 30 minutes, then stir and sprinkle with fresh mint and/or toasted cumin to garnish.

VARIATION
To make a yogurt and garlic salad dressing, omit the cucumber and use 150ml/¼ pint/⅔ cup Greek (US strained plain) yogurt instead. Beat in 1 very finely chopped garlic clove, 5ml/1 tsp French mustard, salt and freshly ground black pepper to taste and a pinch of sugar. Finally, beat in 15–30ml/1–2 tbsp extra virgin olive oil and 15–30ml/1–2 tbsp chopped fresh herbs, such as mint, tarragon and chives, to taste.

Far from being the "poor relations", shallots, spring onions (scallions) and chives are as lively and versatile as any member of the Allium family. There is a lot more to them than extra flavouring for salads, although you might still like to try Salad of Roasted Shallots and Butternut Squash with Feta Cheese, with recipes for soups, fritters, skewers, dressings and a mouth-watering Spring Onion, Chive and Ricotta Bread.

Cooking with Other Alliums

MISO BROTH WITH SPRING ONIONS AND TOFU

THE JAPANESE EAT MISO BROTH, A SIMPLE BUT HIGHLY NUTRITIOUS SOUP, ALMOST EVERY DAY — IT IS STANDARD BREAKFAST FARE AND IT IS EATEN WITH RICE OR NOODLES LATER IN THE DAY.

SERVES FOUR

INGREDIENTS

1 bunch of spring onions (scallions)
   or 5 baby leeks
15g/½oz fresh coriander (cilantro)
3 thin slices fresh root ginger
2 star anise
1 small dried red chilli
1.2 litres/2 pints/5 cups dashi stock
   or vegetable stock
225g/8oz pak choi (bok choy) or
   other Asian greens, thickly sliced
200g/7oz firm tofu, cut into
   2.5cm/1in cubes
60ml/4 tbsp red miso
30–45ml/2–3 tbsp Japanese soy
   sauce (shoyu)
1 fresh red chilli, seeded and
   shredded (optional)

1 Cut the coarse green tops off the spring onions or baby leeks and slice the rest of the spring onions or leeks finely on the diagonal. Place the coarse green tops in a large pan with the coriander stalks, fresh root ginger, star anise, dried red chilli and dashi or vegetable stock.

2 Heat the mixture gently until boiling, then lower the heat and simmer for 10 minutes. Strain, return to the pan and reheat until simmering. Add the green portion of the sliced spring onions or leeks to the soup with the pak choi or greens and tofu. Cook for 2 minutes.

3 Mix 45ml/3 tbsp of the miso with a little of the hot soup in a bowl, then stir it into the soup. Taste the soup and add more miso with soy sauce to taste.

4 Coarsely chop the coriander leaves and stir most of them into the soup with the white part of the spring onions or leeks. Cook for 1 minute, then ladle the soup into warmed serving bowls. Sprinkle with the remaining coriander and the fresh red chilli, if using, and serve immediately.

COOK'S TIP

Dashi powder is available in most Asian and Chinese stores. Alternatively, make your own by gently simmering 10–15cm/4–6in kombu seaweed in 1.2 litres/2 pints/5 cups water for 10 minutes. Do not boil the stock vigorously, as this makes the dashi bitter. Remove the kombu, then add 15g/½oz dried bonito flakes and bring to the boil. Strain immediately through a fine sieve.

COCONUT AND SHELLFISH SOUP WITH GARLIC CHIVES

THE LONG LIST OF INGREDIENTS IN THIS THAI-INSPIRED RECIPE COULD MISLEAD YOU INTO THINKING THAT THIS SOUP IS COMPLICATED. IN FACT, IT IS VERY EASY TO PUT TOGETHER.

SERVES FOUR

INGREDIENTS
600ml/1 pint/2½ cups
    fish stock
5 thin slices fresh galangal or
    fresh root ginger
2 lemon grass stalks, chopped
3 kaffir lime leaves, shredded
25g/1oz garlic chives (1 bunch)
15g/½oz/½ cup fresh
    coriander (cilantro)
15ml/1 tbsp vegetable oil
4 shallots, chopped
400ml/14fl oz can coconut milk
30–45ml/2–3 tbsp Thai fish sauce
45–60ml/3–4 tbsp Thai green
    curry paste
450g/1lb raw large prawns (jumbo
    shrimp), peeled and deveined
450g/1lb prepared squid
a little lime juice (optional)
salt and ground black pepper
60ml/4 tbsp crisp-fried shallot
    slices, to serve

1 Pour the fish stock into a pan and add the slices of galangal or ginger, the lemon grass and half the shredded kaffir lime leaves.

2 Reserve a few garlic chives for the garnish, then chop the remainder. Add half the chopped garlic chives to the pan with the coriander stalks. Bring to the boil, reduce the heat and cover the pan, then simmer gently for 20 minutes. Strain the stock.

3 Rinse the pan. Add the oil and shallots. Cook over a medium heat for 5–10 minutes, until the shallots are just beginning to brown.

4 Stir in the strained stock, coconut milk, the remaining kaffir lime leaves and 30ml/2 tbsp of the fish sauce. Heat gently until simmering and cook over a low heat for 5–10 minutes.

VARIATIONS
• Instead of squid, you could add 400g/14oz firm white fish, such as monkfish, cut into small pieces.
• You could also replace the squid with mussels. Steam 675g/1½lb closed live mussels in a tightly covered pan for 3–4 minutes, or until the shells have opened. Discard any that remain shut, then remove the mussels from their shells.

5 Stir in the curry paste and prawns, then cook for 3 minutes. Add the squid and cook for a further 2 minutes. Add the lime juice, if using, and season, adding more fish sauce to taste.

6 Stir in the remaining chives and the coriander. Serve in bowls sprinkled with fried shallots and whole garlic chives.

SEAFOOD AND SPRING ONION SKEWERS WITH TARTARE SAUCE

IF YOU MAKE THESE SKEWERS QUITE SMALL, THEY ARE GOOD AS A CANAPÉ TO SERVE AT A DRINKS PARTY OR BEFORE DINNER, WITH THE TARTARE SAUCE OFFERED AS A DIP.

MAKES NINE

INGREDIENTS

675g/1½lb monkfish tail, filleted,
   skinned and membrane removed
1 bunch spring onions (scallions)
75ml/5 tbsp olive oil
1 garlic clove, finely chopped
15ml/1 tbsp lemon juice
5ml/1 tsp dried oregano
30ml/2 tbsp chopped fresh flat
   leaf parsley
12–18 small scallops or large
   raw prawns (shrimp)
75g/3oz/1½ cups fine fresh
   breadcrumbs
salt and ground black pepper
For the tartare sauce
2 egg yolks
300ml/½ pint/1¼ cups olive oil, or
   vegetable oil and olive oil mixed
15–30ml/1–2 tbsp lemon juice
5ml/1 tsp French mustard, preferably
   tarragon mustard
15ml/1 tbsp chopped gherkin or
   pickled cucumber
15ml/1 tbsp chopped capers
30ml/2 tbsp chopped fresh flat
   leaf parsley
30ml/2 tbsp chopped fresh chives
5ml/1 tsp chopped fresh tarragon

2 Whisk in 15ml/1 tbsp lemon juice, then a little more oil. Stir in all the mustard, gherkin or cucumber, capers, parsley, chives and tarragon. Add more lemon juice and seasoning to taste.

4 Mix the breadcrumbs and remaining parsley together. Toss the fish and spring onions in the mixture to coat. Soak nine skewers in cold water.

1 First make the tartare sauce. Whisk the egg yolks with a pinch of salt, then whisk in the oil, a drop at a time. When about half the oil is incorporated, add it in a thin stream, whisking constantly. Stop when the mayonnaise is very thick.

3 Cut the monkfish into 18 pieces and cut the spring onions into 18 pieces about 5–6cm/2–2½in long. Mix the oil, garlic, lemon juice, oregano and half the parsley with seasoning. Add the monkfish, scallops or prawns and spring onions, then marinate for 15 minutes.

5 Preheat the grill (broiler). Drain the skewers and thread the monkfish, scallops or prawns and spring onions on to them. Drizzle with a little marinade then grill (broil) for 5–6 minutes in total, turning once and drizzling with the marinade, until the fish is just cooked. Serve immediately with the sauce.

SPRING ONION AND RICOTTA FRITTERS WITH AVOCADO SALSA

THE FRESH-FLAVOURED SALSA SPIKED WITH A LITTLE RED ONION AND CHILLI IS EXCELLENT WITH THESE MELT-IN-THE-MOUTH HERBY SPRING ONION FRITTERS.

SERVES FOUR TO SIX

INGREDIENTS
250g/9oz/generous 1 cup
  ricotta cheese
1 large (US extra large) egg, beaten
90ml/6 tbsp self-raising (self-
  rising) flour
90ml/6 tbsp milk
1 bunch spring onions (scallions),
  thinly sliced
30ml/2 tbsp chopped fresh coriander
  (cilantro), plus extra to garnish
sunflower oil, for shallow frying
salt and ground black pepper
lime wedges, to garnish
200ml/7fl oz/scant 1 cup crème
  fraîche, to serve
For the salsa
2 ripe, but not soft, avocados
1 small red onion, diced
grated rind and juice of 1 lime
½–1 fresh green or red chilli, seeded
  and finely chopped
225g/8oz tomatoes, peeled, seeded
  and diced
30–45ml/2–3 tbsp chopped mixed
  fresh mint and coriander (cilantro)
pinch of caster (superfine) sugar
5–10ml/1–2 tsp Thai fish sauce

2 Beat the ricotta until smooth, then beat in the egg and flour, followed by the milk to make a smooth, thick batter. Beat in the spring onions and coriander. Season well with pepper and a little salt.

3 Heat a little oil in a non-stick frying pan over a medium heat. Add spoonfuls of the mixture to make fritters about 7.5cm/3in across and fry for about 4–5 minutes each side, until set and browned. The mixture makes 12 fritters.

4 Taste the salsa and adjust the seasoning, adding more lime juice and/or sugar to taste. Serve the fritters immediately, with the salsa and a spoon of crème fraîche. Garnish with coriander and lime wedges.

VARIATION
The fritters are also good served with thinly sliced smoked salmon.

1 Make the salsa first. Peel, stone (pit) and dice the avocados. Place in a bowl with the red onion, lime rind and juice. Add chilli to taste, the tomatoes, mint and coriander. Season with salt, pepper, sugar and Thai fish sauce. Mix well and set aside for 30 minutes.

DEEP-FRIED SPRING ONIONS <u>IN</u> BEER BATTER <u>WITH</u> ROMESCO SAUCE

THIS PIQUANT, BUT NOT HOT, SAUCE FROM TARRAGONA IN SPAIN ADMIRABLY CUTS THE RICHNESS OF DEEP-FRIED FOOD, AND IT IS EXCELLENT WITH DEEP-FRIED SPRING ONIONS IN THEIR CRISP BATTER.

SERVES SIX

INGREDIENTS
  3 bunches plump spring onions
    (scallions), 18–24 in all
  sea salt and ground black pepper
  lemon wedges, to serve
For the batter
  225g/8oz/2 cups self-raising (self-
    rising) flour
  150ml/¼ pint/⅔ cup lager
  175–200ml/6–7fl oz/¾–scant 1 cup
    ice-cold water
  groundnut (peanut) oil, for
    deep-frying
  1 large (US extra large) egg white
  2.5ml/½ tsp cream of tartar
For the sauce
  2–3 large mild dried red chillies
  1 red (bell) pepper, halved and seeded
  2 large tomatoes, halved and seeded
  4–6 large garlic cloves, unpeeled
  75–90ml/5–6 tbsp olive oil
  25g/1oz/¼ cup hazelnuts, blanched
  4 slices French bread, each about
    2cm/¾in thick
  15ml/1 tbsp sherry vinegar
  squeeze of lemon juice (optional)
  chopped fresh parsley, to garnish

1 First prepare the sauce. Soak the dried chillies in hot water for about 30 minutes. Preheat the oven to 220°C/425°F/Gas 7.

2 Place the pepper halves, tomatoes and garlic on a baking sheet and drizzle with 15ml/1 tbsp olive oil.

3 Roast, uncovered, for about 30–40 minutes, until the pepper is blistered and blackened and the garlic is soft. Cool slightly, then peel the pepper, tomatoes and garlic.

4 Heat the remaining oil in a small frying pan and fry the hazelnuts until lightly browned, then transfer them to a plate. Fry the bread in the same oil until light brown on both sides, then transfer to the plate with the nuts and leave to cool. Reserve the oil from cooking.

5 Drain the chillies, discard as many of their seeds as you can, then place them in a food processor. Add the pepper, tomatoes, garlic, hazelnuts and bread with the reserved oil. Add the vinegar and process to a paste. Check the seasoning and thin the sauce with a little more oil or lemon juice, if necessary. Set aside.

6 Trim the roots from the spring onions. Trim the leaves to leave the onions about 15–18cm/6–7in long.

7 To make the batter, sift the flour into a bowl and add a good pinch each of salt and black pepper. Make a well in the centre, then gradually whisk in the lager, followed by the water. The batter should be the consistency of thick cream, so adjust the volume of water to produce this consistency.

8 Heat the oil for deep-frying to 180°C/350°F or until a cube of day-old bread browns in 30–45 seconds. Whisk the egg white with the cream of tartar until stiff, then fold it into the batter.

9 Dip the spring onions individually in the batter, drain off the excess and fry them in batches for 4–5 minutes. Drain thoroughly on kitchen paper and sprinkle with a little sea salt. Keep each batch warm until the next is cooked. Garnish with a little chopped parsley and serve hot with the sauce and lemon wedges.

SALAD OF ROASTED SHALLOTS AND BUTTERNUT SQUASH WITH FETA CHEESE

THIS IS ESPECIALLY GOOD SERVED WITH A GRAIN OR STARCHY SALAD, BASED ON RICE OR COUSCOUS, FOR EXAMPLE. SERVE PLENTY OF GOOD BREAD TO MOP UP THE JUICES.

SERVES FOUR TO SIX

INGREDIENTS
75ml/5 tbsp olive oil
15ml/1 tbsp balsamic vinegar, plus a
  little extra if you like
15ml/1 tbsp sweet soy sauce
350g/12oz shallots, peeled but
  left whole
3 fresh red chillies
1 butternut squash, peeled, seeded
  and cut into chunks
5ml/1 tsp finely chopped fresh thyme
15g/½oz/½ cup flat leaf parsley
1 small garlic clove, finely chopped
75g/3oz/¾ cup walnuts, chopped
150g/5oz feta cheese
salt and ground black pepper

1 Preheat the oven to 200°C/400°F/ Gas 6. Beat the oil, vinegar and soy sauce together in a large bowl, then season with salt and pepper.

2 Toss the shallots and two chillies in the oil mixture and turn into a large roasting pan or ovenproof dish. Roast for 15 minutes, stirring once or twice.

3 Add the butternut squash and roast for a further 30–35 minutes, stirring once, until the squash is tender and browned. Remove from the oven, stir in the chopped thyme and set the vegetables aside to cool.

4 Chop the parsley and garlic together and mix with the walnuts. Seed and finely chop the remaining chilli.

5 Stir the parsley, garlic and walnut mixture into the vegetables. Add chopped chilli to taste and adjust the seasoning, adding a little extra balsamic vinegar if you like. Crumble the feta and add to the salad. Transfer to a serving dish and serve immediately.

POTATO AND MUSSEL SALAD WITH SHALLOT AND CHIVE DRESSING

SHALLOT AND CHIVES IN A CREAMY DRESSING ADD BITE TO THIS SALAD OF POTATO AND SWEET MUSSELS. SERVE WITH A BOWL OF FULL-FLAVOURED WATERCRESS AND PLENTY OF CRUSTY BREAD.

SERVES FOUR

INGREDIENTS

675g/1½lb salad potatoes
1kg/2¼lb mussels, scrubbed and
  beards removed
200ml/7fl oz/ scant 1 cup dry
  white wine
15g/½oz/½ cup fresh parsley, chopped
salt and ground black pepper
chopped fresh chives, to garnish
watercress sprigs, to serve

For the dressing
105ml/7 tbsp mild olive oil
15–30ml/1–2 tbsp white wine vinegar
5ml/1 tsp Dijon mustard
1 large shallot, very finely chopped
15ml/1 tbsp chopped fresh chives
45ml/3 tbsp double (heavy) cream
pinch of caster (superfine) sugar

1 Cook the potatoes in salted, boiling water for 15–20 minutes, or until tender. Drain, cool, then peel. Slice the potatoes into a bowl and toss with 30ml/2 tbsp of the oil for the dressing.

2 Discard any open mussels that do not close when sharply tapped and any with damaged shells. Bring the white wine to the boil in a large, heavy pan. Add the mussels, cover and boil vigorously, shaking the pan occasionally, for 3–4 minutes, until the mussels have opened. Discard any mussels that have not opened after 5 minutes' cooking. Drain and shell the mussels, reserving the cooking liquid.

3 Boil the reserved cooking liquid until reduced to about 45ml/3 tbsp. Strain this through a fine sieve over the potatoes and toss to mix.

4 For the dressing, whisk together the remaining oil, 15ml/1 tbsp vinegar, the mustard, shallot and chives.

5 Add the cream and whisk again to form a thick dressing. Adjust the seasoning, adding more vinegar and a pinch of sugar to taste.

6 Toss the mussels with the potatoes, then mix in the dressing and chopped parsley. Sprinkle with extra chopped chives and serve with watercress sprigs.

COOK'S TIP

Potato salads, such as this one, should not be chilled if at all possible, as the cold alters the texture of the potatoes and of the creamy dressing. For the best flavour and texture, serve this salad just cool or at room temperature.

SEARED SCALLOPS WITH CHIVE SAUCE ON LEEK AND CARROT RICE

SCALLOPS ARE ONE OF THE MOST DELICIOUS SHELLFISH. HERE THEY ARE PARTNERED WITH A DELICATE CHIVE SAUCE AND A PILAFF OF WILD AND WHITE RICE WITH SWEET LEEKS AND CARROTS.

SERVES FOUR

INGREDIENTS
  12–16 shelled scallops
  45ml/3 tbsp olive oil
  50g/2oz/⅓ cup wild rice
  65g/2½ oz/5 tbsp butter
  4 carrots, cut into long thin strips
  2 leeks, cut into thick,
    diagonal slices
  1 small onion, finely chopped
  115g/4oz/⅔ cup long grain rice
  1 fresh bay leaf
  200ml/7fl oz/scant 1 cup white wine
  450ml/¾ pint/scant 2 cups fish stock
  60ml/4 tbsp double (heavy) cream
  a little lemon juice
  25ml/5 tsp chopped fresh chives
  30ml/2 tbsp chervil sprigs
  salt and ground black pepper

1 Lightly season the scallops, brush with 15ml/1 tbsp of the olive oil and set aside.

2 Cook the wild rice in plenty of boiling water for about 30 minutes, until tender, then drain.

3 Melt half the butter in a small frying pan and cook the carrots fairly gently for 4–5 minutes. Add the leeks and cook for another 2 minutes. Season with salt and pepper and add 30–45ml/ 2–3 tbsp water, then cover and cook for a few minutes more. Uncover and cook until the liquid has reduced. Set aside off the heat.

4 Melt half the rest of the butter with 15ml/1 tbsp of the remaining oil in a heavy pan. Add the onion and cook gently for 3–4 minutes, until softened but not browned.

5 Add the long grain rice and bay leaf and cook, stirring constantly, until the rice looks translucent and the grains are coated with oil.

6 Pour in half the wine and half the stock. Season with 2.5ml/½ tsp salt and bring to the boil. Stir, then cover and cook very gently for 15 minutes, or until the liquid is absorbed and the rice is cooked and tender.

7 Reheat the carrots and leeks gently, then stir them into the long grain rice with the wild rice. Add seasoning to taste, if necessary.

8 Meanwhile, pour the remaining wine and stock into a small pan and boil rapidly until reduced by half.

COOK'S TIP
Choose fresh, rather than frozen, scallops as the frozen ones tend to exude water on cooking. Scallops need only the briefest cooking at high heat, just until they turn opaque and brown on each side, so have the pan very hot. Although some people avoid eating the orange-coloured coral, it is delicious and many people consider it to be the best bit.

9 Heat a heavy frying pan over a high heat. Add the remaining butter and oil. Sear the scallops for 1–2 minutes each side, then set aside and keep warm.

10 Pour the reduced stock into the pan and heat until bubbling, then add the cream and boil until thickened. Season with lemon juice, salt and pepper. Stir in the chives and scallops.

11 Stir the chervil into the rice and pile it on to plates. Arrange the scallops on top and spoon the sauce over the rice.

CHICKEN BAKED WITH SHALLOTS AND FENNEL

THIS IS A VERY SIMPLE AND DELICIOUS WAY TO COOK CHICKEN. IF YOU HAVE TIME, LEAVE THE CHICKEN TO MARINATE FOR A FEW HOURS FOR THE BEST FLAVOUR.

SERVES FOUR

INGREDIENTS

1.6–1.8kg/3½–4lb chicken pieces
250g/9oz shallots, peeled
1 head garlic, separated into cloves
  and peeled
60ml/4 tbsp extra virgin olive oil
45ml/3 tbsp tarragon vinegar
45ml/3 tbsp white wine or
  vermouth (optional)
5ml/1 tsp fennel seeds, crushed
2 bulbs fennel, cut into wedges,
  feathery tops reserved
150ml/¼ pint/⅔ cup double
  (heavy) cream
5ml/1 tsp redcurrant jelly
15ml/1 tbsp tarragon mustard
caster (superfine) sugar (optional)
30ml/2 tbsp chopped fresh flat
  leaf parsley
salt and ground black pepper

1 Place the chicken pieces, shallots and all but one of the garlic cloves in a flameproof dish or roasting pan. Add the oil, vinegar, wine or vermouth, if using, and fennel seeds. Season with pepper, then marinate for 2–3 hours.

2 Preheat the oven to 190°C/375°F/ Gas 5. Add the fennel to the chicken, season with salt and stir to mix.

3 Cook the chicken in the oven for 50–60 minutes, stirring once or twice. The chicken juices should run clear, not pink, when the thick thigh meat is pierced with a skewer.

4 Transfer the chicken and vegetables to a serving dish and keep them warm. Skim off some of the fat and bring the cooking juices to the boil, then pour in the cream. Stir, scraping up all the delicious juices. Whisk in the redcurrant jelly, followed by the tarragon mustard. Check the seasoning, adding a little sugar if you like.

5 Chop the remaining garlic with the fennel tops and mix with the parsley. Pour the sauce over the chicken and sprinkle the chopped garlic and herb mixture over the top. Serve immediately.

COOK'S TIPS
• If possible, use the fresh new season's garlic for this dish, as it is plump, moist and full of flavour. Purple-skinned garlic is considered by many cooks to have the best flavour.
• The cut surfaces of fennel quickly discolour, so do not prepare it much in advance of using it. If you must prepare it beforehand, then put the wedges into a bowl of cold water acidulated with a little lemon juice.

STIR-FRIED BEEF AND MUSHROOMS WITH BLACK BEANS AND SPRING ONIONS

THE COMBINATION OF GARLIC AND SALTED BLACK BEANS IS A CLASSIC CANTONESE SEASONING FOR BEEF. SERVE RICE AND SIMPLE BRAISED CHINESE GREENS AS ACCOMPANIMENTS.

SERVES FOUR

INGREDIENTS
    30ml/2 tbsp soy sauce
    30ml/2 tbsp Chinese rice wine or
      dry sherry
    10ml/2 tsp cornflour (cornstarch)
    10ml/2 tsp sesame oil
    450g/1lb fillet or rump (round) steak,
      trimmed of fat
    12 dried shiitake mushrooms
      (Chinese black mushrooms)
    25ml/1½ tbsp salted black beans
    5ml/1 tsp caster (superfine) sugar
    120ml/4fl oz/½ cup groundnut
      (peanut) oil
    4 garlic cloves, thinly sliced
    2.5cm/1in piece fresh root ginger,
      cut into fine strips
    200g/7oz open cap
      mushrooms, sliced
    1 bunch spring onions (scallions),
      sliced diagonally
    1 fresh red chilli, seeded and
      finely shredded
  salt and ground black pepper

1 Mix half the soy sauce, half the rice wine or sherry, half the cornflour and all the sesame oil with 15ml/1 tbsp cold water until smooth. Add a good pinch of salt and pepper.

2 Cut the beef into very thin slices, no more than 5mm/¼in thick. Add the slices to the cornflour mixture and rub the mixture into the beef with your fingers. Set aside for 30 minutes.

3 Pour boiling water over the dried mushrooms and soak for 25 minutes. Drain, reserving 45ml/3 tbsp of the soaking water. Remove and discard the hard stalks and cut the caps in half.

4 Using a fork, mash the black beans with the caster sugar in a small bowl. Stir the remaining cornflour, soy sauce and rice wine or sherry together in another small bowl.

5 Heat the oil in a wok until very hot, then stir-fry the beef for 30–45 seconds, until just brown. Use a slotted spoon to transfer it to a plate. Pour off some oil to leave about 45ml/3 tbsp in the wok.

6 Add the garlic and ginger, stir-fry for 1 minute, then add the shiitake and fresh mushrooms and stir-fry for 2 minutes. Set aside a few tablespoons of the green part of the spring onions, then add the rest to the wok. Stir, add the mashed black beans and stir-fry for another 1–2 minutes.

7 Stir the beef back into the mixture in the wok, then add 45ml/3 tbsp of the shiitake soaking water. Let the mixture bubble. Stir the cornflour mixture to mix it well, pour it into the wok, stirring, and simmer until the sauce thickens. Sprinkle the chilli and reserved spring onions over the beef and serve.

GARLIC CHIVE RICE <u>WITH</u> MUSHROOMS

RICE IS READILY INFUSED WITH THE PUNGENT AROMA AND FLAVOUR OF GARLIC CHIVES, CREATING A DISH WITH AN EXCELLENT FLAVOUR. SERVE WITH VEGETARIAN DISHES, FISH OR CHICKEN.

3 Add the rice to the onions and fry over a low heat, stirring frequently, for 4–5 minutes. Pour in the stock mixture, then stir in 5ml/1 tsp salt and a good grinding of black pepper. Bring to the boil, stir and reduce the heat to very low. Cover tightly and cook for 15–20 minutes, until the rice has absorbed all the liquid.

4 Lay a clean, folded dishtowel over the pan under the lid and press on the lid to wedge it firmly in place. Leave to stand for 10 minutes, allowing the towel to absorb the steam while the rice becomes completely tender.

5 Meanwhile, heat the remaining oil in a frying pan and cook the mushrooms for 5–6 minutes, until tender and browned. Add the remaining chives and cook for another 1–2 minutes.

6 Stir the mushrooms and chopped coriander leaves into the rice. Adjust the seasoning, transfer to a warmed serving dish and serve immediately, sprinkled with the cashew nuts.

SERVES FOUR

INGREDIENTS
350g/12oz/generous 1½ cups
    long grain rice
60ml/4 tbsp groundnut (peanut) oil
1 small onion, finely chopped
2 green chillies, seeded and
    finely chopped
25g/1oz garlic chives, chopped
15g/½oz/½ cup fresh
    coriander (cilantro)
600ml/1 pint/2½ cups vegetable or
    mushroom stock
5ml/1 tsp salt
250g/9oz mixed mushrooms, sliced
50g/2oz cashew nuts, fried in 15ml/
    1 tbsp oil until golden brown
ground black pepper

1 Wash and drain the rice. Heat half the oil in a pan and cook the onion and chillies over a gentle heat, stirring occasionally, for 10–12 minutes, until soft but not browned.

2 Set half the garlic chives aside. Cut the stalks off the coriander and set the leaves aside. Purée the remaining chives and the coriander stalks with the stock in a blender or food processor.

COOK'S TIP
Wild mushrooms are often expensive, but they do have distinctive flavours. Mixing them with cultivated mushrooms is an economical way of using them. Look for oyster mushrooms, ceps, chanterelles, morels, and horse mushrooms.

SPRING ONION, CHIVE AND RICOTTA BREAD

RICOTTA CHEESE AND CHIVES MAKE A MOIST, WELL-FLAVOURED LOAF THAT IS EXCELLENT FOR SANDWICHES. SHAPE THE DOUGH INTO ROLLS, LOAVES, A COTTAGE LOAF, OR EVEN A PLAIT.

MAKES ONE LOAF OR SIXTEEN ROLLS

INGREDIENTS

   15g/½oz fresh yeast or 10ml/2 tsp
     active dried yeast
   5ml/1 tsp caster (superfine) sugar
   270ml/9fl oz/generous 1 cup
     lukewarm water
   450g/1lb unbleached strong white
     bread flour, plus a little extra
   7.5ml/1½ tsp salt
   1 large (US extra large) egg, beaten
   115g/4oz/½ cup ricotta cheese
   1 bunch spring onions (scallions),
     thinly sliced
   30ml/2 tbsp extra virgin olive oil
   45ml/3 tbsp chopped fresh chives
   15ml/1 tbsp milk
   10ml/2 tsp poppy seeds (optional)
   coarse sea salt

1 Cream fresh yeast with the sugar and stir in 120ml/4fl oz/½ cup of the water. For dried yeast, stir the sugar into the water, then sprinkle it over the surface. Leave in a warm place for 10 minutes.

2 Sift the flour and salt into a warmed bowl. Make a well in the centre and pour in the yeast liquid and the remaining water. Save a little beaten egg, then put the rest in the bowl. Add the ricotta and mix to form a dough, adding a little more flour if the mixture is very sticky.

3 Knead the dough on a floured work surface until smooth and elastic. Set aside in a greased bowl, inside a plastic bag, in a warm place for 1–2 hours, until doubled in size.

4 Meanwhile, cook the spring onions in the oil for 3–4 minutes, until soft but not browned. Set aside to cool.

5 Knock back (punch down) the risen dough and knead in the spring onions, with their oil from cooking, and the chives. Shape the dough into rolls or a large or small loaf.

6 Grease a baking sheet or loaf tin (pan) and place the rolls or bread on it. Cover with greased plastic or oiled clear film (plastic wrap) and leave in a warm place to rise for about 1 hour. Preheat the oven to 200°C/400°F/Gas 6.

7 Beat the milk into the reserved beaten egg and use to glaze the rolls or loaf. Sprinkle with poppy seeds, if using, and a little coarse sea salt, then bake rolls for about 15 minutes or a loaf for 30–40 minutes or until golden and well risen. When tapped firmly on the base, the bread should feel and sound firm. Cool on a wire rack.

COOK'S TIP
To make a plait (braid), divide the dough into three sausage-shaped pieces about 40cm/16in long. Press them together at one end and then plait, pressing the ends together when completed.

INDEX

ACKNOWLEDGEMENTS

Photographs are all by William Lingwood except those on the following pages: p6, p7b, p18 The Anthony Blake Photo Library; p7t, p19b Cephas; p8, p13tr, p14t, p17b, p20 The Bridgeman Art Library; p9t, p10t, p10b The Ancient Egypt Picture Library; p9b, p10b, p11l, p11b, p13tl, p14b, p16t, p16b, p21t, p21b, p22b, p23t Mary Evans Picture Library; p12, p14b, p15 e.t. archive; p13b, p22t, p23b AKG Photographic Library; p17t Hulton Getty Picture Library; p19t Food Features; p24,

p28b John Freeman; p28r, p36l, A–Z Botanical Collection Ltd; p37tl Michelle Garrett.
  The author would like to acknowledge the following for their inspiration and information: John Ayto, A Gourmet's Guide (Oxford, 1994); Lindsey Bareham, Onions Without Tears (London, 1995); Barbara Ciletti, The Onion Harvest Cookbook (Newtown, CT, 1998); Bruce Cost, Foods from the Far East (London, 1990); William J. Darby and Paul Ghalioungui, Food: The Gift of Osiris, 2 volumes (London, 1977); Alan Davidson, The

Oxford Companion to Food (Oxford, 1999); John Edwards, The Roman Cookery of Apicius (London, 1984); John Evelyn, Acetaria: A Discourse of Sallets (1699), edited by Christopher Driver and Tom Jaine (Totnes, 1996); Four Seasons of the House of Cerruti, edited and translated by Judith Spencer (New York, NY, 1983); M. Grieve, A Modern Herbal, edited by C. F. Leyel (London, 1931, 1998); Dorothy Hartley, Food in England (1954, 1996); Katy Holder and Gail Duff, A Clove of Garlic (London, 1996);

C. F. Leyel and Olga Hartley, The Gentle Art of Cookery (London, 1925, 1974); Harold McGee, On Food and Cooking: The Science and Lore of the Kitchen (London, 1991); Charmaine Solomon, The Encyclopedia of Asian Food (London, 1998); Colin Spencer, Vegetable Book (London, 1995); Tom Stobart, The Cook's Encyclopaedia (London, 1998); Waverley Root, Food (New York, NY, 1980); J. G. Vaughan and C. A. Geissler, The New Oxford Book of Food Plants (Oxford, 1997).

NOTES

NOTES

NOTES

NOTES